RAINER MARIA RILKE:
THE YEARS IN SWITZERLAND

RAINER MARIA RILKE:
The Years in Switzerland

A Contribution to the Biography of
Rilke's Later Life

BY

J. R. von SALIS

TRANSLATED BY
N. K. CRUICKSHANK

1964
THE HOGARTH PRESS
LONDON

Published by
The Hogarth Press
42 William IV Street
London W.C.2

*

Clarke, Irwin and Co Ltd
Toronto

TRANSLATED FROM
Rainer Maria Rilkes Schweizer Jahre
Verlag Huber, Frauenfeld, Switzerland
First Published 1936

Printed in Great Britain by
T. & A. Constable Ltd
Hopetoun Street
Edinburgh 7

DEDICATED
in Gratitude and Friendship to
Nanny Wunderly-Volkart

CONTENTS

CONTENTS

ILLUSTRATIONS

TRANSLATOR'S NOTE

ALL the English versions of Rilke's poems used in this translation are by Mr. J. B. Leishman, and all, except the stanzas on p. 90, are to be found either in *Rainer Maria Rilke : Selected Works Volume II, Poetry*, or in *Rainer Maria Rilke : Poems 1906-1926* (both published by The Hogarth Press). I should like to express my thanks to him and to the publishers for allowing me to use them.

I am greatly indebted to my friend Mrs Martha Schulz, who has kept a vigilant eye on the translation as it progressed, saving me from not a few careless slips and idiomatic pitfalls.

N. K. C.

FOREWORD TO THE THIRD EDITION

THE present book was published for the first time in 1936, and in 1938 a second edition appeared. It has now been out of print for many years. The author and publisher have been persuaded that there is a need for a new edition. This cannot be entirely identical with the former editions, because, since they appeared, new light has been thrown on Rilke's life, thought and work, the letters published by the Insel-Verlag and through the wealth of his own comment made available to us through the Max Niehans Verlag. At the same time the publications concerned with Rilke have become very numerous; during the last twenty years more than 200 books about him, as well as countless essays and articles, have appeared in various countries and languages. This new edition of an old book does not attempt to give a systematic account of Rilke literature. We have, however, had to take into consideration many of the post-1938 publications by and about Rilke, and bring them up to date in the notes at the end of the book.

When I decided soon after Rilke's death, in response to a suggestion made by my former teacher, Professor Harry Maync, to write an account, based on some unpublished material, of Rilke's years in Switzerland – and consequently of his so-called late period – Rilke was famous principally on account of his great early works: the *Stundenbuch*, the *Neue Gedichte* and the *Aufzeichnungen des Malte Laurids Brigge*. Since then the limelight of public attention has shifted to the poet's late and mature periods, corresponding in time with the years of his life presented here, during which he produced work that was for long considered esoteric by the general public. Those were the years of the *Duineser Elegien*, the *Sonette an Orpheus*, the versions of Valéry's poems and prose, and the French poems. As the complete edition of Rilke's poems is not yet available, our knowledge of the German poems written in the creative period 1919-26, apart from the Elegies and Sonnets, is still incomplete. It should be added that only during recent years have good French and English translations of the great poem-cycles written at Muzot been available to readers of Rilke outside the German-speaking countries.

It is, however, these poems above all, as Holthusen says, 'which in the opinion of the most serious critics of the western cultural world place Rilke, as the greatest contemporary German lyric poet, alongside such writers as Yeats, Eliot, Valéry and Claudel'. Holthusen continues: 'For the younger generation of American intellectuals Rilke's place is in the company of Kafka, Proust, Eliot and Joyce as one of the authoritative interpreters of the consciousness of modern man; even for the modern poets of this country he rivals Eliot as the most influential contemporary figure. . . . Not as the spokesman of a hostile, denying attitude to time and world, of isolation, but as the true opposite of the contemporary, mass- and machine-minded, ideological man, a poet separated by a positively sidereal distance from all those throughout the world who want to be in the foreground as representatives of "public opinion" and fashionable thought – yet a poet who, for all that, belongs inseparably to this world of ours as the seer and interpreter of its other side, its hidden character.'

It is highly remarkable that a poet as solitary as Rilke, as far removed from the literary and other busy-ness of the modern world, should have been one of those 'who', in the opinion of the French critic Edmond Jaloux, 'had the most profound influence on the higher life of their time'. And it is not less remarkable that during the quarter of a century since his death his very solitude should have been recognised as a 'genuine, sober confrontation of reality' and also as the 'preliminary condition of a serious, loving encounter with one's neighbour' (Holthusen). But even from the purely artistic point of view, which is above all the one from which a poet should be judged, Rilke's gift for language, his enhancement of expression beyond anything possible in German poetry before him, his extraordinarily mobile, fluid lines, his conquest of new areas of sensibility and his powers of seizing his impressions in metre and rhyme, were things that brought his literary achievement to the very limit of the formable and expressible, as they had hitherto been conceived. One can understand that his late poem-cycles were thought 'difficult' and 'obscure' when they were published, and even after his death.

Time did its work here too, awakening and refining contemporary sensibility, and so making it more capable of receiving such poetry: a truly original artist is always ahead of his time, and not until the shadows of death have descended do the times catch up with him.

It was not part of my task to include in my book the latest findings of analysis and criticism; it remains on the whole, even though parts of it have been enlarged and refashioned, what it was when it was published: a contribution to the biography of Rainer Maria Rilke's later years. Of his life's pilgrimage, which led him through so many realms of this and of a higher spiritual world, the seven and a half years in Switzerland represent the final station. The poet lived in that country from June 1919 until his death on December 29th, 1926, finding a dwelling-place and home in the medieval Castle of Muzot in the Valais, where his last great works were written. We know from Rilke's will that he did not consider any of his portraits to be really good likenesses, except those 'existing in thought and feeling, transitorily'. I have tried to give a faithful account of my own memories of Rilke, but over and above that it has been necessary in the first place to mould this short, fragmentary account of my meetings and conversations with the poet upon the foundation of published and unpublished sources, in order to give a complete and, as it were, animated picture of the final period of his life and work. Oral tradition is, of course, one of the unpublished sources, and here I may draw attention to the fact that in the years immediately following Rilke's death, I had long conversations with the men and women who were his most intimate friends during his last years, so that it was not difficult to verify the truth and authenticity of what was learned in that way. One had to make sure that even the most apparently trivial details corresponded to fact. Rilke abhorred the approximate in everything, and I have continually confronted myself in his posthumous presence, if I may so put it, with the question: could whatever I was recounting or stating claim to be exact and honest?

Anton Kippenberg, Rilke's friend and publisher, who many years ago gave my undertaking his kindly assistance, was of the opinion that the four greatest and most revealing series of correspondence in Rilke's life were those with Lou Andreas-Salomé (from 1897), with the Kippenbergs (from 1906), with the Princess Marie von Thurn und Taxis (from 1909), and with Mme Nanny Wunderly-Volkart (from 1919). All four continued without a break until the poet's death in 1926. The first three have been published in part, or are soon to be published; the letters to Katharina Kippenberg are not yet available*; all those concerned are now dead. In 1952 Mme Nanny Wunderly-Volkart of Meilen on Lake Geneva, whom Rilke left as his executrix, gave the 420 letters which she had received from Rilke during his last seven years, together with all his literary remains so far in her possession, to the Schweizerischen Landesbibliothek, where, with other MSS., letters, pictures and relics, they form the nucleus of a Swiss Rilke Archive. As Rilke did not keep a proper journal, his letters have somewhat the same importance for students of his life and work as the journal of his great contemporary and friend André Gide. When I was preparing the first edition of this book I received Mme Wunderly's permission to see about 80 letters written to her by the poet, and to copy passages relevant to my subject. As, according to the conditions of the gift, Rilke's letters to Mme Wunderly now in the Schweizerischen Rilke-Archiv are not allowed to be shown to researchers, it goes without saying that I have not consulted that source again in preparing the present edition. For all the help and valuable information given to me by Mme Wunderly I repeat here the friendly thanks expressed in the first two editions of my book. I was also allowed to use Rilke's letters to Frau Lily Ziegler, which are now in the same archive. Useful, too, was the permission I had from Herr Paul Obermüller of Heidelberg, to see the MS. of Rilke's letters to Frau G. Nölke, appearing shortly from the Insel-Verlag,† and to quote passages from them. Some passages from Rilke's letters to me are published in this edition for the first time. To all who have helped with this revision of my book I express my sincere thanks.

J. R. v. S.

Schloss Brunegg, September 1952

---

* *Briefwechsel mit Katharina von Kippenberg*, Insel-Verlag Wiesbaden (1954).
† *Briefwechsel mit Frau G. Nölke*, Insel-Verlag Wiesbaden (1953).

Rainer Maria Rilke in Switzerland

We must work at the future as weavers work at high-warp
tapestry: without seeing it.

ANATOLE FRANCE

1

PRELUDE

In 1914 Rainer Maria Rilke was living in Paris, where he had rented a small flat. When war broke out, however, he happened to be in Germany and, as he was an Austrian subject and his country was at war with France, it was impossible for him to return. The manuscripts on which he was working, his books and correspondence, as well as a number of personal possessions, had been left behind in Paris. He found temporary quarters in Munich that August, and from then on he regarded the whole period of the war as a break in the continuity of his life. He awaited the end of hostilities living in quiet seclusion in Munich, where he remained during the November Revolution of 1918. This existence was interrupted by visits to the country, by repeated journeys to Berlin and by a time of military service in Vienna. When at last, in June 1919, he left for Switzerland, it was not in order to look for a permanent home in that country nor in the hope of finding conditions favourable to the resumption of his poetic work, interrupted by the war, his call-up to the army and the collapse of his inner world. The main reason for his departure from Munich was simply dislike for a place and a country which he associated with his unutterable mental sufferings during the war. Dependent as he was on a free, harmonious relationship with his environment, he was unable to think of the city of Munich apart from the oppression and confinement of those years, the atmosphere of war psychoses and chauvinism, and for that reason he could not bear to stay there any longer.

It is typical of Rilke's whole personality that he never arrived at any political standpoint with regard to the war. 'Everything visible has once again been flung into the boiling abysses to be melted down', he wrote in November 1914 to his friends Karl and Elisabeth von der Heydt. 'The past is left behind, the future hesitates, the present is without foundation, but hearts – shouldn't they have the power to hang suspended, to preserve themselves in the great cloud?' He confesses that during those first August days he was moved by the spectacle of war, by 'the war-god'; from this experience a few poems were born, but

for a long time now the war has been invisible to me, a spirit of visitation, no longer a god, but something a god has unleashed upon mankind. More cannot be accomplished even now than that the soul should survive, and the misery and evil are perhaps no more present than they used to be, only more graspable, active, visible. For the misery in which mankind has lived from the beginning cannot really be increased by any outward circumstance.[1]

Influenced by deeper realities than war and its alarms, he held throughout to this unpolitical attitude with admirable straight-forwardness and constancy, his profound, sure knowledge of human affairs helping him from the first to look the horrible unleashed events full in the face, disfigured as those faces were. He felt the war years as a breach and a fracture in his life and there was hardly any question of literary work. He was, however, not so much distressed by the suffocation of his creative impulse as by his spiritual loneliness. Speaking to an acquaintance in Switzerland after crossing the frontier in the summer of 1919, he described the war period as 'five impenetrable, sterile years, interrupting all genuine life'.[2] Rilke had lost contact with human beings and with the world. The development of his life before 1914 had been so closely related to a wide, spacious, frontier-free world, the attitude to life which he had formed on his travels and while living abroad had been so much influenced by the idea of the open, that he felt imprisoned during the enforced confine-ment in a belligerent country which he had never, in a higher sense, regarded as other than his own. *'Cinq ans de prison allemande'*, was how he described the experience in retrospect, almost as soon as he had entered Switzerland.[3]

Rilke's wartime letters show clearly his increasing tendency to observe the happenings of those years from their least compre-hensible side, as something brutal, formless, bogus and horrible. The upward flight of the soul, the 'saying', the 'praising', the 'outsinging' (*Aufsingen*) which he thought of as his poetic vocation, needed quite different circumstances: they called for a physical and spiritual environment as free and wide open as that which had existed before 1914 – existed, at any rate, in the imagination of the guileless. In 1915 he wrote to the Princess Thurn und Taxis from Munich:

Was it this? I ask myself a hundred times, was it this that lay on top of us as a monstrous weight, this monstrous future which has now become our cruel present? I must remember what I once said to Marthe: '*Marthe, il n'y aura devant moi que des désastres, des terreurs, des angoisses indicibles; c'est avec vous que finissent les bontés de ma vie*' – that burst from me as though, in the midst of calm, a sudden storm had torn it out of me, I listened when I heard myself saying it, I thought only of my own fate, so strangely collapsing, and had no idea that the world as a whole was big with destruction. . . . Come what may, the worst is that a certain innocence in which we grew up will never be there again for any of us. The years ahead, many or few, what will they be but a descent, with trembling knees, from this mountain of pain up which we are always being dragged further and further?[4]

The same note is sounded when he writes to the Princess in April 1918: 'I at least have no intention as long as the war lasts of taking up again tasks which have been interrupted, it is a life *en parenthèses*, and only when you have closed the brackets can you carry on with the main sentence.'[5] And some weeks later: '. . . it is a spell in which I stand ever more petrified, pillar of salt or stone, I don't know what it is that I am turning into'.[6] In these circumstances it is hardly to be wondered at that Rilke could not be persuaded to speak publicly about current events. They caused him deep suffering, and the only way he could remain firm and dignified at such a time was to keep completely silent and avoid having anything to do with dilettanti street-corner politics. The poetess Regina Ullmann, with whom he was on intimate terms and in daily contact during his time in Munich, tells how a reporter once forced his way into Rilke's presence, without warning or introduction, and asked the astonished poet about his political views. The victim of this surprise attack answered: 'You've come to the wrong door, I'm not interested in politics.' Rilke refused courageously to be drawn into the never-ending daily discussions or to accept the dogmatic, generalised, grotesque picture of the world as reflected in the minds of newspaper readers swimming with the stream of the war. This refusal sprang simply from being true to himself, and it appears again in a confession that for months on end in Munich he could not bear to see Rudolf Kassner, with whom he had been friendly since their days together at Duino. 'Even with him', he wrote to the Princess, 'conversation always tends to come back to the present, of which I understand nothing, and when one suddenly discovers that one is using newspaper expressions (for what else have we?) one feels disgust and horror at one's own mouth.'[7]

Rilke was in the widest sense a mid-European, and of course, unpolitically speaking, a German poet, just as the Austrians Adalbert Stifter and Grillparzer and the Swiss subjects Gottfried Keller and Conrad Ferdinand Meyer were German poets, viewed unpolitically. But owing to Rilke's launching out into the world, his severance of ties with his homeland, there is little, indeed hardly any, sign of the native and the national on his involved, eccentric itinerary – on what he once called 'the map of my life'. On this map, however, 'capitals' were marked, places to which he responded with a feeling of deep kinship, even of joyful recognition; and these halting places on his pilgrimage were without number. Permanent features of the poet's world-wandering life, and intrinsic to it, were his estrangement as a young man from his native city, Prague, which survived gloomily in his memory as the scene of early horrors; his antipathy towards everything Austrian, rightly mentioned by his friends Lou Andreas-Salomé and L. Albert-Lasard in their books of reminiscences and repeatedly expressed in conversation during his later years; and his animosity towards nationalistic and patriotic Germans – a steady dislike which resulted from his war experiences (and which, showing itself only rarely, would leap from hiding in the form of tetchy outbursts). We look in vain in Rilke's letters and utterances for any mention of the break-up of the Austro-Hungarian Empire, which fell apart after the defeat of 1918. He thought of State and Church as merely abode and setting for the human collective; as such neither attracted him, neither could count on his willing obedience and co-operation. For him the spirit blew where it listed. Here, incidentally, we see one of the differences between Hofmannsthal and Rilke – who have often been named together as Austrian poets of almost the same age, and between whose reputations there was a kind of rivalry during the first quarter of the century. They had little to say to each other, although they were polite and friendly when their ways happened to cross. But Hofmannsthal was attached to all that was time honoured in Austrian social and cultural life, to aesthetic conventions, in short to a traditional, stylised provincialism which claimed his heart both as citizen and artist. There was thus a gulf between the sphere he lived in and the boundless, visionary world view of Rilke. The latter looked in quite a different direction for the fulfilment of his art: in the direction of giving expression to the things of the soul, the direction of pure human inwardness. Rilke's later works composed in Switzerland are witness and monument to the fidelity with which he carried out his survey of the soul's inner space, 'inner-world-space' (*Weltinnenraum*) as he called it. Not the outer, only the inner ways of men were important to him. His mature artistic endeavour resulted in literary works of a most personal stamp, in which the objective material used before the war in *New Poems* (*Neue Gedichte*) appears again, now uniquely sublimated as image and symbol for things that could no longer be expressed. This movement towards pure being (of which there had been signs in Rilke's work as long ago as 1912, when he was writing the first two Elegies at Duino and fragments of others in Spain and Portugal), this struggle with poetic expression, to which he turned from the traditional aesthetics of the day, explains how he came to write the sentence: 'The terrible thing about art is that the further you go into it the more you are pledged to attempt the uttermost, the almost impossible.'[8]

As we read the many lamentations in Rilke's wartime letters, and recall the uncanny fact that the war reduced the poet in him to silence, we cannot help suspecting that the real cause of the trouble lies further back, before the war period; and indeed the war did not create his difficulties, only increased them to an infinite extent. When he finished writing *The Notebooks of Malte Laurids Brigge* (*Aufzeichnungen des Malte Laurids Brigge*), in January 1912, he felt that he had reached 'a great watershed' in his life. After finishing this piece of work, which had indeed called for a supreme effort, he found it intensely difficult to return again to a state of readiness for beginning something new. 'Works of art are always the result of having been in danger', he had written when he was still a young man.[9] In completing his clear, truthful account of Malte's destruction the poet had escaped from danger. A reaction followed, bringing with it, as always in his case, physical symptoms. He was depressed to feel himself a beginner again, one of those who have to go right back to the beginning before they can start anything new. As we can see with astonishing clearness when we study his writings in chronological order, Rilke's 'beginning' takes place always at a deeper, more inaccessible level, a stratum nearer to the core of things and to the frontiers of what is expressible in art; thus each repetition of the experience tended to be more painful than the last and harder to face. His spiritual difficulties were increased enormously by the total exposure to life which resulted from his lack of any sheltering social or professional duty; for he regarded it as an indispensable condition of his creativeness that he should be able to put his 'work', as he called it, uncompromisingly at the centre of his existence. But in obeying this inner compulsion to break free from everything he took upon himself a defencelessness that he found hard to bear. Perhaps no one of his generation or the next lived the life of a poet quite as completely as Rilke did, and it is obvious that after 1914 such a work-centred way of life was attended by all sorts of risks and perils. The special kind of danger that threatened Rilke, the peril which (quite apart from wars and other discordant events) hung over him all his life, sapping his vitality, has been described by Dieter Bassermann in his excellent book *The Later Rilke* (*Der Späte Rilke*): 'That which destroys Malte and from which Rilke suffers to the verge of self-destruction, is the inability to find an adequate attitude to the things and people around him.'[10] In fact, Rilke's attitude was never at any time 'adequate', never quite adapted to the requirements of the ordinary, that is to say, to the rules and conventions governing the behaviour of people born into a certain social environment. For this reason the suffering which life caused him ended only with life itself.

Rilke's life becomes clear and coherent only if we measure it against the poetic vocation which he always obeyed. There was nothing else that he ever wanted to obey, and his inability from time to time to carry out its demands afflicted him with the only deep sorrow of his life, the only real sense of guilt and failure.

From this point of view alone does the itinerary on the map of his life begin to make sense. It turned always in the direction of work, towards whatever circumstances favoured the execution of that work. He had constantly before him, as the goal and justification of his life, the day to day labour in the artist's workshop. Almost the only signpost we have to the poet's innumerable journeys through many lands is the persistent search for surroundings able to provide him with a few daily needs and with the feeling of being close to work and capable of it. He never expressed this more clearly than in a New Year letter for 1914 to the Princess Thurn und Taxis. After the disappointing months in Venice and Spain during 1912 and 1913, he was back in Paris again, in his own flat, having his peace shattered by a neighbour's exasperating piano practice. He wrote:

If God has any understanding, he will let me before long find a room or two in the country where I can rage to my heart's content and where the Elegies can bay at the moon from every side. Then there should be the possibility of going for long lonely walks, and even of a human being, the one like a sister!!! (ah, me) who would run the house and have either no love at all or else so much that she would ask for nothing except just to be there, working and warding at the frontiers of the invisible. Here is the essence of my wishes for 1914, 15, 16, 17 etc.[11]

We can almost feel physically the ruinous shock dealt by the years he enumerates – the years of the world war – to Rilke's existence.

Rilke was not able to do any work during the war, except for some translations (Michelangelo) and – in November 1915 – the Fourth Elegy followed by the *Requiem on the Death of a Boy* and a few short poems, a burst of creative activity which caused him to write to his publisher that 'work is rapidly on the upgrade'. At this moment his call-up papers arrived, and at the beginning of January 1916 the forty-year-old poet had to go to Vienna to train as an army recruit. It was twenty-five years since the boy René Rilke had been given his freedom again after five years as a cadet at St Pölten. Since then this far from strong man had seen no military service. But the life-long effects of the Military School on Rilke were described by him again and again in letters and conversation. A 'horror primer' he called it once, and even during his time in Switzerland we find him writing to one of his former professors explaining, in terms that were perfectly restrained but also full of bitterness, how he left the Military High School at St Pölten

exhausted, mentally and physically misused, retarded, sixteen years old, standing before my life's gigantic task cheated of the most innocent part of my strength, together with the unrecoverable training time which would have cut clean steps for me in the precipitous walls of my future which now, enfeebled and damaged as I was, I had to start climbing.[12]

It seemed to Rilke that an outrage had been committed on his nature when, an awkward, middle-aged recruit, being drilled and shouted at and taught to slope and shoulder arms by a sergeant-major on a Vienna parade-ground, he was thrust back again among boyhood terrors which he had imagined to be outlived. He suffered as a tree might if it were turned upside down and buried crown deep in the earth from which, a forest lifetime ago, it had grown into the sunlight. After a short while, thanks to the help of influential friends, Rilke was posted to the more comfortable, suitable surroundings of a so-called Government records office. There, clad in the grey uniform of an infantryman, he was expected to carry out the (for him) quite impossible duty of using his pen in the service of patriotism and for the glorification of war. He called this 'a perverse and irresponsible misuse of the writer's craft' – his Austrian fellow soldier penmen, with grim humour, called it 'hero-bedizening' (*Heldenfrisieren*) – and felt that the mindless life in barracks was enviable compared to his present lot.[13] After these compulsory months in Vienna Rilke never visited the city again. Nevertheless, it should be noted that during these months there were pleasant as well as trying hours: secluded evenings spent quietly in his hotel room at Hietzing, meetings with his friends Thurn und Taxis and their circle and many with the painter Kokoschka, whose personality he found extraordinarily attractive. It was in wartime Vienna that he first heard Arnold Schönberg's music, and there that he became acquainted with the famous periodical *Fackel* (Torch) and its editor Karl Kraus, of whom he said appreciatively 'he distils a very pure poison'. He was seen occasionally in the theatre, and lived for a time near Hugo von Hofmannsthal in Rodaun, until his final release from military service set him free to return to Munich.[13a]

While he was living in Vienna Rilke had news of a loss which he took with the utmost calmness – not surprisingly, at a time when he treated even his immediate miseries as though they were a long way off: all the belongings, including books, which he had left behind in his Paris flat in the rue Campagne-Première when war broke out had been sold by auction. He had lost clothes and furniture, everything, for the landlord, having no confidence in absentee enemy alien tenants, had put the whole lot under the hammer, realising thereby the princely sum of 538 francs! Details of the circumstances surrounding this unwarrantable and needless sacrifice of Rilke's possessions are given in a diary kept by Romain Rolland, who lived only a few steps from Rilke's former lodgings in Montparnasse. Early in 1916 Stefan Zweig had written to Romain Rolland from Vienna, telling him of this unfortunate affair; Romain Rolland in his turn brought it to the notice of Jacques Copeau, who put the matter into the hands of Rilke's friend André Gide. The steps that Gide took to try and save Rilke's books and personal belongings were quite unsuccessful, for by that time everything had been scattered to the winds. But Rilke's Paris caretaker had collected the unsaleable manuscripts and letters and stored them in suitcases, meaning to return them to their owner after the war. It is clear from Stefan Zweig's letter to Romain Rolland that this affair weighed on Rilke's mind during his time of military service in Vienna (he did not know then that any of his personal things had been saved); and Rolland's and Gide's letters show even more clearly the pains so honourably taken by them and by Copeau to make restitution for a piece of interference and injustice of which, as Frenchmen, they felt ashamed. This restitution was made to Rainer Maria Rilke in the coin of personal friendship and literary esteem. It was André Gide who first introduced *Malte Laurids Brigge* to literary France, by publishing long translated extracts from the novel in the *Nouvelle Revue française* for July 1st 1911.[14]

Little worth recording happened in the poet's life during the three years between his departure from Vienna in the summer of 1916 and his exodus from Germany in June 1919 – those years when the events of war, post-war and revolution were rolling wearisomely and chaotically over the land. Munich was the unloved haven where he anchored his little boat. He spent the summer months of 1917 on an estate in Westfalen as the guest of Frau Hertha König, to whom he was later to dedicate one of his Elegies. In the course of this journey he paid two short visits to Berlin, to which city he had often returned since staying as a young man at the Schmargendorf home of the Andreas-Salomés, 'Waldfrieden', where he wrote *The Lay of the Love and Death of Cornet Christoph Rilke* (*Die Weise von Liebe und Tod des Cornet Christoph Rilke*). The 1917 summer visit to Berlin was dominated by an exhibition of Max Liebermann's work and a birthday party at the famous painter's house, to which Rilke went with Gerhart Hauptmann, first met during the youthful time at Schmargendorf. The autumn days in the capital are memorable on account of a meeting with Bernhard von der Marwitz, a young poet who admired and understood Rilke's work. Marwitz, like Georg Träkl in Austria and Alain Fournier and Peguy in France – and, alas, so many other of the most gifted and remarkable young writers of that generation, was to lose his life in the war. Between the mature, already famous poet and the young man whose genius was ripening but as yet unacclaimed, there sprang up, perhaps for the first time in Rilke's life, a mutually stimulating friendship – only to be ended abruptly by the younger man's death on the battlefield.

As with Vienna and Munich, Rilke did not visit Berlin again after the Great War. The relationship with Gerhart Hauptmann, in which Rainer had once been the admiring youngster (Hauptmann, twelve years Rilke's senior, survived him by nineteen years) was no longer cultivated on either side. Hauptmann's greed for fame, his craving to be acclaimed, to be a representative figure, was distasteful to Rilke, to whom worldly honour meant nothing and fame only an accumulation of misunderstandings. We discussed these matters some years later at Muzot, when I was on my way back from Berlin after attending the celebrations of Gerhart Hauptmann's sixtieth birthday, and was giving Rilke an account of that function. The thought of all the fuss and formality surrounding such an occasion only made Rilke feel sorry for Hauptmann – which is worth noting, because, as Lou Andreas-Salomé truly remarked, Rilke's reaction to fame was quite without vanity. Whether the reason was a natural modesty averse to any pedestal, or a publicity-hating shyness; whether it was spiritual honesty, aware that all fame tends to coarsen and make superficial; or that genuine humility with which no vain and worldly attitude can coexist – whatever the reason, Rilke never allowed himself to be fêted, never entered the limelight of publicity except on the rare occasions when he gave readings from his works. He spent his fiftieth birthday (1925) alone, deep within the walls of snowbound Muzot, looking with mild alarm at the countless letters and telegrams which kept pouring in. It followed that he had no liking for the noise, as he called it, made during the war about the *Cornet* – that little production of his youth which by a strange chance first made him famous. It was not the first time that a thinker or artist has owed fame to a piece of work quite unrepresentative of his output as a whole; but perhaps that is only a trick of the writer's destiny, which by getting a hold on prospective readers in this way gains a wider circle for his more difficult work. The *Cornet* had already been set to music by a composer (since then this has been done many times) and performed in Vienna and Leipzig at charity concerts for the wounded. When Rilke was approached from Vienna, where they had an urgent need of the heroic, with a request to turn the Cornet into a fighter pilot his reply was anything but affable. 'The answer I sent to Vienna goes without saying' he wrote on March 30th to the Princess Taxis, 'but they wouldn't accept it. The zealous gentleman there demanded a flying Cornet from me – such a transposition was beyond even Almighty God himself, the result of his decision to make a flying dog was just a sadly exaggerated bat'.[15]

The world war – no one was to know then that it was only the first – brought about many changes in Rilke's life, as in the lives of most thoughtful and sensitive people. He may, as he said, have put these years between mental brackets, in order to be able, when the brackets were closed again, to go on with the main sentence which the war had interrupted; but in fact the main sentence was never again quite the same as the one he had been uttering before 1914. The only thing that survived unchanged was his unshakeable determination to continue the unfinished Elegies. In spite of years of silence, which distressed him and diminished him in his own eyes, he never ceased to believe steadfastly in the possibility of being able to go on with these poems. For Rilke remained obdurate when his publisher tried to persuade him to agree to the publication of the Elegies already in existence. (Three of them had been finished, including number four of the final sequence.) He was rightly afraid that if a fragment were to be prematurely exposed to the public, there might be a lessening of that unique tension, at once helpful and tormenting, which work in progress generates in the creative mind. The birth of the Elegies was closely bound up with the Castle of Duino on the Adriatic Sea, where Rilke had spent the winter of 1911-12, and we can understand his alarm when during the battles of the Isonzo shells started falling on that noble residence mounted on a cliff jutting out into the sea. But again it is typical of him that he never mentioned the castle's final destruction by artillery fire in any of his letters, even those to the mistress of Duino, although the event must have affected him profoundly. At that time Rainer Maria Rilke struck one of his Munich friends, a psychiatrist, as being inwardly restless and tormented though outwardly disciplined. He seemed to be concentrating all his spiritual strength on the effort to make progress with tasks begun before the war, and Bassermann strikingly remarks that Rilke's later poems and letters – i.e. those written in the post-war years–show that the overwhelming avalanche of war had not interrupted the flow of his work, only slowed it down.[16]

During November 1918, those days which brought the defeat of the Central Powers and the revolutionary cataclysm in Central Europe, Rilke was on his own evidence occupied 'in looking and listening, no, above all in hoping' – and yet: 'at every hesitation in the step of that which is at last on its way, one's heart stands still, as though this future, coming so slowly on foot through the crowd, might trip up, or, once again, turn round'.[17] It is remarkable that Rilke should have attended the people's meetings in the brewery halls, to listen to the talk, and that he said of them:

Although people were packed so closely round the beer-tables and between the tables that the waitresses had to eat their way like woodworms through the solid human structure – it was not oppressive, not even the atmosphere; one did not find the reek of beer and smoke and bodies disagreeable, one hardly noticed it, so important was it, and so preeminently and immediately clear, that the things being discussed, the things whose turn had come at last, could happen, and that the easiest and most valid of these things, in so far as they were more or less clearly presented, would be grasped by the gigantic multitude with heavy, massive applause.[18]

There had been wonderful moments – he wrote in this same account, addressed to his wife – which up till now people had had to do without in Germany 'where there was only verbal protest, or else acquiescence which in a way simply meant a share of power for the subjected'.[19] What had oppressed Rilke in the attitude of those around him during the war now becomes clear: clear from his joy and hope at suddenly seeing a free humanity rising up to express itself freely, and at hearing it speak of the things 'whose turn had come at last'. We learn from one of those present that Rilke made a fine and impressive speech at a meeting of intellectuals which he attended in Munich soon after the Revolution. At about the same time – in November 1918 – he took part in a discussion regarding the reception of homecoming troops, and wrote to one of the organisations concerned a letter which was thoroughly practical and to the point. All the same: Rilke reacted to force in its revolutionary shape almost as strongly as he did to the brutalities of war. As early as November 15th he was writing to a Munich acquaintance who seemed to have asked for his co-operation: 'Then, violence is a clumsy tool and an unusable one, and that is why the spirit always lags behind it, the spirit which knows nothing of force, whose conquests are won by the power of invincible gentleness.' He refused to associate spirit with the activities of war and revolution, in which it could only lose and betray itself.[20] In fact, Rilke was not so unpolitical as he appeared to be. When he applied his critical intelligence, enlightened by an intuitive clearsightedness, to political matters, his views were more penetrating and often sounder than those of the politically minded newspaper reader and the 'well-informed man'. The observation he made at the end of December 1918 is first rate and full of shrewdness:

. . . Under the pretext of a great revolution the old dishonesties are still working and are making a show of themselves under the red flag.

It is terrible to have to say it: but all this is just as *untrue* as the propaganda when war is declared; neither the one nor the other is born of the spirit. The so-called spirit first came after these events and, exactly as in 1914, could not do otherwise than put itself at their disposal, which one must admit was not very grand for the spirit.[21]

As a witness with an all but infallible eye for the true nature of things, Rilke could not help 'concluding with deepest sorrow' that men had been freed from the oppression of war only to be plunged into new forms of oppression,

and that, while the names War and Freedom are simultaneously disappearing, an unknown unnameable event has occurred, at the very moment when it was most necessary for us to establish ourselves in confidence and security. At the same time, people are being tempted to political dilettanti-ism, to trying their hand at generalities outside their knowledge and experience, and introducing experiment where only what is wisest and most pondered over should come into effect.[22]

He adds, returning to personal matters, that his own little bit of confidence in a new, pure beginning has not vanished completely, 'but I have to cultivate it like a small, very fragile seedling, which makes me realise how cold and sunless my inner climate has become'.

As it was in the war, so now: there is still the anxious yet stubborn adherence to the personal – which does not in his case mean family, profession or earnings, but work – work at self-imposed tasks in the unworldly territory of his art. Rilke rejected the violence of revolution as emphatically as he did that of war; even from Switzerland he wrote disagreeing with a German acquaintance, a radical, who had expressed the opinion that the first thing to be done in Germany was to make a *tabula rasa* with regard to the past. Rilke held that nature, which is also active in the political sphere, knows of no such thing as a *tabula rasa*. His conservatism, if one can call it that, was not troubled about the break up of the old order – he had never for an instant mourned his one-time fatherland, the Hapsburg Empire. He had not condemned the Russian Revolution either, only – in conversation – said that the West could not understand what was happening in Russia. But Rilke thought in too natural or creaturely a fashion to imagine that something could come out of nothing, that healthy living could emerge from experiment or man be made honest by the enforced construction of better roads. About the perplexities and distortions which these years brought to mankind, and especially to Germany, he had a very definite feeling, which expressed itself for years as profound anxiety about the future. What he missed right from the first, and looked for in vain in the ferment of the Revolution was – as he said in the letter quoted above – 'the wisest, the most pondered over'.

When at the end of May an invitation arrived from Switzerland, Rilke accepted it eagerly. The Countess Dobrzensky had offered him hospitality at her house on the Lake of Geneva, and then the Zürich Readers' Circle at Hottingen wanted him to give a reading from his work. He had already decided in January to abandon his present surroundings. He only wanted to finish the work he had begun in Munich, and then he would be ready to escape from the scene of his wartime existence. 'Then, going away – this is, I realise, not altogether a trivial matter for me, it would, directly after these difficult Munich years, be not so much an interruption as a total break, I don't suppose (between you and me) that I should ever come back to Munich again.'[23] Obviously, however, Rilke had a return visit to Germany in mind at the time when he left Munich; for he and Lou Andreas-Salomé, who was staying with him during the last days, planned to meet in Germany that October, and he even reminded her of this when she was seeing him off on the platform. It was a Wednesday – June 11th 1919 – when Rilke said goodbye to Lou Andreas, his wife Clara and several other friends at Munich station, before boarding the express which was to take him to Lindau, from where he would reach Zürich the same day. It was for the poet a more thorough 'going away', a deeper farewell, than his most intimate friends had any idea of at the time. Lou Andreas-Salomé, in the book she dedicated to her friend, tells how at that moment 'an ominous remark from one of his old Paris letters' flashed through her mind: '. . . but I am going as animals go when the close season is over'.[24]

What Rilke was looking for becomes clear as, stage by stage, he begins to find, gradually making good the losses of his long silent period and winning through to happiness and the completion of his work. But he soon realises that a short beneficial change such as unscathed neutral Switzerland can offer him will not be enough unless, with the hoped-for return to health, a real return into the world, his own world, is going to be possible. What the exiled poet needs after the first trial of his new host country is, so to speak, a patch of fertile soil and a kindly climate in which to cultivate the work lying before him. When, at the end of 1919, depressed and at a loss after the first rather disconnected and unsettled months in Switzerland, he writes from the Tessin to his publisher Kippenberg and his wife: 'Order and security! Dear friends, when shall I find these things, so necessary to my great task, and where?' and goes on to tell them in moving words of his need for a year of seclusion in the quiet of the country, in some congenial spot, we entirely see the sense of his searching and striving.[25]

2

OUTSIDE

RILKE'S restless search during his nomadic years for a home and a plot of ground where he could cultivate his work had for its real aim 'the obtainment of an inner refuge'. He admits this repeatedly, with a candour that shows his self-knowledge to have been without illusions; 'only' – so the postscript runs – 'anyone as impressionable as I am is always imagining that the right outward setting can improve the state of affairs within'.[26] To begin with, the departure for Switzerland meant a journey into freedom, a step in the direction of *outside*; and it is not to be wondered at that at first, and for quite a time, Rilke hardly knew what to do with his recovered freedom. That he chose to go to Switzerland at all is remarkable and surprising: he had 'thought of it in former years as a country to pass through, . . . suspicious in a way of its famous "beauty", which seemed too obvious, too pretentious'.[27] When travelling through that country it had been his habit to draw the curtains in the compartment, leaving the fine view to his fellow travellers! It was certainly not outward impressions that the poet was now looking for, although – sometimes with wholehearted appreciation, sometimes with ironic disapproval – he could not fail to encounter them. After barely three months in Switzerland he refers in an almost frivolously derisive tone to the country's exaggerated natural beauties, which had apparently found an ally in the imagination of grand- and great-grandparents, coming as they did from lands where there was 'nothing' and finding here 'everything', in luxury editions, 'a nature with ups and downs, full of abundance, full of repetition, full of underlined objects'.[28] Rilke was not a man who felt at home among mountains: he did not really understand them, and there were far too many of them in Switzerland for his liking. He found the Swiss landscape 'eclectic'. He himself explains this hostile attitude when he says that less striking surroundings would not have made any impression on him at all; since Spain he has not been able to take in anything new; his nature is being driven from within, by the work banked up inside him, 'so powerfully and so constantly that it cannot be "impressed" any more'.[29] As we accompany Rilke on his way we should not forget that it is this banked-up work, impatient to burst from its confinement and pour into poems, this work waiting for liberation and redemption, by which he is driven.

A little book called *Letters to a Travelling Companion* (*Briefe an eine Reisegefährtin*) gives a very faithful account of Rilke's journey to Switzerland in the summer of 1919. He shared a demicompartment of the train from Munich to Lindau with a pretty young woman, a cabaret singer on her way to an engagement in Zürich. They got into conversation, and the young woman's experience and practical good sense were a help to her somewhat nervous travelling companion in dealing with customs and frontier formalities. The companion felt that he had to learn all over again how to travel, after being shut in for so long. They continued their journey together in the express from the Lake of Constance to Zürich, where Rilke was met at the station by emissaries of the Reader's Circle, the young lady by her friends and her dog. It goes without saying that this fleeting encounter – but was anything 'fleeting' to Rilke? – led to an acquaintance and an exchange of letters. These did not last very long, though long enough for Rilke's letters to give us his first impressions of Switzerland. He ate his first breakfast on the balcony of the Hotel Eden, 'looking out over the beautiful summer lake', he writes to her on the next day but one.

Already I can see what it means to be 'outside': these two days have been rich and good for me – it started strangely, first I stood looking into the windows of the scent shops – and if anyone had noticed my much happier expression as I walked back later on along the Bahnhof-strasse, they would never have guessed that it was the names *Guerlin* and *Houbigant* reflecting from me. Then came discovery after discovery: the French bookshop (*Crès*), new books, and, up above, on the third floor, some rooms full of pictures and today again a whole exhibition of French drawings and water-colours: to become aware again, after so many famished years, of the wonderful, sure, sensuous faculty of looking! And in addition to this, good and lively, serious and absorbing conversations with friends whom I hardly expected to be here: in short, if you wished me well, wished me a good development of the beginning which, thanks to you, was so good – your wishes have most definitely been fulfilled.[30]

But almost as soon as he had arrived in Zürich Rilke left again for Nyon on the Lake of Geneva, where he wanted to discuss the possibility of remaining in Switzerland with the Countess Mary Dobrzensky, who had asked him to stay with her in her chalet. It was this friend's invitation and her solicitude which had made it possible for him to come to Switzerland and to stay there for a time. His next letter to the 'travelling companion' was written from an hotel in Geneva; from there, as he was tired and in need of quietness and relaxation, he went on to Bern.

Here he really began to get on familiar terms with this new country and with its inhabitants. It was characteristic of him to lay enormous stress upon external things, a tendency to which he was always giving expression in his rejections and acceptances. He now began to take note of the landscape, the houses, the people, and to reach back to their source in the history of Switzerland. Wherever the secret influence of antiquity was still to be found, in stonework, inscriptions, inherited things, wherever historic forces had left their mark on the present, there Rilke felt himself drawn, there he felt on intimate terms with his environment. 'I must be allowed to start a new life wherever I am,' he wrote that summer, 'and to yield to the fancy that in this place or that tremendous events have happened in the past, which want to grow towards me with at least one of their branches, as if they belonged to me or my family. Only so can any place become profitable and familiar to me.'[31] As the months and years went by he continued to take this great interest in his adopted country, renewing it every time he moved from one place to another. He was in fact engaged in a perpetual investigation of everything about him that was rooted in the past, an endeavour to enter into relation with the living and the dead – between whose worlds he had never, all his life, made much distinction. It is not unimportant for the understanding of Rilke's inner life to know that whenever he visited a new place he tried to learn something of its topography, to discover the main dates in its history and the age of its buildings; that he looked for old houses, noticed the coats of arms, and, finally, never left a place without paying a visit to the churchyard, in order to decipher the lettering on the old tombstones. Scores of notes, including copies of epitaphs and other inscriptions as well as rough sketches, bear witness to this loving investigation of his environment. In his letters from Switzerland Rilke is continually describing objects which have struck him, and making notes about them. We learn from these letters that he studied genealogical almanacks and books on heraldry and of course visited historical museums – he was enthusiastic about the so-called Burgundy tapestry in the museum at Bern; they show us too how he discovered connections between these things and brought them into significant relationships with one another, constructing from them a little world in which he became more and more wrapped up and from which, when the time came, he dared to take off into the vastness outside. We see here how constant was the exile's need to strike roots and grow into his alien surroundings.

These surroundings spoke most intimately to him in Bern. He tells his publisher in a letter that this city 'turns out to be what was necessary in order to see more in Switzerland than the usual conspiracy of hotels in which a striking landscape has become innocently (or not so innocently?) involved. Here at last a face, a city with a face, and, in spite of all interferences, what a lineage, what staying power!'[32] He mentions the terrace in front of the Gothic cathedral, the unusual fountains, the 'wonderful situation of the Herren- and Junkerngasse, which gives the aristocratic mansions two faces: the one reserved, steep above the stone arcades, the other, on the terrace side, festive, overlooking the gardens which spread themselves out all the way down to the River Aare and on to the old Matte Quarter'.[33] Rilke soon began to make acquaintances and to gain entrance to some of these houses; he also paid visits to the owners of country mansions in the neighbourhood. The wide view of fields and hills bathed in the light of early summer, the peace of the landscape, aristocratic country houses in French eighteenth-century style, all had something to say to the foreign visitor; even the atmosphere of bourgeois self-confidence emanating from the town appealed to him.

During the last years of his life Rilke often went back to Bern. It was his nearest big town when, later on, he was living in Muzot, and he would go there to shop, to visit his friends and to stroll appreciatively through the old arcades and across the cathedral terrace. There he came to understand Switzerland 'with its unique pervadedness (*Durchdringung*) and its native unity'. Bern, 'in a remarkably clear and transparent way', gave him an insight into 'these countries that nature has built up out of frontiers and obstacles. . . . Their history is full of the power of nature', he continues in this letter to Germany, 'people, when they gathered in crowds here, had something of the consistency and hardness of mountains, and in their most decided moments the rush of their will was a continuation of that irresistibility with which the torrents arrive in the valleys.' By way of a detour through history and nature Rilke came to the people, of whom he said that 'their disposition is moulded out of the most uniform material and cut from one piece: . . . so that in each of them the whole nation is present (a thing one misses so with us, where one is always dealing with the obtuse or even amorphous, or else being confronted with the individual as an exception)".[34]

Only later, when he has come definitely to prefer Geneva and is comparing it with Bern, does Rilke make some detailed and well-founded reservations about the city on the Aare: once he has discovered the Valais he prefers its landscape and atmosphere to those of Bern. When I was walking with him once near Sierre, he called my attention to the subtler light and hazier air of the Valais, and to the wooded slopes which reminded him of tapestry, comparing these surroundings with the harder, more obtrusive Bern landscape, whose contours seemed to him overclear. He said that he found this same hardness of contour in the pictures of Ferdinand Hodler, and in the course of our conversation he remarked on the connection between this feature of Hodler's work and the early impressions made on the painter by the country around Bern.

On July 7th Rilke went back to Zürich, with the intention of undergoing medical treatment in a sanatorium there. He gave up this plan, however, in spite of continuing ill health, staying in the hotel with the garden he liked, dining with Busoni, who was one of the poet's ardent admirers, and going a great deal into society. He was often to enjoy the stimulus of Zürich during his remaining years; but the city's modernity and busyness prevented him from ever finding a personal relationship to it. Throughout the rest of his life he was faithful to the French bookshop in the Rämistrasse, which he had discovered immediately after his arrival from Munich. The bookseller, Paul Morisse, a Parisian, was himself a man of literary judgment and a striking personality. Rilke ordered his books from him and wrote to him frequently over the years, giving his opinion of modern French poets and men of letters.

An acquaintance called Rilke's attention to a place in the Grison Mountains called Soglio, describing it in such a way that it sounded as if it might be the wanderer's promised land. The poet imagined, as he mused on this latest goal of his journeyings, 'a country with the southernest possible sky above it'. To the 'travelling companion' he spoke of this journey as his 'second exodus from Zürich': he had set out on July 24th, had hired a small carriage at St Moritz, in rain and bitter cold, to drive to Sils Baselgia, and had been frozen, 'in spite of Sacharoff's fine Russian fur coat which a guardian angel saw to it that I took with me'. He wanted to see his Danish translator, Inga Junghanns, at Sils-Baselgia, before going on over the Maloja Pass to his destination.[35]

3

THE LIBRARY IN SOGLIO

Six weeks after leaving Munich Rilke decided to settle for some time in a little village on a high-up mountain terrace – the village of Soglio. There, according to his own account, he experienced his first quiet moments in Switzerland; it was also the first time for ages that he had felt a stirring of his creative powers: he wrote in Soglio the 'experiment-proposition' published under the title *Primeval Sound* (*Ur-Geräusch*), a prose work which might perhaps be looked upon as the resumption of the 'main sentence' interrupted by the war. Yet he continued to bewail the dullness of his mental and spiritual faculties, a trouble for which there still seemed to be no cure in sight and which prevented him from re-entering a state of mind 'that once, earlier on, was my usual, everyday one, absolutely natural to me'.[36] In spite of this, as we read the innumerable letters written to his friends from Soglio, we get the impression that an inner thaw has already begun. The liveliness of his descriptions, the clarity and integrity with which he writes, as well as his warm appreciation of his temporary surroundings, all point to the fact that the 'numbness' complained of in Munich during the war has now been replaced by inward movement. Rilke's native innocence and naturalness come out in Inga Junghann's *Personal Reminiscences*, as she describes his arrival in Sils-Baselgia. This is only a brief sketch of the evening of July 24th 1919, made by the Danish author who translated *TheNotebooks of Malte Laurids Brigge*, but in this sketch something is preserved of Rilke's personality, which could not have been more natural and friendly[37]:

Long before he arrived I stood on the stairs leading to our attic and heard the rumble of the carriage as it came into the village. There they were at last. Rilke took hold of both my hands, kissed them, and looked at them for a long time, studying them. Then he smiled at me affectionately, while tears of happiness ran down my cheeks. We were to have our meal in the slant-ceilinged kitchen. I never had any guest at my table who got into the right mood as quickly as Rilke did. That he preferred light dishes I knew from former days. But it was a lucky chance that fried eggs on toast with a Madeira sauce of my own invention pleased him so much, reminding him immediately of Copenhagen. And when, finally, that last remaining jar of olives which I had just found in a Sils Maria shop roused a boyish appetite in Rilke together with a whole lot of cheerful Paris memories – it was more than any housewife had a right to hope for. 'May I take them with my fingers? We used to do that in Paris, where we bought them in the street and ate them straight out of the paper.' And now he started to talk about Paris before the war, about his friends there, about Rodin, André Gide, Trubetskoy, and many others. We sat for a long time at the table as if we had just eaten a big dinner, and when we got up at last it was to go out on to the balcony to look at the last light of sunset on the mountains. After that, indoors, in the small sitting-room, we talked about Scandinavia, about the sea, about Worpswede . . .

And finally we learn that this little party ended in a great deal of hearty laughter, as stories of North-German fishermen and other amusing anecdotes were told.

Features of Rilke's personality emerge here which ought not to be omitted from the picture that posterity forms of him. It would be misleading to think of him as a complicated, tormented, shy individual – which, among many other things, he certainly was – and not to allow that he also had a capacity for enjoying small happinesses and simple pleasures as well as an eye for the down to earth, humourous side of life. All those who shared a genuine relationship with him knew how unselfconscious and communicative he could be, remember his almost childlike gratitude for small acts of kindness, and know that his enjoyment of life would often shed its sunshine upon intimate circles. No one who heard him laugh could ever forget it, any more than the occasion that caused such merriment. His laugh was light, clear as a bell and full of warmth; it was free from spite and constraint, free from any nervousness, bitterness or irony. Not only the wide mouth laughed, under the thin, dark, drooping moustache, but, most remarkably of all, the eyes laughed too. Little, star-shaped wrinkles appeared at the corners of his eyes and these joined in the laughter. In boisterous moments Rilke could play the fool and provoke his companions to a crescendo of mirth; and when the hilarity he felt and aroused had risen to its height he would savour it to the uttermost. All Rilke's friends were familiar with his humour, loved it and thought of it as one of his finest gifts. He could relish comic incidents and funny stories – and occasionally tell such stories himself. In propitious hours his sense of humour would suffuse his conversation, with results that were delightful, never merely witty or clever. Such moments of relaxation were necessary to him as to everyone, but, without meaning to do so, he made them delightful. In many of his letters too – though only when he was writing to intimate friends whose likemindedness he could be sure of – his humour and tendency to satire show themselves. The doctor who attended him during his last illness confirmed to me that Rilke kept his sense of humour until the end of his life. It is true that he usually observed strict moderation as to food and drink, but it is also true that he appreciated careful cooking and good wine. I have seen a copy of a gastronomical guide to Paris – *Le Guide du Gourmet à Paris* – which Rilke once brought back for a Zürich friend: it was inscribed by his own hand and there were marginal notes in his writing on various Paris restaurants.

The fact is that when the poet made a simple human contact with anyone whose personality vibrated in sympathy with his own, and in whose company he could be unconstrained and perfectly open (though never familiar in a cheap way) he had no difficulty in passing from small talk to the discussion of deeper, more vital matters. Inga Junghann's *Reminiscences* of the Sils-Baselgia visit also show how intensely at that time, in spite of complaints about unproductiveness, he was concerned with the creative work which was the centre of his life. On the evening after his arrival he told his hosts with great feeling about the destruction of the Castle of Duino and about the times when he had stayed there with the Princess Thurn und Taxis; then he read some extracts from the unfinished Elegies 'by the light of a single candle flickering in an old iron Engadine candlestick'.

After staying for three days in the Engadine, Rilke set out one cool morning to travel by mail coach over the Maloja Pass. In

Maloja the unknown passengers got out, and now, alone and in good spirits, he enjoyed the ride down into the sunlit Bergell. During the wait at Vicosoprano he occupied himself with looking at the coats of arms on the houses and at 'a certain fountain'. At Promontogno, where a side-road branches off to Soglio on its mountain terrace, only a luggage cart was available to take him to his destination. The distance being short, Rilke got into the rustic vehicle with his luggage and, after a steep climb through a chestnut wood, arrived in Soglio at midday. There he went to the Palazzo Salis, which had now been converted into a guest house.

The poet found much in Soglio that other refuges in other localities were to give him more completely; but for the time being he was well satisfied and quite at home in this mountain village so delightfully imbedded between alpine and southern vegetation. Among the congenial things it had to offer him were: an old house complete with inherited furniture, links with the past, a library room where he could work undisturbed, candle-light on the writing-desk, a path through the garden. During the perplexed, unhappy time that he spent in the Tessin the following winter he was seized with a longing for this haven which had satisfied so many of his deepest needs. To his publisher in Leipzig he sent from Locarno three photographs of the Soglio library, to show him just what it was that he needed and was looking for. . . .[38] That this attachment was not just retrospective can be seen from the letters he wrote to his friends from Soglio. How observantly, how almost tenderly, he describes the garden as he found it on the first day of his visit:

. . . Then I discovered the old garden, which in parts is beautifully wild, in others, alas, disreputably so . . . but the box edgings round the lawns are still trimmed in the traditional way, while pieces of architecture have been made out of the tall box bushes beside the old, tumbled-down wall. In between are masses of wild flowers, half-wild roses, violets, currant-bushes with ripe currants, and a few cherry trees covered with bright red morellas. And everywhere the wonderful grey gneiss, which supports the terraces and forms a flight of (four broken) steps; and above the growth a tranquil, uplifted vase. . . .[39]

So that Rilke should not be disturbed by the noise the children made, the landlord gave him the use of the library, where guests were not in the ordinary way allowed:

The quietest part of the house, with a robust table and a glorious armchair, a spinet, and, on every side, rows of books right up to the ceiling, which I can browse in and dust to my heart's content. The youngest in this book collection dates from Napoleonic times, while the backward age-limit may well reach into the sixteenth century. I've just been shaking the soft dust from a few Alduses and Elzeviers.

The little library became more and more of a work-room for the poet, who was making discoveries in eighteenth-century almanacks and books of verse and reading Linné, and he praised, as he put it, the instinct which had brought him there. In these surroundings he became conscious once more of his 'benign sensitivity', and he asked the friend he was writing to: 'Must I, by the way, reproach myself for being most deeply affected by human influences when they reach me through the vibrations of inherited things?'[40]

Rilke's letters to German and Austrian friends are packed full of descriptions – by means of which he tries to make them understand why it was that he needed 'a thorough outward change', and why it had been essential for him to take a 'journey to a foreign country not immediately affected by the war', a country whose landscapes, cities, rivers, bridges and forests he longed to see: 'for what I missed most sorely during these last painful years was just the old, close communion with nature'.[41] And in the same letter:

A map of Switzerland will show you plainly the position of the Bergell, what a haste this valley is in to reach Italy; and halfway up the mountainside, overlooking the valley, is this little village roofed with grey slabs of gneiss, a (Protestant alas and therefore empty) church on a slope, very narrow lanes; one is living in the midst of it in the old family home of the Salises (Soglio line), even surrounded by their old furniture, and for good measure the Palazzo has a French terrace garden with the old stone edgings, box trimmed in the traditional manner and everywhere a crowd of the gayest summer flowers. I must tell you another time about the chestnut woods on the lower slopes, marching in sublime beauty down towards Italy.[42]

The cue word 'Spain' occurs also in these despatches from Soglio: the mountain village reminds him of his time in Spain before the war – Spain, from which he had had to tear himself away with a painful effort after six months; and to leave Soglio too was going to cost him a painful effort. 'Old houses, old things, can exercise the most powerful influence over me, old cupboards and drawers breathe out such a homely smell, as I told you I have all this sort of thing around me here – I gave you, didn't I? a description of wood carvings, stucco work, my four-poster bed.'[43] And fresh variations on the themes of the garden and the oldfashioned library-room are always cropping up in these letters in which he breathes so freely.

His stay in Soglio was important to Rilke in other, more present and immediate, ways. To begin with, this Grison valley, sloping down to the Italian Lakes and belonging to the Italian language, brought him, for the first time for years, close to Italy and under her sky, so that he felt closer in his mind to Venice, to his friends there, and to his pre-war memories – in a word, to the native land of his unfinished Elegies. Then during this time he discovered a poem which moved him profoundly and to which from now on he was to yield a special place among the literary experiences of his life: this was Carl Spitteler's *Prometheus and Epimetheus*. A book of a very different – political – sort, which he also read at Soglio, was Wilhelm Mühlon's *The Devastation of Europe* (*Die Verheerung Europas*). Coming into his hands as it did in these early post-war days, Mühlon's book, which had been published during the first year of the war, made a special appeal to Rilke. In it he heard, probably for the first time, a German expressing a view of the painful war years which was very close to his own: that view which had isolated him in Munich, making him feel cut off from all communication with his surroundings. In the letter Rilke wrote to Mühlon (whom he met in Bern) we get a deeper understanding of the politics which formed the background to his Munich life, and which he found so distasteful:

If during those first months, when fuel was being added to the lunacy from all sides, I'd had the least idea that somewhere such words of sorrow and conscience were being written what a support, what a help it would have been to me at a time when one was being refuted by everybody and everything, when one was suddenly left alone with one's innermost feelings, learning that there wasn't any, wasn't the slightest, chance of them being shared. This experience happened so far within me, and the five dreadful years made such a thorough job of it, that I still bear the mark of it on me. And that is why these pages of yours are as understandable and important to me today as they would have been in November Fourteen, and I think people ought to read them again now, for although everything you foresaw and feared has happened, the German – inexplicably – is still in need of the same warnings; he has not got over his touchiness, his insularity, his lack of self-reliance; even when he looks at himself critically he is still, after so many changes, confronting himself at the level of his old mistakes, with which he is just as pleased as ever. And that is why the most moving thing which can be said of your book is that it is so thoroughly German: little by little, not all at once (for the German was in fact overwhelmed by that exploitation of the Wilhelmian era,* when his qualities were so misrepresented) – little by little, every German, by reason of the roots he has, should have come to feel and act just so and not otherwise. The quickness of your perceptions, the unusual accuracy of the way you express yourself, make your book a remarkable one: its message is a straightforward answer to the German nature: – woe, woe to it if it does not recognise itself there and find the way back.[44]

Rainer Maria Rilke's prose work – if we leave out the far from artless prose of the volumes of letters – is not bulky. The *Malte* novel was the only book of its kind that he attempted. There, the direct precursor of Proust, Joyce and Musil, he succeeded in breaking down the traditional novel form, replacing the narrative's chain of consecutive happenings by a series of associatively linked inner events, and thus drawing nearer to psychological truth. Lou Andreas-Salomé tells us that he intended to write a 'military novel', using for material his early experiences at the St Pölten Military School and the terrors he endured there. During his later years Rilke often recounted episodes from his boyhood and his time at St Pölten; he wrote down one such reminiscence in September 1914, but it remained a fragment.[45] When he had finished *Malte* and was trying, bewildered and at

* The reign of Wilhelm II, 1888-1918. Translator.

a loss, to find a new beginning, some of his close friends advised him to undergo a course of psycho-analysis. He discussed the possibility of having such treatment, and the likelihood of being helped by it, with a Munich psychiatrist, Count Stauffenberg. 'I quite see', he wrote in 1914,

that those who rely entirely on themselves, on their lives being useful and bearable, may be helped by having a spiritual nausea induced in them, enabling them to vomit up, little by little, the uselessness and misunderstanding of childhood. But I? Do I not depend on making angels, things, animals, even monsters when necessary, precisely out of that which could not be lived because it was too huge, too premature, too horrible?[46]

It is clear from these words that Rilke was fully aware of the connection between his difficult youth and the kind of poetry he wrote, since he expected psychiatry to hinder rather than to help his art. He seems to have been afraid that the application of Freud's analytical methods to his inner life would have a harmful effect on the process (which *is* Rilke's poetry) of transforming the soul's inward space into an imaginary world filled with images.

In this connection the essay called *Primeval Sound* which he wrote at Soglio in August 1919 shows how unique and how thorough was his self-knowledge. Starting from a memory of his schooldays, Rilke here examines the poet's true function – which is, he says, to use the five senses simultaneously.[47] In this strange, closely packed treatise, which is not quite like anything else he wrote, he touches, as Bassermann truly says, 'on the problem he was most conscious of when using language creatively: how to express an experience directly in words, without subjecting it to the supervisory mediation of thought – convey it in all its actuality, undiluted by verbal description'.[48] Rilke spoke some months later, in a letter from Locarno, of the often unsatisfactory behaviour of language, which is outward and superficial when one

means it to be as inward as possible, an innermost speech, not plucked from the top, from the stalk, but gathered as language seed. . . . Oh, how often one longs to speak a few degrees deeper, my prose in the 'Suggested Experiment' does lie deeper, a shade further in the ground than that in *Malte*, but only a thin layer is penetrated and one is left surmising what talk may be like *there*, where the silence is.[49]

(By the 'Suggested Experiment' Rilke means the prose piece *Primeval Sound* written in Soglio; he emphasised repeatedly that this poetic title, under which it was published, did not originate with him.)

When September brought all the signs of approaching autumn to Soglio, Rilke became really apprehensive and dismayed. He did not know where to go next, where to find shelter for the coming months. How often during his nomadic life must he have seen the onset of autumn without knowing in which direction to turn his steps, or where his next dwelling-place would be. Such an unsettled existence may be helpful to an artist when he is young – but Rilke, essentially lonely in spite of all his human ties and contacts, was now in his forty-fourth year. And he was literally not at home anywhere, not able to call any place his own. His relatives – mother, grandmother, wife, daughter – were remote from him, almost strangers; he had lost his possessions in the war, and there was nothing he could regard as his own property. He saw himself as an eternal stranger adrift in a foreign country, yet he could not bring himself to return to Germany. We can imagine what the coming of autumn meant to this delicate man, no longer young, who did not know where his winter was to be spent, and who, for a short while more like dream than durable reality, had been living in an enchanted palace: this man whose life had been a series of emigrations, who had no means of his own, and who for four whole years had been unspeakably tormented by his inability to write. . . . 'It is one of the hardships of these days', he laments, after the first September storm had come down upon Soglio,

that this room (the library), with all its peculiarities, is so right for me; how I would hasten towards it if I knew that somewhere it existed just like this in a house that wasn't a guest-house and where it could be mine for years! Already I am speaking sadly of it, this room that I greeted so joyfully when I found it; nevertheless, it has been a most propitious time, this stay in Soglio.[50]

There were two clues to guide him in planning his immediate future: the chalet at Nyon, to which he could return at any time, and, above all, the readings from his works which he had agreed to give in various Swiss towns. These readings had prompted his journey to Switzerland and were his financial justification for staying there. He planned to travel over the Furker, 'which would have enabled me from Gleitsch onwards, along the Rhone, to follow the route of Goethe's second Swiss journey, albeit in the opposite direction'. However, having left Soglio in pouring rain on September 22nd and encountered a dense snowstorm on the coach journey through the Maloja, he hurried on to Chur, stayed there two days and then took the express train to Lausanne. All further movements were to be decided at Nyon. As a precautionary measure against a return to Munich, Rilke arranged for a young couple to have his flat there – a little trick which served as pretext and excuse for staying away. And then – these words written from the shore of Lake Geneva: 'Saying goodbye to Soglio wasn't easy. Much inner life was interrupted at that parting. And what began as delight – finding the little old library, so suitable, just as though made for me – had to end as sorrow: someday such a room for a long, long time, and, in addition, all the solitude of a house and garden:—God grant it me. *This* only, nothing but this.'[51]

4

THE TROUBADOUR

RILKE'S wandering life was part voluntary, part involuntary. His inner daemon drove him to lead such a life – but on the other hand he is always complaining of the way things are and wishing that they were different. 'By lamplight at the family table' could never be his life's pattern (another difference, incidentally, between Rilke and Hofmannsthal, the good citizen and family man). Rilke did not belong to the Age of the Good Citizen, rather to an imaginary Baroque Age, inhabited by feudal barons and gypsies, where society's orderly and disorderly members lived tolerantly together. The manner of living to which he remained faithful throughout his life was not the manner of the century into which he was born; that he took Bettina's part against Goethe shows which side he was really on. The motive of the ancestor's survival and fulfilment in the descendent, which occurs so often with Rilke, is, romantic though it may seem, a symbol for the presence in himself of a past mode of existence, whereby he seeks to justify his essential unlikeness, his non-conformity. Rilke was the last of the troubadours. When he travelled by train, ate at restaurants and stayed in hotels he was making an unavoidable concession to the century; but when, much more readily, he took a coach or went as a guest to an old *palazzo* or castle he was doing something that seemed to him to be fraught with meaning. We can see now why the last place to make an 'impression' on him was Spain, a country which had not gone in for modern developments, where nobles and beggars lived side by side and took each other for granted. In Switzerland, however, it was not easy to find conditions to satisfy these deeply felt needs. With all the inflexible obstinacy of the gentle, the sensitive, the impressionable, Rilke continued his travels about the country, convinced against every probability that the conditions for finishing his interrupted work would be granted to him there. This painful ordeal of being always on the move, of seeking and not finding, of hesitant starts and fruitless waiting, was to last for fourteen months. The poet's recovery after the six most bewildering and unproductive years of his life was not to begin until the winter spent in Berg Castle, when seeds were sown that would burst into glorious blossom later, about the Tower of Muzot. Only then shall we find him enclosed again mentally and physically in an enchanted circle, with his powers unfolding freely and nothing to hinder his absorption in his work. Even so, the shapeless fourteen months helped him. He was always growing more familiar with his new surroundings, and he formed a number of human relationships many of which developed into firm, reliable friendships.

In striking contrast to the aristocratic women friends and patrons in Rilke's life is the young girl Marthe, the little Parisienne who had meant so much to him in the days before the war and who is so often mentioned in his letters. He found her, he writes, 'when she was seventeen years old and in the last stages of misery, she was my *protégée*, a working-class girl but with those natural gifts of heart and mind which you only find in French girls'.[52] Before going to stay with the Countess Dobrzensky at Nyon he spent a few days with Marthe at a little-place on Lake Geneva. He had hopes that her presence would help him to find his way back into his own real world. He expected the meeting to be 'almost a return to Paris', and was convinced that even a few days in her company 'would repair the fracture in my life, re-uniting past and present'. Once again reality did not come up to expectation. After Marthe had gone, Rilke spent practically the whole of October at Nyon. He occupied his time there in preparing for the reading-tour he was about to embark on, taking in a number of Swiss cities. The first of these readings was given in Zürich on the evening of October 27th.

The tour was an ordeal for Rilke. It was years since he had made a public appearance, and the business of having to read aloud to a large gathering seemed to him the very opposite of what he ought to be doing. These days 'went against the grain' of his nature, he wrote to the 'travelling companion', whom he had found again in Zürich; instead of being occupied with outward affairs and meeting people, he needed 'the exact opposite: . . . the other direction, self-communing, of which the weeks at Soglio were only a small beginning'.[53] This may explain why, in introducing his Work on these occasions, Rilke always started from the assumption that the audience would find his poems difficult to understand. He was afraid that the sense of 'immediate co-operation', so necessary in getting poetry across to a big gathering, would fail to appear. In order to establish contact with his public he had written an introductory address, in which he briefly described the characteristic features of his poems and explained why it was that they so often dealt with the past. He says in the manuscript of this address:

The works of which I am being allowed to show you some examples start somehow from the conviction that it is possible to give a pure demonstration of the width, variety, and even the fullness of the world. For: yes! I hoped to exalt the poem into such a demonstration, and through it to become capable of a lyrical understanding of all appearances, not only those with an emotional appeal: of setting each thing – animal, plant, every happening – in its own special domain of feeling. Do not be misled by my frequent invocation of images from the past. *The past too is alive in the profusion of happenings, if we think of it in terms of its intensity, not its content.* We are members of a world which, producing movement upon movement, force upon force, seems to be plunging irresistibly into a less and less visible state; and we are dependent on that superior visibility of the past if we want to present an image of the muted splendour that still surrounds us.[54]

The poet would enter the halls where he gave his readings – and where there was never a vacant seat – nervously, almost reluctantly, wearing evening-dress and white gloves. His fame was great, but he had never been able to do much with the outward manifestations of it. He was very conscious in those days of having 'no fixed abode', and his Zürich lecture's great public success – an audience of 600 was a big one for a reading of lyric poetry – did nothing to ward off the 'sudden disconsolateness . . . which often overwhelmed (him), especially in restaurants and hotels'.[55] He would have liked to cancel the evening at St Gallen, but financial considerations prevailed, and he overcame his reluctance. (He had to give a second reading in Zürich, after which he read in St Gallen on November 7th, in Lucerne on the 12th, in Basle on November 14th, in Bern on the 18th, and finally in Winterthur on November 28th.) The rapid sale of his books in Swiss bookshops at that time gave solid evidence of the reverberations his voice had aroused. His letters describing the tour report that his confidence in the project increased with every city that he visited, and that, on the whole, those evenings brought him some satisfaction. The account sent to Anton Kippenberg, his publisher, is revealing. He has thought up, he says, a method of introducing his readings which has worked exceptionally well with

the Swiss, who are often stolid, dry and difficult to penetrate . . . I don't just give them poems, I start with a general introduction, always more or less the same – and then I begin the second part of the evening with an impromptu *causerie*, the theme always being adapted to the place and designed to lead back to my work. (For example, at St Gallen there was a little dissertation on Regina Ullmann, in Basle I introduced the important name of Bachofen in an unexpected connection; and I wound up in Winterthur, where they have a first-rate collection of pictures, by making Cézanne the centre of my observations.) Without anyone noticing it, these talks did such a lot of preparing and enlightening that afterwards even very personal and 'difficult' poems were received with unusual enthusiasm.[56]

Rilke's way of adapting himself to an audience, as well as his habit of making more or less impromptu comments on individual poems before reading them, struck a responsive chord in his listeners, which continued to vibrate. Much appreciated too in this multi-lingual country was the fact that when reading translations of poems he always gave the original French or Italian texts first. 'I believe', he ends his report to Kippenberg, 'I have to thank this inoffensiveness for the favourable notices given to my readings–so I'm told–by the Geneva papers and especially the *Gazette de Lausanne*. I myself never read criticisms in the press.'

It is only right to dwell in some detail on this tour because it was in such complete contrast to Rainer Maria Rilke's usual habits; he had not given any public readings for ten years, and the Swiss *tournée* was the last occasion of its kind in his life. He was an excellent interpreter of his own poems; in his pure German and spoken by his warm, virile baritone voice, the lines, firmly stressed, supple and clear, sounded magnificent. But however well such performances went, Rilke usually read, and liked to read, only in private, in homely surroundings, to one other person or a few familiar friends. It did give him a real feeling of triumph, however, to be able to bring a hallful of people under the spell of his voice – controlling and driving them 'like a four-in-hand'! (How significant too is this image: conveying the necessary idea of power, but conveying it by means of an allusion to the past.) Afterwards Rilke refused a request that he would publish the manuscript of his general introduction in a journal. He had an idea that the spoken address, inspired by the circumstances of the moment or prepared in view of them, did not belong to the same sphere as the written word. The difference can be seen if we compare the manuscript of the Zürich address, or as much of it as we have in Basserman's book, with the 'Suggested Experiment', written at about the same time.

In the way Rilke courted his audience we see again how pliable and adaptable was his mode of expression. He shows this adaptability, not in his poetry, where he is independent of relationship, but every time that he turns towards a particular person or a particular milieu and tries to establish a close connection with them. These modifications of style and dialectic, which naturally come out most clearly in his conversations and lectures, can also be seen when we compare his letters written to different people. Light is then thrown on the finer shades of his relationship with each correspondent. As sometimes happens with poets and artists who have a streak of the feminine in their nature, Rilke's conversation was one thing in male society and quite another when a woman was present: his attitude changed at once and instinctively – not only out of courtesy to the female sex. But the point should be stressed that such dialectic flexibility was only a kind of superstructure on an altogether firm, consistent base.

There were times when Rilke was so much inclined for talk that his work, and even his correspondence, suffered almost to the point of coming to a temporary full stop. Even though such lectures as those mentioned above were exceptions, he could in times of intense sociability direct all his communicativeness into conversation and burn it up there. It was perhaps due even more to the fascination of his personality than to his literary fame that he was so often endangered by the excessive claims that people made on him. He cultivated human relationships with such intensity that sometimes his sympathy for other people, his sharing of their lives and problems, turned into a painful, helpless bewilderment – until the effect on his own delicate health drove him to flight. Anyone who is surprised by Rilke's search for refuges and hermitages where he could concentrate quietly on his work overlooks the fact that not only his many personal and social involvements but also public intrusiveness allowed him no peace for work as long as he was living in or near a town. Only the strictest solitude, the most complete seclusion in an out-of-the-way place, could save him from becoming a prey to people, from being emotionally drained and annihilated by exposure to their claims, their love, their restlessness. For the poet put his work before everything that was purely human and personal. Katharina Kippenberg says of him that he was a 'work-addict', not a 'self-addict'.

However, Rilke was fundamentally resilient enough to be able for a short while not only to put up with being prevented from following his vocation but to find some positive good in his condition as a homeless wanderer. His 'curious public behaviour' – as he sometimes called his reading tour – brought him much closer to this new country and its new people, especially perhaps to the people of Basle. Of them he said:

They behaved to me in a specially welcoming and understanding way; I'm not sure that the evening there wasn't the best of them all. Then one of the most beautiful of the aristocratic houses (belonging to the Burkhardts) opened to me in hospitality, even in friendship. . . . There followed unexpectedly rich hours, when even the well-known Swiss obstacles did not make themselves felt. (And what beautiful things, what a combination of intimacy and dignity in those cultivated, quietly inhabited houses!) There was, besides, the circle around the painter Nikolaus Stöcklin, his sister Francisca and a few young artists of the friendliest disposition: they gave a little party for me in Stöcklin's studio, which I must tell you about. . . .[57]

In Basle too he was delighted to meet Wanda Landowska again, the famous harpsichord player, whose interpretative art he admired and with whom he had the bond of personal memories of Tolstoy. In Lucerne he admired the ancient bridges with their painted gables, but seems to have been disappointed that no one

from 'the old families' came to his lecture.[58] (How he keeps
harking back to this theme of the local, the hereditary, the
traditional!) His reception in Zürich, and even more in Winterthur, did not lead to any closer ties with local literary circles, but
it brought him the hospitality of certain families and people
from which specially intimate friendships developed: the story
of Rilke's last years can never be told without mention of the
Reinhart family at Winterthur and the old Wunderly-Volkart
house at Meilen on Lake Zürich. Rilke never had much to say
about Zürich, whose former self-contained unity at the mouth
of the lake had of recent years been sacrificed to an encroaching
modernisation which had changed the city's whole appearance.
His innate courtesy kept him silent where he could not find
anything appreciative to say, and it is perhaps not far wrong to
conjecture that he never quite overcame the feeling of being a
stranger in Zürich, because for him the city lacked a recognisable,
genial face. He owed good, restorative hours to the painter Marie
Laurencin, who passed through Zürich in December: her pictures
appealed to him and called up memories of French painting. We
do well not to forget those psychological 'obstacles' which the
sensitive, cosmopolitan poet had to overcome, no doubt oftener
than he mentions them, in approaching the Swiss people, whom
he found so 'difficult to penetrate': otherwise it might seem that
the wanderer had simply made up to Switzerland with the idea
of spending the rest of his life there in modest comfort.

As we read Rilke's letters we are continually surprised to find
his responses of joy and pain, approval and disapproval, comfort
and complaint, existing so close together, to the extent that there
are sometimes contradictory reactions to one and the same object.
This makes the letters confusing but also remarkably genuine
and spontaneous. Their writer would seem to have had the
curious power of being able to entertain contradictory feelings
and moods simultaneously, or else to have been capable of passing
with extraordinary speed from one mood or feeling to another, a
sort of psychological interchangeableness. He found people, cities,
landscapes, environments at once delightful and hateful. Who
can explain it? We recall – one instance of many – how sinister
and terrible Paris could seem to him, and then how wonderful,
invigorating, enjoyable. It is surprising too that during the few

days between his lectures in Zürich and St Gallen, Rilke should have written to the 'travelling companion' complaining about his 'homelessness' and the 'sudden disconsolateness' which kept seizing him, and then have gone on to compose the glorious sonnet which, on November 3rd 1919, he wrote as an inscription in Mme Nanny Wunderly-Volkart's copy of his translation of Elizabeth Barrett-Browning's *Sonnets from the Portuguese*.[58a] According to the dates given by Ernst Zinn in the *Selected Works*, this was the first poem that Rilke had written since November 1915 (there may possibly have been a few others, as yet unpublished, during the long silent period between his army call-up and his first winter in Switzerland, but certainly nothing important was written during that time). It is most essential that those censorious critics who take the poet to task for his 'complaining letters' should be confronted with the work, the marvellous achievement of the poetry; for, as he well knew, his dreadfully perturbed nature was justified only by his creative work. In the poems which he now and then inscribed in copies of his books, or wrote in visitors' books, he took very little interest; in most cases he did not keep a copy. They had to be laboriously collected after the poet's death, and there are enough of them to fill about two hundred printed pages. Needless to say, many are of less importance than others, written when his powers had begun to fail, but there are, too, some very beautiful poems among them. One of these is certainly the sonnet already mentioned, written on November 3rd 1919: 'When a heart's long made giving-up a duty'. Since, as far as we know, this is Rilke's first post-war poem, it may be given here, as an indication of his state of mind at the time, and also as showing the masterly craftsmanship of this rich poet, even when so prodigally scattering his gifts:

> When a heart's long made giving-up a duty,
> and laid all hope and confidence aside,
> and then awakes to hear itself accried:
> 'You overflowing fountain of all beauty!' –
>
> How hard for it to bound on being unbound,
> to hasten to returning happiness!
> That heart, accustomed to a mute distress,
> transmuting love is forcing into sound.

Here sounds a heart that sorrowed silently,
and fears to handle, as beyond its due,
the wealth of its victorious poverty.

Who's full? whose giving is most unconfined? –
One who goes on seducing: for flesh, too,
achieves its incarnation in the mind.

Although this sonnet is about the poetess Elizabeth Barrett-Browning, it quite obviously reflects Rilke's own subjective state: it is he who has long made giving-up a duty, laying hope and confidence aside; he is the one accustomed to a mute distress, and it is his heart which has learned from love how to sound again and which fears 'the wealth of its victorious poverty'.

Longing whole-heartedly for quietness and seclusion, Rilke went at the beginning of December to Locarno in the Tessin. But the three winter months that he spent in a pension there disappointed all his hopes. Nowhere could he succeed in making contact with his surroundings and with his real self. The letters written during this visit speak continually of the inner discord he feels and of his tormenting inability to adapt himself to the new place. Even letter-writing was painful to him. The obligation that he set himself in his artistic work, to do every task well, dominated his life like a strict law, and now made even dealing with big arrears of correspondence seem a hard and responsible undertaking. He admitted that on days when the right words would not come he preferred not to use any at all – 'and as many, many days will be like this, a general standstill looks like setting in'.[59] On another occasion he laments about it being 'a sign of hidden, inward weariness, that so many things stare me in the face, as though I could never get above and beyond them'.[60] Nothing seemed easy to him. All day long he kept asking himself 'Can I do it?' as though before an examination. He admitted that this was 'a ridiculous state of affairs, a kind of illness', but a year of solitude, he thought, would rid him of it.

In spite of the state he was in – which they make so evident – the letters he wrote from Locarno bear moving witness to the poet's great powers of self-criticism and to his sense of inner direction. He realised that, in contrast to the complexity of his psychical make-up, his physical needs were simple, and that the fulfilment of a few trivial, primitive conditions would suffice to re-unite him to his own true nature. He remembered the time when walking barefoot had given him intense pleasure, the contact of the naked sole with the ground bringing a thrill that was quite unique and no less delightful than the finest spiritual experience. He was longing to find a doctor – a wish that he had mentioned to his friend the doctor-poet Hans Carossa in Munich during the war. Now Rilke said that he needed a doctor 'who would help me towards a new beginning with my body, so that I could, as it were, serve a noviciate in it, and use it more wisely for as long as it retains some flexibility – but doctors, when one comes to the more subtle of the invisible complaints – doctors, as Malte discovered, simply do not exist'.[61]

What Rilke, all his life, expected of his ideal doctor was neither remedies nor drugs, not any arbitrary interference with the natural course of organic processes. He had an almost mystical belief in nature's wisdom and healing power. He believed that discordances between a man and his body can only be resolved when the man complies obediently with the creaturely tendencies of nature, instead of arrogantly attempting to turn them in another direction. We have it on good evidence that Rilke put this conviction into practice, refusing to take medicine when he was ill. 'We used to be such good friends, my body and I', he said once to a doctor when he was suffering from his incurable illness. Rilke was convinced that he could only be fully himself when in perfect health, a state of unclouded physical well-being, and that if he were to fall seriously ill he would turn into a completely different person and have to begin a new, unknown, incomprehensible life. He was certain that he would never be able, like some others, to turn illness to advantage for his creative work.

These ideas of Rilke's link up with his practice of never seeking poetic inspiration outside the framework of his own existence. He led a regular life, normal in all respects, and never took narcotics or stimulants. The 'artificial paradise' was something quite unknown to him. We have already mentioned his moderation in eating and drinking. He did not smoke at all, which was most unusual for an Austrian. When I expressed surprise at this one day, he told me with a smile that his father had forbidden him to do it when he was very young and that by the time the ban was lifted he, Rainer, had lost all inclination for it, so that his father, who earlier on had worried in case his son should disobey him, ended up by worrying even more about the latter's refusal to smoke!

Rilke had good reason to feel cheerless and harassed, not to say bewildered, during that winter in Locarno. A woman in all sorts of interior and exterior difficulties had attached herself to him, exploiting his good nature and his weakness. But he never rebelled or lost his temper as a result of this predicament. At the worst he got irritable, but when this happened he would at once try to dispel the mood gracefully by giving it a humourous turn. For example, he refused to occupy a hotel room because the wall-paper, with its pattern of endlessly repeated little flowers, annoyed him. He said it reminded him of someone who kept on using a meaningless, silly word like 'please' or 'of course'; he could not stand these 'of course' wallpapers with their little posies of flowers. . . . But apart from such passing moods, Rilke's attitude to life at that time was characterised by submissive patience, as he waited for nature to cure him. There was something slavonic about this pious passivity with its refusal of outward action and its scorn of artificial remedies. 'As to myself', he wrote from Locarno,

sometimes I excuse my dreadful labile touchiness by attributing it to the all-too-precocious horrors and accomplishments of my childhood (oh, at that time I would have lain on stones if I'd thought God would reveal himself to me any sooner that way) – now I'm waiting for much about me to be set right, a certain stubborn human effort has become strange to me – the plant, the thing – they aren't ashamed of themselves either, when all goes right and well with them they simply thrive, full of joy at being what they are meant to be.[62]

However, what Rilke calls disinclination for work and unim-pressibility might well be called by another union with nature and a more-than-ordinary power of describing impressions. So relative are these things when looked at objectively. In his diary-like letters to Mme Nanny Wunderly-Volkart there are such wonderful accounts of what he is doing and reading, and, above all, of the natural world around him, that we are left asking ourselves who else could describe, for instance, a starry night as Rainer Maria Rilke sometimes does. . . . And those lines from a letter dated Christmas Day – are they not among the most vivid pieces of descriptive writing to come out of Rilke's years in Switzerland? They may be given here:

The chimes ring out continuously, they unravel all the hours, you think you hear an hour striking, and then the chimes play with it, it's as though little John had got hold of time and made a toy of it for the Child Jesus, up and down, little ladders for the heart, upwards and downwards, not going anywhere, already in a celestial place. I haven't heard such carillons since Belgium, there they were more remote, oldener, like pure rosary-beads slipping through the ears instead of through the fingers, here it is sweeter, more pagan or childlike, I don't know, here it is berries that ring when they are ripe. Yesterday, sweet sweet, they ripened in the night, I thought it must be in Losone at lovely St George's, for I was walking up the winding path towards the stars which is always my path of consolation when smallish troubles are trying to get the better of me. . . .' [63]

And then, at the end of February, listening for the first bird-voices announcing the spring, those voices that the poet likened to musicians tuning and practising – until he became aware of

one of the dark sort, more mature, a song already full of inwardness, which was to the others as a poem to a few words – how it shone towards God, already already, how devout it was, how full of itself, a song-bud still in the calyx of its sound, but already aware of its irrepressible fullness, pre-blissful, pre-afraid. Or rather, the fear was already there in its entirety, the pain common to all creatures, which cannot be divided, and which is as simple as the blissfulness over there, on the other side where all has been surmounted. [64]

Even so, Rilke says in the same letter that he is not sorry to be missing the spring in Locarno, where it is 'sure to behave like the teacher's darling, sitting on the front bench and knowing by heart all the homework set by Almighty God for next Monday. Round Basle there must be a spring that gets many an answer wrong, one that is often defiant and says *sha'n't*. – I've always preferred that sort.'

On March 4th 1920 Rilke left Locarno for the Schönenberg

estate near Prattel in Basle-Land, a new and welcome resting-place on that zig-zag journey through Switzerland which one hardly knows whether to call a pilgrimage, a flight, a voyage of discovery, or a mixture of all three. At last he was to be a guest again in a country house, and one that was an old family seat into the bargain – a thing the refuge-seeking poet particularly valued after months in hotels and pensions: friends from Basle were lending it to him.[65]

After a difficult start, for he did not find it easy to settle down in his new work-place, he stayed in Schönenberg throughout the spring: that more capricious, reluctant spring of the region, which, with all its sudden vagaries of weather and changes of temperature, he professed to like better than the too-beautiful southern variety. He did not, however, subject himself to the strict seclusion that he was to insist on later at Berg and Muzot. He had visitors, and went in and out of Basle, where he attended a performance of the St Matthew Passion in the cathedral and listened raptly to Karl Erb as the Evangelist, completely carried away by the impression that the singer made on him. The letters – there are surprisingly few of them – that Rilke wrote during the two months at Schönenberg hint discreetly at the anxiety and unhappiness from which he was suffering. A cold brought on 'a *malaise* which has had a far-reaching effect on my spirits',[66] but he admits that his persistent bad health 'is not the most deplor-able thing; what upsets me more is this: that my time in Switzer-land is coming to an end, irrevocably, on May 15th'.[67]

His position at this time was indeed rather desperate. His Austrian passport was about to expire while the new Czechoslovak one had failed as yet to arrive; and until this 'desirable document', as he called it, had been received from the Czech ambassador in Bern, the Swiss authorities could not renew his resident's permit. At the same time word came from Munich that the flats of all foreigners who had moved into the Bavarian capital after August 1st 1914 were to be confiscated. 'The sensation of being between two expulsions added considerably to my discomfort and disquiet', Rilke remarks although, incidentally, he had never intended 'to stay in Munich for ever'.[68] Meanwhile he asks the Princess Taxis whether he ought to take his new citizenship *à la lettre* and return to Bohemia. At any rate, he thinks, this would make a return to

Paris easier in the future. It is no exaggeration to say that during these years this homeless soul's homeless plight was officially recognised: in France, where all his possessions were confiscated during the war; in Austria, where he lost his citizenship as a result of the break-up of the Austro-Hungarian Empire; in Germany, where, as a foreigner, he lost his Munich flat, after being explicitly told by the authorities that no exception could be made for him; and in Switzerland, where, as a stateless alien, he was temporarily in danger of losing his residence-permit. . . . Rilke adds that whatever the decision of the Bern authorities might be, 'my financial state makes it impossible for me to remain abroad any longer'. He had been living in Switzerland on a sum of money paid to him in advance; this was now exhausted, and owing to the progressive devaluation of the German mark he could not change any further payments arriving from Germany into Swiss francs. 'Without the hospitality of Schönenberg,' he writes, 'I should have been over the frontier by now.'[69]

In the middle of May, after the Czech passport had arrived and been sent to Bern along with Rilke's application for an extention of his permit, the poet went for a few days to his friends at Meilen on Lake Zürich, then, over Whitsuntide, to Baden in the Aargau, and from there to Schönenberg again for a brief visit. At the home of mutual Basle friends he met Hofmannsthal and his wife and daughter. One is involuntarily reminded of the coolness between Gottfried Keller and C. F. Meyer on discovering that this re-encounter with the Vienna poet was regarded by Rilke purely and simply as an opportunity for making a malicious remark.[70] At last, before the middle of June, he found courage to launch out in the direction of Venice, where the Princess Taxis was expecting him.

5

VENICE — GENEVA — BERN — PARIS

A PLUNGE back into his past, his former life, his own great
outside world – that was what Rilke's journey to Venice meant to
him after that first year in Switzerland. He had known the City
of Lagoons since 1897; he had lived for some time during 1913
in the Princess Taxis' *mezzanine* in the Palazzo Valmarana, where,
surrounded by a wealth of roses, he had seen the Duse almost
daily. Memory after memory now confronted him, each in the
shape of some object – something that, before the war, he had
given to the Princess to complete the furnishing of her rooms.
He had last seen all these things – pictures, a small Italian
library with books in old bindings, a writing-desk – six years ago,
at the time when his re-union with the Thurn and Taxis couple,
after the dreary months of military service in Vienna, had given
him so much happiness. Now, once again, these friends left the
poet in possession of their *mezzanine* on their departure. Its
proportions delighted him, and he spent five weeks marvelling
at how little everything had changed, even the writing-desk that
he was using again after those long years. But while his highest
hopes were realised at finding these objects from the past so
unchanged, it surprised and distressed him to discover that he
was just as unchanged himself. 'At least,' he wrote,

that's how it seems to me – and it ought not to be like this after six
years, which after all must be considered as years of one's life, years
that have gone. Holding my breath has preserved me to some extent
throughout the ruinous time, and the numbness and immobility of
my heart really stood me in good stead – but now that I can test my
interior state on things I once loved it frightens me to find it so
undisturbed and unchanged, it is contrary to nature.[71]

Switzerland had felt to him like a 'waiting-room', an impression
which was heightened by the absence of any threads of memory
waiting there to be picked up. But the longer he stayed in Venice
the more alarmed he became at the standstill he found both in

himself and in his environment. Only now did Rilke realise that there is no going back in life, 'that life cannot be joined up again, in the way I thought it could, at the spot where it was fractured by the war – everything has changed, and travelling "for pleasure", for the sake of absorbing superficial, somewhat lazy impressions, in short the travelling of the "cultured" traveller, is over once and for all'.[72] Clearly Rilke had reached a real turning-point in his life through coming to see the senselessness of spending years in aimless travel and 'aesthetic contemplation'. A new power of discernment took possession of him, which made him exclaim: 'You have no idea, Princess, how different, *how different* the world has become, one must try to understand it. If anyone imagines that from now on he can live "in the way he is accustomed to" he will find himself continually faced with pure and simple repetition, with mere once-againness in all its dreadful sterility.'[73] The too-exact fulfilment of his wish for re-union with his former life now had a bewildering, almost a frightening, effect on Rilke. The abyss torn open by the war could never disappear completely, and the illusion created by this wing of the Venetian palace at once made him realise how profoundly things had altered. When he had left Venice he wrote as follows to his life-long friend, Lou Andreas: 'When, to crown all, I heard that the Duse had come to Venice, ill, to look for a flat, then it seemed to me that this too was going to be repetition, so terribly, that I left the very next day and came back to Switzerland.'[74]

In Venice Rilke came to see how necessary it was for him to arrive at some definite plan with regard to his life, which was going to be unbearable without a permanent home. He asks where he can turn in order *'to be able to expose myself to the whole danger of my work'*.[75] He feels the urge to live in some place where a foreign tongue is spoken, to live there as a stranger, alone with his native language which, during creative periods, he would like to guard as the raw material of his poetry, preserving it from contact with everyday life and from use simply as an instrument of meaning. In these circumstances, it seemed to him, he would be able to reserve the German language exclusively for his work.[76] Moreover, at that time immediately after the convulsions of the war, a return to Germany did not seem advisable, or likely to be helpful for his work. 'On the other hand', he tells his publisher, 'it becomes clearer and clearer to me that my stay in Switzerland is only a time of waiting, and I understand that I can't take off from this springboard into the open, but must "go back" – if only that backward direction were a bit more obvious and natural I would not have indulged in so many postponements.'[77] Again he has thoughts of visiting Soglio, 'the only place in Switzerland where I have felt close to my work'[78]; but he abandons this plan immediately, because of his dread of 'mere once-againness' and the unhappy experience of repetition which he had had in Venice; also because, after Venice, Soglio no longer meant Italy to the extent that it had done a year before. Furthermore, Rilke was afraid that on financial grounds he would only be able to spend a few days in Switzerland after his return from Venice. All that summer and autumn he was worried lest his circumstances might force him to go back to Germany, especially after the Austrian ambassador had succeeded in saving his Munich flat from being requisitioned.

Venice turned the poet's thoughts towards both his past and his future. In a letter he wrote at that time to Mme Nanny Wunderly-Volkart there are some significant lines which now seem like a premonition, even a foreknowledge, of what lay in store for him during the years ahead. He complains of being oppressed by a feeling of insecurity,

because I could not or would not consider that any of the places where I might have come finally to rest was the right bit of ground for me, and consequently have to live with restrained roots, for I dare not put them down into the temporary, especially as my root-system would not now stand up to re-planting. So much is certain: I shall not be a traveller again for many years, all my needs come together in a single longing for stability – if only I do not pass by the place which would promise it to me, and if only everything in me can be alive enough to transform a long and protected solitude into uninterrupted, unquenchable praise of heaven and earth![79]

Never, even when he was beset with money worries or distracted by people, did Rilke abate in the least his devotion to his work, nor did he ever suppose that the disjointed to-ing and fro-ing of that year was a normal state of affairs; for, as he wrote from Geneva that summer: 'I can't go on taking the future in table-spoonfuls, a spoonful every three weeks. I am longing to have it in front of me all at once "in the piece": *un bloc d'avenir, soit-il même dur a travailler.*[80]

After his return from Italy, Rilke had his passport visaed for Germany. Yet he could not bring himself to leave Switzerland. He did not after all go to Munich, but visited instead some of his old haunts: Schönenberg near Basle at the end of July (1920), and at the beginning of August Zürich and Winterthur; from there he went – for the first time – to the nearby Castle Berg by the Irschel; then on to Nyon and Geneva, in which two places he spent practically the whole of September and from where he paid repeated visits to Bern, Zürich and Meilen. But he always reckoned with the possibility or even likelihood of having to return before long to Munich. In that event he thought he might go on to Bohemia, where the Princess Taxis had offered him a little house on her Lautschin estate. He had the chance of a châlet in the neighbourhood of Geneva, but decided against it because once again the arrangement would only have been temporary; and in the late autumn he also gave up the plan – already far advanced – to rent a small flat in the old quarter of Geneva, though the reason this time was that he had accepted an invitation to spend the winter at Castle Berg by the Irschel (in Canton Zürich).

Geneva became an important landmark in Rilke's life during his last years. The city delighted him. He felt 'tremendously irresponsible' as he spent, instead of the intended four days of leave-taking, day after day at the Hôtel des Bergues, always finding new reasons for postponing his departure. 'Geneva was never so beautiful, so wide, so airy, blowing, almost floating, and so much of it recalling what I summarise *vaguement* under the name Paris: so that I am bidding farewell not only to Switzerland but also to all hopes of seeing my old surroundings again', Rilke wrote on August 18th, from the city to which he was yet to return so often. It was there that the decision was taken which led the poet, who had longed to settle in a country where a foreign language was spoken, to turn for the remainder of his life to French-speaking Switzerland, after his fruitless search in Italian Switzerland and in Italy, and although he had not yet given up the plan (only dropped in 1921) of settling in Czechoslovakia. There too, needless to say, Rilke made himself familiar

with the old lanes around the Cathedral of Saint-Pierre and with
the history still present in the Cathedral atmosphere. He enjoyed
Philippe Monnier's *Tœpffer's Geneva*, also Tœpffer's own work.
In two directions Geneva became a gateway for him in his search
for spiritual freedom: it opened on the one side towards France,
helping him to prepare for renewing his old ties with Paris, and
on the other towards the Valais, where his life was, though not
for a while yet, to become stabilised, and which he visited from
Geneva for the first time. In Geneva also he met the painter
Baladine Klossowska, whom he had known slightly in former
years, and to whom he now became closely attached. Off and on
during the last phase of his life Rilke's emotions were deeply
involved in this love-relationship, of which we hear in the letters
to 'Merline'. It also brought him much distress and perplexity.[81]

Another reason for staying in Geneva longer than he had
intended was the theatre, later to become famous, belonging to
the Russians Georges and Ludmilla Pitoëff, which aroused all
the enthusiasm of his ardent nature. 'How I love him, how I
admire him', he wrote of Pitoëff.

What a piece of luck is genius, how far-reaching it is, what immediate
happiness it can give to anyone who is able to be present at one of its
manifestations, even if only as a quite silent, tired and barely capable
spectator! The day before yesterday I found the Pitoëffs at Madame
Blumer's. All that day P. had been producing in his head a play by
Chavannes. . . . Now he told us about his vision of this play, how
wonderful, how deep and light, how completely and entirely play . . .
it made one breathless to listen to him. And when he, P., gets up from
an imaginary bench, moves away from an imaginary wall, wall and
bench come tumbling out of his eyes, one experiences his mental
picture of them! If I'd been staying on in *Genève* I'd have engaged
myself to P. and served him as secretary or something . . . if only he
had the means to carry out his plans – he has to do too much himself –
he lacks (just as Rodin lacked!) the right pupils and helpers, who would
submit to him *pour l'amour de métier accompli*! I should know how
to do that, and I could learn a lot. For every perfect mastery helps
mastery in general.[82]

So writes the 'tired and barely capable spectator'! In spite of
his own burdens and worries, he used to delight the people about

him and the distant friends to whom he wrote with his wonderful capacity for receiving and communicating impressions. He enriched his friends by his presence, by his gentle, forceful personality and by his inimitable words! One can only feel full of admiration for a man who remained mentally so receptive in such insecure circumstances, keeping the hyper-sensitive antennae of his soul constantly on the alert. Although at this time disharmonies and distractions made it impossible for him to collect his powers and focus them on his work, we have to marvel at the maturity, freshness and integrity of his mind, and at the close, accurate prose with its fine craftsmanship and tempered purity in which the letters are written. At this time of his life summer was his favourite season, and it made him melancholy every year to watch it drawing to an end, alarmed to see the first leaves changing colour. The poet would now seem to have been at the high summer of his life, pregnant with his inner world and his work, his frequent anxieties to have sprung only from uncertainty as to how and where the approaching harvest was to be gathered. He was convinced that arbitrary willing and doing were now out of place, that there was growth within him and that the time for reaping was imminent. For Rilke's complaints and weariness should not be interpreted as signs of any lack of confidence in himself, in his powers as an artist. He was sure that the gift of 'praising' – which he was later to extol so musically in his *Sonnets to Orpheus* – was still his, and to an even greater extent than before. The genius and vocation of a Pitoëff were only the pure note calling out a powerful answering vibration from his own most resonant string. All the same, the great danger of this free-and-easy way of life must not be overlooked. It was a danger of dissipating his energies in personal relationships and sociability, in conversation and letter-writing, almost to the point of self-immolation.

Rilke's nature was badly in need of healing: the vessel had to be made ready at last to receive the poem. The new impressions, whether of cities, landscapes, artists or books, could be no more than nourishment, sun, soil, a favourable climate, for the blossom and fruit once again taking form within him. But during the whole turbulent course of Rilke's life, and especially after he finished *Malte*, one keeps realising how incredibly difficult he found it to collect and prepare himself – in a way that tolerated no compromise, half-heartedness or distraction – quite apart from the 'impossibility of aloneness'. His tormenting self-criticism, his 'daemons', his restless impulsiveness, led to terrible hours and days. He longed to find peace in associating only with nature and with things – to put an end to this business of being distracted, confused and consumed by people. Rilke was the most considerate, attentive and irresistible of friends, but he could if need be subordinate every other consideration to the claims of his literary work; it was this that he lived for, and not family, friendship or love. Ever since his youth and the break up, after so short a time, of his much-too-early marriage, he had put his poetic vocation before both happiness in love and fidelity to any individual or community. Whenever he sensed the danger of being enchained by a woman he took fright, and on these occasions he would be painfully torn between his desires for bondage and for freedom. No love-affair could dissolve his basic sense of aloneness, or his need for being alone. Ardent and susceptible, prone to be quickly enthusiastic over new acquaintances, a captivating captive, boyishly inclined to admire where he was attracted and to project upon the beloved qualities originating in himself, Rilke could be just as swift to retreat, to weigh his partner up coolly and critically, inwardly setting himself free from her. Then he would be in a position to say once more that people had no idea how little they interested him. That this was so was the harder to guess because of his tendency to overwhelm his friends in an incomparable way with proofs of his sympathy, with practical help and with the most tender consideration, and spoil them with showers of luxurious presents. We have to accept this ambivalence as one of the permanent features of his make-up, or, at any rate, of his typical behaviour; an ambivalent attitude to his surroundings, and especially to people, was the almost inevitable outcome of his hyper-sensitive constitution, which was never in a state of robust health. Friendship with a woman, if it was to continue bearable and free from misunderstanding, was only possible for Rilke when no element of compulsion entered into it, when the relationship did not confront him with claims and pretensions. He looked to his women friends for support, care and protection, while at the same time refusing to let them impinge on his inner world, which he regarded as belonging to his poetic vocation. Hence the longing for the 'sisterly human being', and the idea that union between two people could have for its object 'the protection by each of the other's solitude'. He himself was much more of the brother than the lover. He felt a need all his life for women friends and companions; but, knowing well how great was the danger of squandering himself into which his weakness and aptitude for devotion kept leading him, he never gave in to the demands of human love for exclusiveness and permanence. Human relationships and the human presence affected him so strongly that he always feared the power they had over him. In the same way he would never share his solitude with a dog lest the dog should end up by being master. This attitude, which only confirms that Rilke's adjustment to his environment was not 'adequate', often brought him conflicts and unhappiness; for a relationship which became too close could distract him to such an extent that he would be forced to interrupt the association for long and frequent intervals, or even to break it off altogether.

We have to bear in mind that during that summer and autumn of 1920 Rilke was forever on the verge of departure, a perpetual leave-taker. This made the whole atmosphere of his life one of unrest and impermanence, and his state of mind melancholy. When he left Geneva on August 21st he had no thought whatever of returning – as he was to do – on September 4th; he went, as he definitely stated, on a short 'hail-and-farewell' visit to the Bund capital and then via Zürich to Meilen, as a prelude to leaving at last for Munich, where he wanted to clear the things out of his flat (a service which others did for him later).

Rilke had no sooner arrived in Bern than he started thinking about Geneva; and here we must not fail to mention the change in the poet's reactions to Bern which took place when he visited it the year before. 'I know', he wrote,

that I love Bern, but this time I can't feel it – yesterday evening when I arrived I was even a little frightened by the hardness in the air (*je voudrais tant encore de la chaleur et de l'été, de l'été*) – then, too, by this separateness of sky and earth, and, suddenly again, by the fallow-coloured, fragmentary and (alas!) bourgeois appearance of things, their heaviness, their impenetrability, their density, their 'object'-

iveness, objecting to what? To the sky. In *Genève*, almost as in Paris, everything comes over you in waves. The atmosphere, as it goes on its penetrating way, floats towards you from trees and slopes – there is only *one thing*, the bearing, billowing light, through it, through the spirituality of this element, one apprehends the near and the far, and even solid bodies are instilled into the seeing eye like a fluid, like an event, an idea, not so thickly laid on, not so prompted, so pushed into you as facts which have to be known and learned by heart.[83]

But for all that he revisited his favourite walks, through the old town past the Gothic cathedral, and over the Aare bridge to the 'rose garden', those high-situated gardens whose old avenues he loved and whose roses and water-lilies he describes so charmingly in the same letter. When he discovered, on another walk outside the gates of the town, a little castle in a garden – it was called Holligen – he was seized with a mood of deep melancholy at not having found, after all the months of fruitless searching and waiting, some such place to protect him and his work. Like a poor child gazing hopelessly through a garden fence at the paradise enjoyed by the rich and fortunate, the afflicted poet stood in front of this garden which his longing transformed into a wonderland:

The tall old chestnut-trees lining the drive, and at the end, behind the iron gate, the upright little castle, and to one side, under the trees' edge, a wide view of the sunlit landscape, it made the tears come into my eyes again – such an avenue, such a house for a year and I should be saved. I felt that if only I could go inside and into a quiet study which was expecting me I should be able to work that very evening! I tell myself it's all imagination, that there too I'd find drawbacks, hindrances, interruptions, difficulties. . . . And yet, why do such avenues move me in this way. . . . You can see it, can't you?: how high it was – protective, dark, solemn, how it sang on both sides like a choir, and how the castle stood at the end in a subdued light . . . I went up close to the park fence. . . . People passed, out for their Sunday walk, all moved away, and from the old trees of the park an evening bird whistled, a single one, as though questioning whether the silence was deep enough for the feeling in its song: . . . it was.[84]

During those last ten August days in Bern – which according to a later report were 'beautiful . . . especially the mornings, and the nights full of moonshine' – Rilke conceived the idea of writing a series of 'window-poems': poems springing from the conception of the window as the measure and frame of human domestic life; as the measure – he calls it 'a windowful' – from which we really get our idea of the world, whose shape influences our thoughts, whether it be 'that of the prison grating, the palace *croisée*, the ship's porthole, the attic skylight, or the rose window in a cathedral'.[85] This subject occupied the poet's mind a great deal. He thought that a history of windows ought to be written one day. As he walked along the old streets of Bern and Fribourg he kept looking at the windows and thinking about them. The window was soon to join the mirror, the fountain and the rose in the universe of Rilke's lyrical motives.

It was on one of his outings to nearby Fribourg with Mme Klossowska that he and his companion formed the plan of collaborating on an illustrated book of window poems. The outcome of this project was issued some years later by a Polish publisher: a self-contained volume of French poems, *Les Fenêtres*, with etchings by Baladine (the pseudonym of Rilke's friend).[86]

And now followed, in rapid succession, three important dates in Rilke's life, which were suddenly to restore a congenial shape and a secure frame to his existence, and to open a new window, a 'windowful' of creativity, on that personal future which had been obstructed for so long. On October 4th he went for some days into the Valais, to Sion and Sierre, where he became enthusiastic about the landscape, having an immediate intuition that this was the place he had been looking for, the place truly destined to be his home. Then on the 17th, in Bern, he decided to spend the coming winter in a château which had been offered to him, Berg by the Irschel. Finally, on the 22nd, he set off to stay for a short, happy time in Paris, revisiting his old haunts.

The discovery of the Valais, which he first saw when on an excursion from Geneva with some friends, was an event of the utmost importance for Rilke's later years. He at once felt powerfully drawn to this region, whose landscape he drank in with sheer delight. As yet he had not seen the Tower of Muzot, near Sierre, into which he was to move the following year. It was not until those ancient walls on the southern alpine slopes took him into their protection that his longing for new, enduring roots was to find its fulfilment. Fate had cast the Upper-Rhone valley to be this poet-pilgrim's final home and resting-place.

However, before he found his way back to the Valais later on, the prospect opened up for him – at last – of having his old wish for a home of his own fulfilled in another part of the country. Acquaintances had offered him – in keeping with the luck of those days – the use of their old country house for the winter : Castle Berg by the Irschel, in the distant neighbourhood of Winterthur. Rilke finally decided on this abode rather than Lautschin in Bohemia which was – literally as well as figuratively – too far out of his way.[87] The house by the Irschel was not as grand as Duino, but it was more openly and pleasantly situated than the château near Bern which had been the object of his mournful admiration. Joyfully he made up his mind to accept the hospitality of Berg, 'this extraordinary, quite wonderful refuge'.[88] But before entering his *retrait* in East Switzerland he set off for Paris, via Bern, where he picked up his Czech passport from the embassy, and Basle. 'The object of this journey', he said, 'is to prepare my mind for being made whole again, at the very point where the evil break occurred. . . .'[89] Rilke started out in the confident hope that, later on in Berg, he would be able to complete his spiritual recovery through the benign influence of uninterrupted solitude and seclusion.

Paris. . . . What those six autumn days meant to him was, in his own words, 'indescribable . . ., indescribable'.[90] It was his first visit after the six-year absence forced upon him by the war – a time of continuous self-discovery, when everything was a goal in itself, each shape had a meaning. That city, still there just as he had always known it, became for him a symbol of survival, of steadfast endurance, a witness to life's healing powers. The 'universal fruitfulness, bearing-capacity and resilience of the ground which supports an all-outriding city as easily as if it were a growing crop',[91] the light of that sky, the autumnal Luxembourg Gardens spread out right in front of his door, glorious with a thousand flowers – how shall he call all this, how describe it? He cannot find words: the poet is struck dumb with happiness. In the Odeon Arcades he buys a notebook, with the intention of recording his impressions of these Paris days; however, much unavailing effort to write something in it results only in the statement: *'ici commence l'indicible'*. Perhaps, he says, in a letter to Mme Wunderly-Volkart written entirely in French, this will be the only sentence to come home with him from Paris: 'Car comment, comment exprimer ces moments? c'est tellement familier et si grand, cela étonne et satisfait, cela exalte et cela fait pleurer tour à tour et presqu'en même temps, ça réunit tous les contrastes: c'est tout: – comment l'exprimer, même à vous qui comprendriez à mi-parole, même devant mon propre cœur crédule, soumis, croyant!'[32]

Paris, too, perhaps even more emphatically than other places, confirms the impression that Rilke is far more moved and influenced by whatever is enduring and universal in his surroundings than by transient, variable human relationships. He did not seek out his old friends and acquaintances, but contented himself with following in the steps of Malte Laurids Brigge: to and fro in the Latin Quarter, along the Seine quays, to the beloved park in front of the Senate House, with its octagonal pool and the Medici fountain under the old plane trees.

We encountered a curious fact when we came to compare the letter mentioned above with another, part of which was also in French, addressed by Rilke to the same correspondent eleven days previously in Geneva. In the earlier of the two documents the foreign language is still really foreign, clumsy syntax and style showing that the sentences have been translated from German, and not thought or felt in French. Then, in the second, Rilke suddenly starts to write a much purer French, already breathing the spirit of the other language. This is not simply a proof of the poet's great gift for languages, nor yet – more generally – of the unusual adaptability and openness to the world which enables him to step so lightly over cultural barriers; it shows above all how greatly those few days in Paris heightened his mental faculties. It is an objective manifestation of the wholly subjective enthusiasm released in him by that renewed sight of the beloved city.

Healing and New Beginning

The vigilant see the hour of their departure coming.
(Inscription on the gate-tower of Saint-Prex)

1

CASTLE BERG BY THE IRSCHEL

RILKE'S desire for seclusion was fulfilled at last. And so completely, in conditions so utterly congenial to him, that the reports sent out from his hermitage overflow with praise for the new dwelling and cast a reflection of his happiness upon the friends to whom they are addressed.[1] Phrases such as 'the indescribable healing of my nature after the fearful fracture of the year Fourteen' keep on recurring in these letters like a refrain.[2] The process had begun in Paris, but, as the days spent there had been too few to work a fundamental cure and as the German currency position made it impossible for him to stay longer, he had accepted the proferred hospitality at Castle Berg by the Irschel. He called it 'the miracle — for which I have been waiting for years (with that long, long patience which has been proved right after all). Without my doing the least thing about it (and what could one do for the sovereignty of the miracle!) this little, ancient Berg Castle has been put at my disposal. . . .'[3]

After spending three days in Geneva on his way back from Paris, Rilke moved into his new home on November 12th. This date remained in his memory long enough for him to send a telegram a year later, when he was already settled elsewhere, to his hosts Richard and Lily Ziegler, the owners of Berg. Everything combined to emphasise his longed-for isolation: the remote position of this estate, in a hilly and well-wooded district; the slight mist enveloping the house and garden on the day he arrived — even the 'contagion sentry', standing outside the gate to prevent the new occupant from leaving the grounds: a precautionary measure against spreading the foot-and-mouth disease prevalent in the village but not, as yet, in the neighbourhood. The village clergyman acted as intermediary between Rilke and the village during this time of blockade; he brought the mail and the milk every day, and frequently this led to a confidential chat about the affairs of the parish and the district, or about the castle's history and former occupants; but religious matters were

F   81

discussed as well. Rilke got the clergyman to take his passport to the mayor, before he sent it to his host, asking him to forward it to the Aliens' Department in Bern, together with a request for an extension of his resident's permit, due to expire on November 17th. The poet asked his friend to back up his application to these authorities.

At last, at last Rilke could again report that

all is well, a thing that I, strictly speaking, have not been able to say since Soglio, except when I was simply thinking of and referring to a general kind of pleasurable diversion vouchsafed to me at times, and not of *that* which deep down is required of me, with which I've been lagging behind for six years, a straggler not altogether faithless but dog-tired.[4]

At last he found life homely again; the house was comfortable, and concentration on his work became a possibility. This stroke of good fortune – which he called 'one of the most opportune that ever befell me'[5] – overwhelms him 'with a continuous sense of obligation to take up again in good earnest, under these wonderfully favourable conditions, everything which the bad years destroyed or interrupted'.[6]

Rilke cannot praise enough the 'miracle', happening so naturally, which bestowed upon him 'the very *retraite* for which the chaos of six destructive years had left me almost desperate. But that it existed!' he wrote from Berg to Nanny von Escher:

I am amazed – and that it should really have been there all ready for me, in that moment of extremity, when I was already standing, as it were, at the Swiss frontier, beyond which only a crowd of intrusive uncertainties could be expecting me. And for more than a fortunate year Switzerland has known how to spoil me, with so many good friends and agreeable places – I really had no right to keep on asking more from her: but lo and behold! she had been saving up for me the best of all her gifts, a complete fulfilment, this place of perfect refuge which will always be marked as a capital on the map of my life. . . . Of course, in such entirely congenial surroundings, where there can be no shadow of excuse, the obligation has become inexorable to produce at last, from a restored existence, something worthy of one's concentrated powers. This then is the resolution that I make daily in my Berg-protected retirement. . .[7]

These words express everything that Berg had come to mean to Rilke. With this orientation towards inwardness, towards the real centre of his life, he began to find the way back to himself. In this new, peaceful environment he wanted to address himself again to those vocational tasks which had been left undone for far too long. Even if Rilke had not been given just then to speaking of his 'cell' from time to time – in his imagination he saw the words: *'cella continuata dulcescit'* inscribed over his door – there was no mistaking the monk-like expression on his face, the look of obedient austerity, of severe unworldliness. 'I am the caterpillar in the *cocon*, spinning myself more and more into my growing beard.'[8] His real activity began only when, safeguarded by the old walls, he was left to himself. He was emphatic that his delight at seeing no one for months on end did not spring from misanthropy, but from the exact opposite. For him there was only one thing needful and important: to serve his work under a self-imposed, almost monastic rule. He told the Princess Taxis that he had not felt like this since Duino; he could not have imagined, particularly during recent years, that every requirement of his 'exaggerated isolation' could be fulfilled, even down to the last, most trivial detail.[9] In a letter to Frau Lily Ziegler, the owner of Berg at that time, he said that it did not require any great talent to discover that his new surroundings were highly suitable. But with what intense enthusiasm he describes the harmony between himself and these same surroundings, as he continues:

already it really surrounds me, already it has given its heart to me, already I am strengthened by the strength of its walls, already its silence overflows into my own, already there is, from moment to moment, an equalizing exchange between us in which, for a long time to come, my part will have to be a simple taking and using. It is not boastful to speak of the response that things make to one: – these here requite the love that I brought them with such a happy natural-ness that, without any need to adapt myself, I felt at once at the centre of tasks waiting to be begun.[10]

It was not only these objects' peaceful yet lively silence that responded to the cheerful mood of the castle's extraordinary tenant, but also their music and their appearance. The clock's familiar sound seemed to him a welcome interruption of the silence; he said that the hall clock when it struck had a voice which knew 'how to report on a, so to speak, roomy time'. And the clear sky which, on the day after his arrival, had dissolved into warm sunshine the mist shrouding the park, beamed in on him through the open window. As he installed himself in his new home and conversed with it until dusk, Rilke kept looking and listening through the window. Of impressions received by delightedly expectant ear and eye he says in the same letter: [11]

Now the garden's stillness was translated into the murmur of the fountain, which I never tire of analysing, and which I follow in all its variations: what an exciting moment it always is when an encroachment of the air tugs the falling jet from one side of the pool to the other, right through its own ascent, so that for a fraction of a hesitant minute it falls silently into itself: and then, after every deviation, the fall sounded different, with such a wealth of variations that I grew envious of my hearing and looked out at it too. The shape of the jet was no less astonishing than its music. Almost feminine, it stood there on the round, dazzlingly bright circle of water, about which the remaining circle of the pool spread out, dark and openly reflecting; in the depths the park, solemn almost, opening towards the paling Irschel, then, even paler above it and quite abandoned to evening, the sky, the narrow quarter of the new moon gleaming above the edge of the pine tree. . . .[11]

Rilke suddenly saw the waxing moon as 'a symbol of beginning', a discreet allusion on the part of the sky to his newly-begun life – so strongly in those first days at Berg did he feel the solidity of this place in which he had settled.

Two other things were important to him – things that were always among his never excessive but very precise basic requirements: the books and the housekeeper. He was delighted to find, right away, a Moliére and two volumes of Stendhal in the bookcase, and he lost no time in extracting them from their hiding-place. But he was particularly pleased with the quiet housekeeper, a local peasant girl called Leni: '. . . so completely right for me, *she too*–like a friendly climate, there and not there, just as you wish. . .'. [12]The great importance he attached to this being who for weeks on end was, apart from the village clergyman, his only associate, and the kindly way he thought of the girl, can be gathered from another letter where he says:

I am constantly surprised by her composure, her refinement, even by what one might call her 'tact', something which in the last resort cannot be learned, and which is so rarely found in serving people, who do not have the freedom necessary for the cultivation of these intimate qualities, for getting to know themselves, as it were! – If I could get fixed up with a creature like Leni for the rest of my hazardous life, what progress there would be for its security and regularity![13]

It is not to be wondered at that Rilke started to do some research on the history and curious architecture of the unique house he was living in. He was disappointed to be able to get so little information about the history of Berg and its inhabitants, and remarked regretfully that there was no mention of either in Nanny von Escher's little book *Old Zürich* which he was reading at the time. To this authoress, whose family had once owned the property, and whom he asked to make a study of it, he wrote:

Doubtless you know the big panelled room in which I work (the drawing-room); the whitewashed sculptured pillars flanking the midmost of three broad windows carry two coats of arms in similar colours, one of which is the von Eschers', the other unknown to me (red stag reposing in white erected tent on blue ground).[14] Among other things recalling the Eschers' time is a portrait which we have brought from the hall into this room which appreciates it more. It represents a child, a little girl, who in a certain upright, almost refusing *tenue d'apparat*, and with her little white lap-dog, looks so happy and self-sufficiently gay that she seems to discourage any participation of the viewer as a piece of tiresome intrusiveness. This attitude ought to have been entirely enclosed within the picture, but it happens that the eyes of the little self-sufficient person are continually full of a minutely observant look, which has an effect on the space one is living in, such a powerful and persistent effect that at times one seems to feel it on one's back.[15]

Strange enough: the presence in the study of the 'little Escher girl', as Rilke called the picture, often kept his imagination busy during his time at Berg. How he would have loved to know something about this child, to guess her secret, to learn the story of her life! 'Thus', the poet's letter goes on,

the strong old house is still full of bygone people and events; on the other hand, the harmonious proportions of the park grounds bear lasting witness to how well its founder gauged the effect on its surroundings of the dignified, gabled house. . . . How easily a small castle can overestimate and disgrace itself in relation to its grounds: here all the proportions are as pure and as sure as possible.[16]

When he found one day that the contagion sentry, with his fire and kettle, had disappeared from the park gate, Rilke was almost frightened, as if here was the first threat to his chosen, cherished way of life. His work did not even allow him his usual hour off for afternoon tea. Going for his evening walk in the park, between five and six, he invariably took the same path, pacing up and down the length of the kitchen garden, 121 steps each way. When the moon became bright enough for him to see his own shadow walking in front of him he returned to the study, regretting the time that he had spent out of it. He explained his invariable routine, even with regard to this walk, by his need for concentration.

He did not dare to expose himself to the influence of the peaceful landscape around Berg, in which he did not feel the same confidence as in the rooms of his house. In fact, he was finding it more difficult than he had hoped to enter completely into himself again; to set a firm foot on the shaken foundation of his inner life. One thing was certain: he was 'wholeheartedly determined not to see people'.[17]

That the completion of the Duino Elegies was the ultimate goal of this 'protected, secure winter' cannot be doubted. It is equally clear that the journey into his innermost self was not possible without transitional stages. Letter writing fitted into Rilke's working life as a means of getting closer to himself and to his own centre. As he was not in the way of keeping a regular diary, and needed a non-corporeal ear in which to confide, his incredibly extensive correspondence must be regarded as taking the place of the journal kept by other writers, André Gide for example. At the same time, letter writing was for him the ideal way of being sociable, since he could not endure any kind of social tie. With such a wealth of very different correspondents – the

majority of whom were always women – infinite variations were
possible on what could be told and what was worth telling. It is
significant that Rilke started his new life at Berg by dutifully, carefully and lovingly fulfilling this task. According to his own account,
he regarded the mastering of his correspondence as practice for his
'long-neglected pen'; it was a sort of intermediate stage between
oral communication and the work writing (*Schriftlichkeit der
Arbeit*) no longer addressed to any particular person. ('Work' to him
meant always and only literary creation.) When the pile of letters
he had to deal with became quite small he felt as though 'there has
been a tidying-up of my mind, reaching right into the depths'.[18]

The conscientiousness, the meticulous care that Rainer Maria
Rilke brought to his letter writing was excessive. On the small,
four-sided sheets of greyish-blue notepaper that he liked to use
the characters are as graceful, firm and clear as if they were
etched on copper. Each turn of his sentences is carefully thought
out, every word exactly right. Nothing in form or content is left
to chance. Haste or carelessness would have been incompatible
with the deliberately precise, sometimes sophisticated style and
handwriting with which he curbed his teeming thoughts. It is
only in the copiousness of the letters and the length of some of
the sentences that he now and then allows his communicativeness
to overflow its banks, breaking free from the discipline which
makes his poetry so compact and finished. In the prose of his
letters Rilke permits himself certain liberties: accumulations of
subordinate clauses, sprinklings of French words and idioms, and
sometimes flourishes and distortions which perhaps have their
roots in his early memories of Prague baroque. (One must never
forget how strong was the early influence of the baroque atmosphere on poets and artists from the Danube and Moldava
countries.) Not only in his poetry, but in his letters as well, Rilke
makes the utmost use of the German language's extreme supple-
ness and adaptability. His stylistic liberties and ornamentations
are simply the result of using his astonishing, original gift for
words to explore to the fullest extent all the possibilities of
language. Rilke's letters are surprising in our century because
they form such a complete contrast to the sober, utilitarian style
of letter-writing which is now the fashion. At a time when the
typewriter's mechanical script has advanced right into the

personal realm of private correspondence, and when this correspondence is becoming more and more limited to short statements
excluding all finer shades and any touch of contemplation, the art
of letter writing as Rainer Maria Rilke practised it – compact of
handwriting, style and content, luxurious as a flower-bed in
summer – is indeed bound to be looked upon as an exception,
almost as an anachronism. It is not Rilke who is not at fault for
having the courage to write like this, but our age, which has lost
the desire and capacity to do so.[19]

One thing will never be said of Rilke, even when the last,
shortest scrap of his immense correspondence has come to light:
that he was ever, even when tired, less than scrupulously careful
in carrying out this task to which he attached so much importance.
We do not know of a single occasion when he used a postcard.
But we do know that when he sent a telegram he never employed
the notorious 'telegram style'. Instead, with a perfect, touching
courtesy towards language and recipient, he refused to save one
unnecessary word in his message or in the address. On the
envelopes of his letters he would write names and addresses in a
highly individual but almost calligraphic hand, so that the
balanced, elegant design makes a striking aesthetic impression.
Usually these letters were sealed with grey sealing-wax on which
the poet imprinted his family crest with a small seal. Very
important letters he usually registered or sent by express. He kept
his correspondents' replies in their envelopes, arranging them
methodically under the names of the senders. They were found
after his death preserved in dark-green envelopes each of which
bore the sender's name in his handwriting. As Rilke often let his
correspondence accumulate over a long period, it was his habit
when a letter arrived to jot down the sender's name on a writing-
pad kept for the purpose. Having answered the letter he crossed
out the name; and during letter-writing periods he would
contemplate the many horizontal strokes on his pad with relief
and pride. He hints at this habit when he writes to a woman
friend: 'The letter list is before me, looking quite praiseworthy,
like a page of music, with all its horizontal lines, heaven grant
that I shall soon be able to sight-read the finale.'[20]

'A trifle', Rilke calls the foreword which, during the early
days in Berg, he wrote for a book of cat-drawings by his gifted

little friend Baltusz – Mme Klossowska's twelve-year-old son. *Mitsou* related the adventures and death of a little cat, events which had taken place in Nyon when Rilke was staying there with his friend and her boy. This '*préface*' – of only a few pages – is worth mentioning because it was his first French work to be published, and created some stir.[21] He sent the short manuscript to the poet Charles Vildrac in Paris, to be looked over and, if need be, 'mercilessly corrected'.

I should never dare to make a public appearance with this little improvisation, which obviously cannot come under the judgment of my artistic conscience. I feel myself too much of a 'professional' to be willing to misuse that supreme instrument, your language, and am almost frightened at having touched its strings, ignorant as I perhaps am of its hiddenmost sensibility. Save me, please, from the censure with which my work might deservedly be met.[22]

Rilke had hardly been in Berg for a fortnight when he had a strange experience. What was it that happened in his solitude to make him write the sequence of poems to which he gave the title *From the Remains of Count C. W.*? In that stratum of consciousness which was the meeting-point of his awakening creative energy, his introspective thoughts and his inadequate powers of concentration on his work, verses sprang into being. They were curious, alien verses which Rilke recited and found astonishing, and which would not let him alone: verses which, it seemed to him, did not originate in himself. As, one evening, he was sitting at his writing-desk in the big drawing-room he suddenly became aware of a figure in a chair by the fireplace, deep in the shadows of the twilit room. It was a gentleman in eighteenth-century dress, gazing silently into the fire, his head supported on his hand. To this man Rilke attributed the authorship of the poems whose rhymes and rhythms haunted him continually in those days, and which he now began to write down, just as they had been dictated to him. From now on Rilke called the mysterious figure 'Count C. W.'. No one ever learned his full name, but we gather from one of the poems that his Christian name was 'Charles'.[23] The first lines that Rilke heard in this way were:

> Nightly my wild heart alone has tendered
> harbourage to everlastingness.

They are now the last in the short cycle. Here is the poem of which they are part:

> Passing time – oh, unreflective saying!
> *Keeping* it is where the problem is.
> Who's not shuddered: is there any staying,
> Any final *being* in all this?
>
> Look, the day has slackened pace on nighing
> That last lap that leads to evening:
> rising stood, now standing turns to lying,
> and the lief down-lier's vanishing.
>
> Mountains rest, by great stars over-splendoured;
> time in them, though, twinkles none the less.
> Nightly my wild heart alone has tendered
> harbourage to everlastingness.[24]

Most of the poems *From the Remains of Count C. W.* consist, like that just quoted, of four-line stanzas, each line being a five-foot trochee; but there is a variation in the seventh poem, where five- and four-foot trochees alternate. The longest poem consists of seventeen four-line stanzas. One of the few with a metre differing from the others ('Karnak. We'd ridden') was published anonymously in the Insel Almanack for 1923; it would seem to be founded on memories of Rilke's Egyptian visit. But he still refused to acknowledge the authorship of these poems. Whether he was imagining it or not, he had the impression that the cycle was dictated by a dead man, a stranger, who used him as a mouth-piece. He himself always spoke of the author of these poems in the third person, now and then expressing surprise at 'how well he puts it!'

Rilke's story of the fireside apparition, which he does not explicitly mention in the letters discussing this affair, need neither be taken literally nor as a deliberate invention inspired by his delight in the fabulous. Flat realism can never be enough for poets, who make no great distinction between the natural and the supernatural and in whose imagination the two spheres intermingle. The incident of 'Count C. W.' is not at all unique among Rilke's stories of his experiences; but it is remarkable in calling attention to his practice of recounting the extraordinary happenings of his life by word of mouth only (except when he makes a fictitious character, Malte Laurids Brigge, responsible for them). We learn from the Princess Taxis's *Reminiscences* that Rilke was already taking an interest in occult phenomena in the years before the war. We know that during his time in Switzerland he took part in spiritualist séances at C. House in Basle, and that he read Schrenck-Notzing. Occasionally – very occasionally! – he did discuss these questions in letters, but only when the subject had been brought up by someone else (the Princess Taxis or Nora Purtscher). For all that, it must be emphasised that he was never anything but a very reserved spectator of spiritualism. He never let himself be used as a medium, although, or perhaps because, he was capable of psychic experiences, lived on familiar terms with the fantastic, and, presumably, had mediumistic gifts. Nine years before going to Berg Rilke had a similar experience in the garden at Castle Duino, when he remained transfixed for some seconds in the expectation of seeing one of the castle's deceased occupants come round a bend in the path.[25] But in both instances it was more a case of half-fearfully, half-hopefully, feeling it *possible* that a *revenant* might appear. (In Muzot, too, Rilke felt this possibility.) In spite of such experiences it must be stated that his attitude to the occult remained ambiguous and cautious. Lou Andreas-Salomé, whose verdicts on her friend's states of mind are always well considered and full of insight writes:

Into the same category, to my way of thinking, comes Rainer's intermittent pre-occupation with the occult and mediumistic, supernatural meaning of dreams, influence of the dead, which he proceeded to elevate, as it were, into imagery for abundant being and knowing, and with which he tried in vain to identify himself. In good times he brusquely rejected such things, even thought of them with loathing.[26]

Incidentally, Rilke comes to our help with a plausible explanation of his own. Immediately after writing down the 'C. W.' poems, he sent a light-hearted account of the incident to Mme Wunderly:

. . . It was strange, by the way. I was too much alone, didn't know enough about the house, about its past, about those who lived here (I'm a bit frightened of the little Escher girl, she's not very com-

municative and has an understanding with her little dog in which I'm
not allowed to participate) – in short: I wanted to find something
like a footprint of one of Berg's previous occupants, i.e. a notebook
discovered one evening in a bookcase, just look: who could it have
been? I imagined, quite superficially, a figure – the situation helped –
but in spite of all my imagining the said notebook failed to turn up,
what remained for me to do but to invent it? And there it lay, closed,
in front of me . . . *Poems*, just think – on the first page you will read:
'From the Remains of Count C. W.'. Strange things, for which I,
most agreeably, have no responsibility whatsoever. No but, joking
apart, I didn't know what it meant, this game – it was charming and
so it charmed me on – (by the way, the whole was the work of three
days and done as one knits – I presume).

Only now do I understand how it kept turning up day after day: as I
was not really quite in the mood or quite fit for my own work I had,
it seems, to invent a 'pretext' figure, someone to take responsibility
for whatever could be formed at this highly insufficient level of
concentration: this was Count C. W. . . .[27]

One has to admit, as one reads this cycle of poems, that the
old nobleman's rhymed 'Remains' cannot be considered as
belonging to the main body of Rainer Maria Rilke's poetic work.
Not only do they differ in kind from his own poems but, more
important still, they simply are not good enough to be recognised
as his. Hints and echoes of the poet's voice are not lacking; but the
verse does not sing, it merely tinkles, it has not grown naturally
but been made; these poems are exercises which Rilke enjoyed
doing, as he knew well enough when he was in a more sunlit
mood. He himself rejected the series as the work of an often
unskilful, often all-too-skilful 'dilettante': . . . 'sometimes
though', he ends his account, 'he scores a hit which I thoroughly
approve, which, to be honest, even makes me envious – and often
he gets quite close to me (the good Count had certain presentiments in his leisure hours) – and the affair ends with a lot of
bowing on my part, I respect, I venerate him – it's a pity that he's
dead. *Voilà l'aventure!*'[28]

But apparently the adventure had not ended, even yet. According to Rilke the voice now started dictating to him in Italian!
But when Count C. W. took to Italian Rilke revolted against his

dictation and gave him notice, most energetically. He wanted to be himself again and not somebody else's mouthpiece. That his thoughts were still occupied with the strange experience is evident from the fact that he recounted the story of the fireside apparition to Anton Kippenberg when the publisher visited him at Berg some weeks later, at the end of January. Copies of the 'strangely-discovered *Remains of Count C. W.*' were sent by him to Mme Wunderly-Volkart, the Princess Taxis and the Kippenbergs. He did not, however, want to see these poems in print (except for the solitary one which remained anonymous). Later on, in the very early spring of 1921, Rilke composed another sequence of eleven poems, on the MS. of which he wrote 'From the Poems of Count C. W.'.[29] The tone here is somewhat different from that of the earlier, November, cycle, and nearer to Rilke's own. But his ever-alert faculty of self-criticism stepped in once more and would not allow him to own up to their authorship.

Later on, after May 1921, when he had finally turned his back on the enchanted castle and was living in different surroundings, Rilke made the admission, speaking of Count C. W.: 'His connection with Berg, by the way, has become clear, that he should dictate to me again seems quite unthinkable since I left.'[30] When he wrote these words Rilke was drawing his breath once more on the sunlit side of life, where he vigorously rejected things that appealed to him in certain places and moods.

'Unforseen circumstances', which he called 'disastrous', tore Rilke from the sheltering walls of his hermitage soon after the New Year. He had to go to Geneva, to deal with a serious personal affair 'the management of which I could not delegate to anyone else, and which contained a threat for the whole of my future'. This letter goes on:

. . . and even though I have brought it to a kind of temporary assuagement, I am still suffering from the after-effects of the most profound sorrow and perturbation and feel that I have been thrust far away from the centre where the entrance to my innermost self is to be found. Journeys right across Switzerland became necessary – but the outward happenings, for all the disturbance they brought, were negligible compared to the inner torment of not being able to hold on to the essential.[31]

Rilke was away from Berg for a fortnight, but after this shrill interruption from life, which had torn him so cruelly from his preparedness to restart his 'work, barren for years', it took weeks before he could calm himself again and repair his 'shattered concentration . . . I have to start right from the beginning again now – and I watch the approach of full spring with horror, like someone going to bed towards morning, who would like to hold up daybreak and prolong the night'.[32]

In the several accounts that Rilke gave of this episode, he asserted that it had interrupted his long preparatory run towards the hurdle when he was almost there, just as his call-up had done some years before in Munich, when he was on the point of reaching the Elegies. The rough grasp of fate had intervened between him and his work; 'it's as though there were a secret hostility against this big work which is so indispensable to me – and in the end it is always the same irreconcileable conflict between life and work through whose untold variations I have to pass, barely surviving'.[33] Rilke never found a solution to the conflict between the demands of life and those of artistic creation; it was a tension that, sometimes loosening its grip but always tightening it again, never ceased to harass him as long as he drew breath. He would not have suffered so much from it, or been so helpless when confronted with it, if his nature had not given a complete assent to these demands and held them to be absolute. He wanted to do justice to both, life in all its abundance and sensuous glory, which filled him with admiration, astonishment and enthusiasm, and the art which he felt to be his vocation, and which seemed to ask of him an entire, almost impossible, apparently unutterable, surrender. This extravagance in Rilke's nature prevented him from settling down, as other writers and artists have succeeded in doing, to an orderly working life, the broad, steady flow of an harmonious day-to-day existence. Naturally he felt himself drawn, again and again, to other excessive natures – to such visual artists as Rodin, Cézanne and Picasso, and to writers like Dostoevsky, Hölderlin, Büchner, Strindberg, Kafka and Proust. No one without some excess in his make-up can be a visionary, can desire and dare to give spontaneous, uninhibited utterance to his innermost thoughts, without any regard for conventionality. Since, on the other hand,

Rilke was conscientious and punctilious, also too soft-hearted and polite to turn unfeelingly aside from his human obligations of the moment, he was always finding himself in situations where, at a summons from life, his work had to be disturbed; he was always having to interrupt it at a request from someone or other who needed his presence, his help, his time. Bassermann says of the occurrence which so suddenly tore into his time at Berg:

We do not know what the circumstances were which made him at that time 'wholly needed'; we only know the deeply disturbing, long-lasting effects of which he writes. . . . This particular case makes it quite evident that in the conflict between life and art Rilke did not fail in his duty to life (or, as has sometimes been said, fail in regard to life). He measured up to circumstances which really called for his help, even at a critical moment like this, when the work for which he had waited so painfully and patiently for ten years 'was there'.[34]

After his return from Geneva and Zürich, Rilke remained at Berg, apart from short outings, until May 10th. On January 22nd Kippenberg visited him in his cell, staying until the 24th. He came apparently to give the poet encouragement and to console him about the unfortunate circumstances which had upset him so badly. The wonders performed for German publishing by his Insel-Verlag were not Kippenberg's only claim to singularity: his relationship with Rilke, too, was unique. It would not be easy to imagine two men less like each other than this poet and his publisher. Kippenberg was the typically forceful, efficient German citizen and patriot, a tremendous worker, a businessman who had built up his famous publishing house by his own labours and initiative. Goethe was his god, and he had erected a monument to him at his Leipzig house in the shape of a Goethe collection which he would show to his guests with justifiable pride. By and large his outlook was that of the Wilhelmian German, basically simple and rather humdrum. He worked for the honour of Germany as he and his generation understood it. He had a touching admiration for his wife Katharina, who came from a more distinguished social background than her self-made husband. She was well educated, rather sentimental, fond of poetry in a somewhat gushing, affected way, and had ambitions to be a writer herself. This couple played a decisive part in Rilke's life, and it is greatly to the credit of them both that they published his work and did all in their power to support and further it, helping him with understanding, true friendship, enormous patience and an unfaltering belief in his greatness. Since 1905, when the *Book of Hours* appeared, the Insel-Verlag had published all Rilke's books, and the years had cemented the poet's friendship with Kippenberg and his wife. Rilke called the latter 'the mistress and book-keeper', as Anton Kippenberg listened to Katharina's advice on literary matters, and she had a good head for business. It was in their Leipzig house that Rilke finished the *Notebooks of Malte Laurids Brigge*, and he happened to be staying with them in 1914 when war broke out. Naturally it distressed Rilke that, after so many years, he was still unable to deliver the promised Elegies to his publisher. A ten-year silence is hard for a poet to endure, but it is also a most discomforting thing for his publisher. During his stay at Berg, however, Kippenberg did not allow Rilke to feel anything of this, so that the poet could write to a friend in Geneva:

The 'fatherly friend' brought nothing but good-will, and left no other odour behind him than that of his strong cigars. Seldom, it seems to me, can a publisher have had such a soothing effect as this one of mine, to whom I haven't been able to present any work for a decade. He even consoled me about it (in so far as I still have consolable places in me). It is a source of such good-natured pride to him that the old books are still going strong, that, for example, the little production of my youth, the *Cornet Rilke*, has sold 200,000 copies, this he praises with such innocent delight – and he has calculated that if all these copies were set out in a row back to back, it would take me almost a quarter of an hour to pass them, walking briskly – and that is only one of my books! 'Practical' as I am (!), I thought at once: is this going to help me to keep my feet warm?[35]

This human, decent relationship between poet and publisher, Rilke's kindly, grateful humour, Kippenberg's pride and good nature, shine in a genial light during those winter hours spent together in the big old drawing-room at Berg Castle.

Rilke also discussed with Kippenberg the problem of his future. He would have liked most of all to return to Paris in the spring,

but the rapid deterioration of the German mark put this out of
the question. That wretched business of the German inflation
caused Rilke a great deal of worry during his first years in
Switzerland, for even when the Insel-Verlag sent him large sums
of money they were not enough for him to live on. Without any
doubt Kippenberg wanted Rilke to settle in Germany, but to this
idea the latter remained resolutely opposed. He recommended
Berg to his publisher as the model home, the place that he himself
would have loved to live and work in for years. 'My publisher
beamed', Rilke informed his hosts,

to find me in such seclusion – not only as the shrewd businessman,
who could hope for a manuscript from these conditions, but also as the
unselfish-honest friend that he has been to me for more than a
decade and a half; in this second capacity it quite simply made him
happy to see me in surroundings so helpful and favourable to the slow
recovery of my inner life, especially after the devastation of the war
years. . . . 'This is what I need', I kept repeating to my good attentive
friend, holding up Berg as an example, Leni being, as you can well
understand, included, as indispensable and altogether ideal. Let's
hope he has taken it to heart.[36]

As during later years Rilke often spoke in this way, blessing
Providence for leading him to the old house, we may surely see
more than the expression of a transitory contentment in the
remark that 'Berg Castle is already shown as a capital on the map
of my destiny, and has its place in this intimate topography close
to Moscow, Paris, Toleda, Ronda and the friendly Castle of
Duino'.[37] Yet even this favour, received by the troubadour with
such touching gratitude, came to an end. It had certainly helped
him a great deal, for the early summer of 1921 found him staying
on with renewed hope in the country which had given him this
sheltering refuge. Was it obstinacy, faith or instinct which made
Rilke stand firm in the face of every persuasion to leave that
country, which had seemed to him first a place of transit and then
a waiting-room? He himself admitted in a letter from Berg: 'But
since coming to Switzerland I have gone about with the often
repressed, often freely admitted hope that some arrangement,
some compensation, was waiting for me precisely in this land.'[38]

2

THE MAIDS' ROOM AT THE PRIORY

ONCE again – for the last time in his life – Rainer Maria Rilke turned his steps towards the unknown. Once again he set out to look for a permanent home, or rather, as was his way, prepared to wait patiently until a kind Providence should enable him to find one. That the problem of his future and of where to live never left him goes without saying, but he was no longer tormented by it as he had been previously. A note of inward stability and cheerfulness sounds in the journal which the poet kept during the weeks after he left Berg.[39] While thinking of his uncertain future he recalled a sentence he had read in Anatole France's *Monsieur Bergeret à Paris*; it ran: '*L'avenir il y faut travailler comme les tisseurs de haute lice travaillent à leur tapisserie, sans le voir.*' ('We must work at the future as highloom weavers work at their tapestry: without seeing it.') This sentence he wrote on a card and preserved carefully among his notes in a little envelope. At that time, when he was looking for a gentle hint from fate, he was struck by some inscriptions under the clock on the gate-tower of Saint Prex, which he took to be the first oracles of his new surroundings. One of these read: '*Celui qui veille voit venir l'heure de son départ.*' ('The vigilant see the hour of their departure coming.')

On leaving his Berg hermitage, Rilke had gone by car to West Switzerland, accompanied by Mme Wunderly-Volkart and her son. He had no use for covering long distances rapidly in a car, but liked to progress in an old-fashioned way, making detours to unknown or out-of-the-way places and stopping whenever he saw, or thought he might see, something that appealed to him. . . . After a detour through Solothurn he came in this way to Lake Geneva, where he took lodgings in the Pays de Vaud district, at Etoy near Morges. The *pension* in which for several weeks he had a friendly room was a simple house which had been an Augustan priory in the Middle Ages, and was still called *Prieuré d'Etoy*. He stayed from mid-May in the neighbourhood of Lake Geneva, visiting its lovely places, without realising that he was following in the footsteps of great poets such as Jean-Jacques Rousseau, Lord Byron, Shelley and Lamartine, all of whom had loved these shores.

Rainer Maria Rilke has added an important chapter to the literary history of this delightful lake country by his repeated visits and the many meetings he had, especially in his later years, with Edmond Jaloux, Paul Valéry and others. But his quiet, unnoticed sojourn in Etoy is perhaps the most beautiful episode of them all. No doubt the move from Berg seemed to him lamentable at first. Immediately after he arrived he wrote in a letter which he himself marked *Journal*:

We die to one set of surroundings and awake to another which we have to 'bring into the world' ourselves, at first it seems difficult to find a connection with our own consciousness, then all at once we 'continue to live' – though it is inexplicable as yet there are signs to indicate that he who is now dealing with the maids' room at the Priory is the same who enjoyed the favour and confidence of the old château by the Irschel. Already the mail forwarded by Frl. A . . . gives a proof of continuity. . . .[40]

And, as usual, he made an effort to come to terms with the small things about him, touching the unfamiliar objects almost shyly and taking possession of them.

On one of his first walks there he discovered the village rubbish heaps, hidden in a little wood near by. Was it Rilke or Malte Laurids Brigge who wrote that detailed description of refuse in his notebook? One of the subterranean aspects of Rilke's sensibility comes into the light here, forcing him to notice the useless, revolting left-overs of domestic life. One is involuntarily reminded of that horrible passage in *Malte* where the upstanding, sole surviving end wall of a house is described. Commenting on the episode, Rilke confesses:

How often, when I think of it (Strindberg would have described and explained it in his 'Blue Books' with all the '*Schadenfreude*' of his superstition), how often has my longing for lonely places led me to ashpits and rubbish dumps – the worst were in Tunis and the neighbourhood of Cairo, where these precipitations and 'dregs' of life formed whole mountain ranges and ravines, haunted by a ghostlike population of yellow, ravenous dogs which were continually derided by the hard grins of sharp, pointed objects, displaying such toothlike teeth that one could have imagined the ground was snapping and snarling at those nervous, desperate dogs.

– That is what Rilke is reminded of in the Etoy woods, which 'are of course completely innocent for all their *débris*'. He goes on: 'We do well to stay on the open roads in the breath of the meadows, in spite of the burning sunlight.'[41] The solitary wanderer seems to have stuck to this plan from now on, for as far as we know this reminder of one of the horrors of Malte's world is unique among his notes of the time.

Strange to say, this sudden hark back to an old inner discord did not cast any lingering shadow on his time by Lake Geneva – for he experienced some increasingly happy, serene, almost carefree weeks. He looked upon Etoy as a holiday, a time of freedom from duties to himself and his work. In such a frame of mind he managed to lead an agreeable life, and to avoid melancholy and perplexing thoughts. His reading consisted mostly of works by modern French writers: a novel by Jean Schlumberger, about which he wrote to the author, the fourth volume of Proust's *À la Recherche du Temps Perdu*: how early he was to recognise the importance of this writer we know from his pre-war letters to his publisher and the Princess Taxis.[42] He came across the *Cahiers Verts*,[43] a new series published by Daniel Halévy, and advised the Princess to give up her subscription to the *Literarische Echo* and subscribe to this instead. He was delighted to receive letters from André Gide and Charles Vildrac. At Berg during the winter Rilke had seen one of Paul Valéry's poems in a periodical, and had immediately been greatly impressed by him. And as though to emphasise these links with his former life, he heard from Mme Landowska – mother of Wanda Landowska, the harpsichord player – that two boxfuls of his belongings, saved from the wartime auction, had turned up in Paris and were being kept safely for him.

Almost with the impatience of a child on holiday who is reminded of his homework, Rilke shook off the religious questions about which he had been corresponding with the Berg clergyman, Rudolf Zimmerman. He even made play in one of his letters with the humourous thought of what it would be like if he, Rilke, became 'Vicar of Flaach' (by the Irschel). And after he had exercised his high spirits sufficiently on this comic idea, he went on, more seriously:

There was no need to mention God. It often gives me an immense satisfaction to spare him – to be deeply disturbed and *yet not trouble him. Qu'il ce repose. C'est assez encombrant d'avoir faire le monde*, it would be a *courtoisie* on the part of this world to refrain from mentioning God, at least for a time, his name, in all languages, has something indescribably evadeable about it – (which is what prevented me from becoming Vicar of Flaach).[44]

It was not difficult for Rilke to introduce an idyllic note into his life at Etoy: his immediate surroundings gave him every help. Two children, girls of eleven and fifteen, fellow guests at the Priory, were a source of endless delight to him, their doings captured his attention every day. His stories of the stone-deaf maid who looked after him were devastatingly funny. The animal lover in him was touched by the friendship of a cat, and by the trust that some pigeons showed him. We are told of another important matter: that the coffee which he had brought to his room was first rate! His pleasure in an innocent enjoyment of life had been aroused once more, and the brightness and kindliness of the season scared away the winter's ghosts. To the Princess Taxis, from whom he was expecting a visit, Rilke wrote on May 22nd:

If the loss of Berg and the *dépit* that I could not welcome you there were not in the background, I should have to call Etoy wonderful. It will delight you, it is the happiest season for this lake, the broom is in flower, the yellow, fragrant kind that I haven't seen since Brittany – and how much else. And roses, roses – thousands are making ready – there is an old, prodigal *Gloire de Dijon* climbing up to my window, and the view from that includes the lake (in the distance) and the Savoy Mountains – beneath it bloom the two terraces of a pleasant garden. . . .[45]

In another letter written on the same day Rilke remarks: 'If these really are my last days in Switzerland, it is rather strange that I have almost the same view from my window that I had at the *Ferme* near Nyon, where I stayed as the guest of Countess Dobrensky when I first came to Switzerland.'[46]

Naturally, in the course of adapting himself to his new surroundings, Rilke did not fail to have his usual intimate dialogue with local scenery and history: he always had to know what sort of ground he was treading on. In the course of the past two years he had selected for himself those aspects of his adopted country that most appealed to him, satisfying his need for order and protection: in the old lanes of Bern, under the Soglio sky which was already Italy's, within the sound of Tessin's pealing bells, in the cultured houses of Basle, in the midst of Berg by the Irschel's gentle hill country, in the floating atmosphere of Geneva which so recalled Paris. Now he added to these experiences and impressions the glorious Maytime blossom of the Valais coastline. On one of his first days at Etoy Rilke went to Lausanne. At first he 'could not make much of this overcrowded town' – but later, when he was living at Muzot, he often went there. During his last years he enjoyed visiting Lausanne friends, including a circle of local and French writers. He used to sit for long on a seat in front of the cathedral, and found the Place de la Palud and the steps leading from it to the cathedral very pleasing. With the little town of Saint Prex, on the lake between Lausanne and Geneva, he fell in love at once; he preferred it to any other place in the neighbourhood, for the sight of it brought him 'a profound peace'. He wrote:

An old, monastery-like building and a row of houses with wide gardens in front of them leave open a beautiful stretch of shore; at the end of this view, where the peninsula of Saint-Prex reaches its point, there is an old mansion with glorious trees, an old garden wall edging the lake, a garden pavilion right inside the park, and, further back, facing the little town, the wonderful old grey house (which might be an Italian building). A large balcony projects from it, with a simple railing made up of alternating straight and twisted rails, a simple device which has a most charming effect, as if the railing had been made by calm and wind. Of course I sat in front of the wall in a rapture of admiration. . . .[47]

Of the castles round about he admired Vufflens and, even more, Allaman, which seemed to him 'admirablement fier' with its open courtyard and the two mighty plane trees by the entrance.

Over Whitsuntide Rilke, in his little room at Etoy Priory, was immersed in a book. He told his friends that it absorbed him completely and kept him from his bed, and he wrote pages about it in his holiday diary. Who would have guessed that the title of this thrilling work was: *History of the Swiss on Foreign Service*?[48] Some notes that he made in the margins are revealing about the psychological motives for his constant study of local and personal history; they are also a typical example of his bilingual style. '*J'en raffole*,' he says of this book,

et c'est presque aussi dangereux pour moi que l'Almanach,[49] *tout m'interesse, tant de portraits, tant de vies que l'on dévine*, so much fate, so much will to get away – I first opened the book at General Faesi – and all these adventurers, this Moginié from Chésalles p. Moudon, who, as it might have been in the 'Thousand and one Nights,' married the Grand Mogul's daughter, the Princess Neidonne Begoum, *ah les Suisses ne manquement pas du tout de fantaisie s'ils sortent un peu de leur république et si on les laisse faire* – and, worthy of special note, that wonderful old General de Saint-Saphorin, with a castle near Morgues here, who, when Voltaire found him reading his Bible one morning and laughed at him for it, looked up quickly, said: '*Faites atteler pour Monsieur de Voltaire*' and went on reading – I simply must go and look for this castle *pour rendre hommage à ce digne général* – it isn't mentioned anywhere, but according to the picture it must still exist. And find a portrait of Louis Beat de Muralt, I should now like to see one of him in old age, at the time when he undertook the wonderful 'inspired' journey[50] – *oh que des portraits sont amusants à voir, chacun me semble un commencement d'une histoire que l'on devine*. How obstinate and eccentric they look, all these speaking likenesses (not one Planta among them) and how clever the Salis lot! A very noble de Mestral shows up *avantageusement* – but *cela foissonne des Wattenwyl*; they have done best from about the sixteenth century onward as far as the *modelé* of the mouth goes, wonderfully intelligent curves start appearing then, mouths that have been formed by silence, but by keeping closed on graceful or successful ideas, *qu'ils dédaignent de mêler aux incidents communs.* . . .[51]

Having ended these considerations, Rilke remarks that the 'History' has made it impossible for him to leave Switzerland in the immediate future: he wants to remain on her soil in order to examine his new discoveries and pursue them further.

One of the poet's characteristic traits, and one that might very easily be misunderstood, is seen here in a most revealing light. Just as there is no question of attributing his predilection for old houses and castles to social prejudice or any similar motive, so we must not suspect his interest in noble families and historic names of having its roots in ordinary, idle snobbishness. Rilke's commentaries on the lives of the old Swiss soldiers show him, as we take a closer look at his words, as a psychologist and physiogmonist who, in spite of all his enthusiasm about what he has been reading, observes well and judges shrewdly. As he turns these pages, his intense interest in the old portraits – similar to that aroused by the 'little Escher girl' at Berg – suggests that the iconography was much more important to him than the somewhat fantastic historical appendages. His artist's eye delighted in comparing, whenever possible, portraits of the same person made at different times of life, and also portraits of individuals belonging to different generations of the same family; then again he enjoyed tracing likenesses to people of the past in their living descendants. (Among the notes quoted above there is a passage bearing on this which for obvious reasons cannot be quoted here.) I remember once at Muzot Rilke showing me an illustrated work on the history of the Reinharts of Winterthur and commenting on it. This family rose in the course of a few generations from artisans to big business people, owners of a firm engaged in world-wide trade. Turning from one portrait to another in this book, Rilke drew my attention to the way the features gained in refinement, becoming more distinguished and urbane in the grandson and great-grandson; also to the mouths, in the curves of which the gradual improvement could be seen most plainly. It was the slow process of selection that Rilke found so fascinating to study, the generation- or century-long stages in the modelling of social or facial type. He enjoyed visiting the great sculptress History in her studio, questioning her about the secrets of her art, examining and comparing heads and figures in their various stages of development. He wanted to study these historic families as they rose, flourished and declined, as well as all the variations of family likeness appearing in individual members. In the literary world, it was this theme which made him enthusiastic about Thomas Mann's *Buddenbrooks*,[52] and it occurs also in his own *Malte*.

Malte Laurids Brigge is the highly civilised, impoverished scion of a noble Danish family, of whose older members there are some remarkable, penetrating descriptions. From thumbing through an illustrated history book, designed simply to entertain, Rilke found his way easily to a deep study of facial and psychological relationships. It should never be forgotten that during his formative years he went industriously to school with painters and sculptors, and that his own creative work was essentially visual. He had the most extraordinary gift of observation where nature and works of art were concerned. He loved to use in conversation images and comparisons taken from the visual arts – as when he said of a young man whom he had not seen for some time: 'He was a sketch, now he is a portrait.'

His weakness for the nobility sprang from various impulses – and one can say of him as he himself once said of Proust, whom he admired as few writers of his generation did: 'How narrowly he missed being a snob!' Although his own origins were middle class and provincial, Rilke's way of life was never in the least 'bourgeois', and his taste for the unaverage drew him all his life to two different kinds of people: artists and the aristocracy. To these groups all his friends, both male and female, belonged – with, of course, a few exceptions, and important ones at that. What appealed to him in both groups was the absence of a bourgeois outlook; he was equally at home in the artist's studio, the castle or the patrician house. With his highly developed aesthetic sense, he enjoyed the aristocracy's cultured style of living, their beautiful houses and elegant manners. He had a strong feeling for the heraldic style and was, moreover, an expert on matters genealogical. To put it bluntly, the offspring of an ancient line gave him the same sort of aesthetic pleasure that an animal of fine pedigree arouses in a horse or dog lover. On this point Rilke was at one with the great Frenchman Marcel Proust. Like Proust he was attracted by aristocratic society and by its peculiarities: coming as they did from middle-class backgrounds, both writers were all the better fitted to be observers of this alien world. Rilke's admiration for Proust's *Le Côte de Guermantes*, published in 1920 and 1921, knew no bounds. He read this book at Etoy Priory, almost simultaneously with the history of the old military families, and the two were perhaps not so far apart in his mind as one might suppose. He makes a thoroughly Proustian remark when he says that some of the aristocrats portrayed in the history book keep their intelligent mouths closed upon gracious ideas, because they refuse to have them mixed up with everyday affairs. According to Edmond Jaloux, who knew them both well, the Parisian novelist and the Austrian poet were undoubtedly kindred spirits: both had a specially sensitive organ of appreciation for the over-refinements of an ancient culture and of an exclusive layer of society. Their modes of literary expression were quite different because their intellects were very unlike; but for all that, these two writers, among the most individual of their time, are remarkably close in their aesthetic feeling and punctilious behaviour to the people and objects about them, the likeness extending even to their attitude to their work. This correspondence of human and artistic personality goes even further and deeper. H. E. Holthusen says: 'What Marcel Proust did for French prose Rilke did for German lyric poetry: opened up an entirely new microcosmic consciousness, a sort of micro-physic of the heart, through remembering, interiorising and differentiating intellectually.'[52]

Rilke was not in the mood for creative work at Etoy, although he stayed there for over two months. He confined his occupations to reading and letter writing. While he was still at Berg he had received a manuscript of collected poems from the young Austrian poet Alexander Lernet-Holenia, entitled *Kanzonnair*. Rilke had used 'all his influence' with the Insel-Verlag on behalf of these poems; 'it was one of the rare instances where one could do this', he wrote to the Princess Taxis.[53] It was also one of the instances when a poet educated in the school of the Rilkean lyric had succeeded in freeing himself from it to such an extent that his poetry had acquired its own sound and weight. In a letter written at Etoy Rilke said that Lernet in his *Kanzonnair* had achieved a work of 'important coinage and execution. Both dangers', he writes,

the one of preciosity, of simple showing-off, and the other of getting stuck in my 'school' – with him I have felt almost always that conformity was apprenticeship, the good submission of the *apprenti* – both dangers have been overcome, the *Kanzonniar* on the whole breathes wonderfully freely and his vision, always more individually conceived and recognised, gives the poems a direct, even an over-powering strength.[54]

When one thinks of all the verses by young German poets in which Rilkean music and imagery live a ghostly existence because the authors could not emerge from the apprentice and imitator stage, these words uttered by their master sound like a posthumous exhortation, or even disapproval of their under-takings. It was not Rilke's way to found a school or a circle, like Stefan George, setting himself up as a poetic lawgiver. He main-tained that all teaching was simply a pointing in the right direction. And although he knew that many contemporary young people looked to him as a signpost, he had no wish to gather them about him like a schoolmaster and ask them to remain with him. Each must find his own way and walk in it, directed by his own inner law: it was only when one of them attained the freedom to do really individual work that Rilke's appreciation became whole-hearted. Although well aware of his own value as a poet, he never thought of himself as a model, as an 'authority', and even when responding to requests for advice he would proceed most warily, careful not to put any restriction on the freedom of the other.

The time at Etoy produced another example of his readiness to help literary aspirants. Rolf von Ungern-Sternberg had sent him the MS. of his translation of Jean Moréas' *Stanzas*. Rilke knew and admired Moréas and had himself at one time translated some of the stanzas. In Germany he had talked over the problem of translating Moréas very thoroughly with Ungern. In the main he agreed with Ungern's version, on which he congratulated him – except in the case of one poem about which he differed completely. This stanza happened to be one that Rilke had translated, and he sent his own version to Ungern 'as a little gift to celebrate your completion of the work', accompanying it with the request that he would 'dispose of it as if it were entirely your own property'. Ungern gratefully accepted this magnanimous offer, and included Rilke's stanza in his collection, which he dedicated to 'the master of the German language to whose kind advice and warm-hearted assistance this translation from the French owes its conclusion'.[55]

In spite of being mentally so active and buoyant, and in such friendly surroundings, Rilke was not altogether free at Etoy from inward pressures and outward cares. No real turning-point had appeared as yet in his life or in his work. Human attachments had developed into obligations which – as always happened in the case of his love-affairs – distressed and alarmed him with their demands. The Princess Taxis relates how he confided his troubles to her when she came to visit him by the Lake of Geneva. She wrote afterwards in her diary:

I keep worrying about Serafico. Will they never let him alone, will he never find a woman who loves him enough to understand what he needs – to live for him without thinking of her own unimportant little life? Poor Serafico, how anxiously he asked me again and again whether I thought that somewhere there might be a loving person who would be ready to step back in a moment when the voice called him. The answer was difficult. A woman who will give her whole heart without demanding anything for herself – he wants nothing less than that! His question would have seemed more than a little naïve and egotistical if one had not felt in it the imperious will shaping this destiny, which no power whatever can thwart.[56]

The Princess goes on to say that she is often astonished at the extraordinary attraction that women have for him; he has frequently told her that it is only to them he can talk, that they are the only ones he can understand, and that he really likes going about only with women; but then, the Princess adds, comes the moment of flight, when he unties the knot that holds him – and the same old unhappiness begins all over again. This good and clever woman closes the entry in her diary with the words: 'I can see no way out'. [57]

The problem too, of where Rilke was eventually to settle down still remained unsolved. 'What can possibly happen now, after the Berg miracle?' he asked. The possibilities that Switzerland had to offer him seemed to be exhausted, yet he lacked the courage to travel. Paris was not to be thought of because of the currency. A young Austrian couple, the painter Purtscher and his wife Nora Wydenbruck (a relative of the Princess Taxis), invited him to come to Carinthia, where they lived; it was also the home (Klagenfurt) of Alexander Lernet-Holenia. Rilke thought of Carinthia as his family's ancestral home – 'the legendary one' he would add prudently. Genealogists could find no connection between the Rilkes who had once flourished in Carinthia and the Rilkes of Czechoslovakia, in spite of the greyhound coat of arms which they had in common. (This greyhound, which appeared on Klagenfurt town hall, was engraved on the seal which Rilke had inherited from his Czechoslovakian great-grandfather and with which he was in the habit of sealing his letters.) Genealogy was only one of the many paths explored by Rilke in his search for links between himself and the outer world; the study of it had led him as a young man to discover the document about Cornet Christoph Rilke which inspired the famous early work. Excited by the correspondence with Lernet and the Purtschers, he had the strange idea that he 'would link up with the year 1276' – the date, apparently, on Klagenfurt town hall – and carry on from there. The words which follow give us a deep insight into the workings of the poet's mind: '. . . but I wrote 1921 without any real obligation to it, and perhaps I have been trying for a lifetime to escape from tradition only because the tradition was not sufficiently clear to me. Do I recognise it there at last in the oldest connection of all?'[58] Flight from family, home, tradition and love: beyond any doubt that was one of the basic themes of Rilke's life, and the dangers to which it gave rise are obvious. That, at the same time, and especially in his maturer years, he was engaged in a desperate search for tradition, home and love, only proves once again how ambivalent was his attitude to life. He writes to Rolf von Ungern – again from Etoy, which seems to have been a spot conducive to self-criticism – that his lack of a settled place to live in was entirely his own fault. (His Munich flat had been confiscated in February and 'the poor defenceless aftergrowth' of his furniture and books had been moved to Leipzig.) Of his lost native land he says in his letter to Ungern:

The city I grew up in (Prague) did not provide the right soil for it (i.e. for the 'development of a useful "homeland consciousness" ') its air was suited neither to my breath nor to my plough. So it came about that I acquired homelands chosen by myself, according to the degree of their responsiveness, that is to say, I involuntarily pretended to have roots wherever the visible obligingly met my instinctive need for expression with a supply of adequate images. . . .

For as long as the world stood open to him, Rilke continues, there grew from all that he acquired in this way 'something like a hovering and sustaining place, as it were above the countries'.[59]

When, at the beginning of June, the Princess Taxis came to visit her grandchildren in nearby Rolle, there were frequent meetings between her and the poet. The correspondence between the two, which has now been published in its entirety, and is one of the four collections of Rilke's correspondence richest in biographical material, bears splendid witness to the faithful, clear friendship between the older patroness-friend and him to whom she gave the rather too elegant name of 'Dottor Serafico'. Certainly Marie Thurn und Taxis could not penetrate into the labyrinth of Rilke's inner life, into the complications of his nature, nor could she comprehend what was most individual and essential in his work. But she was in the finest sense of the word a great lady, original, intelligent and full of charming common sense. A Maecenas and aristocrat with whom it was a pleasure to read Dante's *Divine Comedy* or correspond about Proust, she had a flair for dealing with literary men, was astonishingly well read in several languages and, though familiar with the tried and traditional, always open to new ideas. She was an old-style princess who kept up with the times, a benevolent princess who gathered round her not only the numerous members of her family circle, her relatives and social equals, but also a court of writers, poets and musicians – whether at Duino overlooking the Adriatic, her Bohemian castle Lautschin, or Vienna. She was convinced that she had had a difficult life, which may well have been true of anyone possessing such lordly wealth in a time of social decline; but she was always eager for education, beauty and travel, surrounded by an army of faithful servants, completely without guile, never weary of social life and conversation, proud of her intellectual acquaintances and friends, whom she counted as her life's finest adornment and to whom she was always touchingly faithful. She was, moreover, capable of translating Rilke's poems into Italian, including the first two Elegies, written at her Castle of Duino. Here, in short, was an individual who had courageously carried over unbroken into a new century and another era the way of life belonging to her rank and social position, and who, in spite of catastrophes, never grumbled or became depressed but remained good-humoured and helpful; who found the point of existence in a civilized enjoyment of life– a sovereign without a realm, a princess without subjects but with many friends, of whom Rilke was her favourite. In the letters she wrote to Rilke and he to her, letters into which both correspondents have put mind, heart and wit, we encounter the good, the sincere and the noble. They are the pure legacy of a time of confusion, an important witness to a culture which has almost vanished.

The Princess writes in her memoirs that she spent a 'glorious time' with Rilke in Etoy and Rolle – but goes on to give an account of all Rilke's troubles, arising from his persistent inability to do creative work, and also from his personal relationships. She urged him to be patient and not to expose the existing poems and fragments to premature publication. He confessed later that her advice had prevented him from doing this, as he had decided on publication in a moment of profound discouragement.

Naturally Rilke discussed with the Princess the still undecided question of a permanent home – Carinthia, Rome, North Italy, or Bohemia, where the Princess again offered him the garden house at Lautschin. As regards Lautschin, he would do no more than promise to visit her and her husband there in the summer, by which time he had discovered Muzot and made the old Valaisian tower ready for occupation. Of Rilke's attitude to Bohemia the Princess wrote: 'He loved its forests but otherwise it was alien to him.'[60] His Venetian friends the V—'s had also offered him the use of a small house in the North of Italy. Apparently Rilke was afraid of being dependent even on such well-meaning noble Maecenas. We are doing no harm to the memory of the Princess Taxis, which lives on in the dedication to the *Duino Elegies*, if we say here why he would not take advantage of her hospitality. He is conscious, he writes from Etoy (before meeting the Princess again),

how little the V—'s are able to understand what I need. And the Princess Taxis *can't either*, she has such a *vague idée* of how few my basic needs are, but how clearly defined are the ten things which have ultimately to fill the frame of this minimum, if my life is to be protected, clear and fruitful: for that she lacks the vision, the love and the patience.[61]

Rilke goes on to remark, with a perception gained from years of associating with aristocratic circles, that such people have for centuries been accustomed to think of the practical problems of life as 'servants' problems', which explains 'that discomfort-in-spite-of-everything in their wonderfully well cared for houses'. If he were to decide on the little house at Lautschin, he would know well 'what not to expect there'. On one occasion at that time he had written to the Princess herself about his '$7\frac{1}{2}$ requirements', which were very precise and on which he depended – but without specifying them. There is no need to doubt Rilke's sincerity when he writes from Muzot, recalling the Princess's Etoy visit: '. . . our meeting has done me good, *indescribably*', and adds that it was only a start of all they had to say to each other, not diminishing in the least 'the necessity for some more weeks in each other's company'.

His misgivings about making a permanent home on the Taxis estate in Czechoslovakia sprang from his dread of the immense amount of social activity going on there; he was apprehensive too about his prospective hosts' somewhat casual treatment of domestic affairs, that indifference to life's small necessities characteristic of people who are suspended above the lowlands of everyday existence. There was no question of any dimming of his old friendship with Marie Thurn und Taxis, to whom he was devoted, although he could look at her with a critical eye.

On the subject of Rilke's failure to visit Bohemia – for he never went back there – the Princess wrote in her memoirs: 'It was his destiny to remain in Switzerland, and in spite of being anxious about his continual wanderings to and fro, I could not rid myself of the strange belief that his way would not again bring him to us; in fact we were not to see him in his native land again.[62] In July 1921 Rilke left Lake Geneva for the neighbourhood of Sierre in the Valais, the district which had appealed to him so much in the autumn of the previous year. There he found the home that was to shelter him until he died.

Rainer Maria Rilke, Greifensee, 1923

Photograph: H. Wyss

The Château of Muzot

The Château of Muzot and the Completion of the *Duino Elegies*

What is epochal and epoch making about Rilke's poetry, especially his later poetry, is above all the fact that he is not concerned with the half problems or half realities of this world of ours, much less with staking out a poetic plot on which to build the ivory tower of pure beauty; instead, he puts the epoch's cardinal question, the really truth seeking question. He is thus the opponent of the '*terribles simplificateurs*', as Jacob Burckhardt calls them, the terrible simplifiers who believe that they can understand and dominate this world by applying some of their poor half truths and half errors which they call '*Weltanschauungen*'. He is their opponent, but he stands in secret correspondence to them.

HANS EGON HOLTHUSEN

H

1

RILKE IN MUZOT

THE sheltering roof, the permanent home, were not for Rainer Maria Rilke an end in themselves. Loudly as the cry for both came from his tormented soul, it was not the eternal pilgrim's dearest wish to own a house, to be able to call some place his own. Even when fulfilment was granted him and he had settled down inside the walls of a medieval tower high in the mountains, he was filled with horror at the thought that this arrangement might be bound up with an obligation to remain there permanently. In order that he might be able to leave at any time, to shake the dust from his shoes if he grew weary of staying there, he had expressly stipulated that he would take over the Château of Muzot only as a 'fief'.

It was not his, the poet's, business to fulfil a social task and to govern a household. Son, husband, father, friend, lover, householder: he had been all of these, but he had drawn back from each rôle at the summons of his daemon, whenever creative work called or detained him. This was only the most extreme, most honest consequence of his artistic vocation; the man who is obsessed by such a vocation uncompromisingly orders his behaviour according to the law of 'inspiration' – devotion to his work. He listens with Prometheus in Spitteler's poem to the commands of the 'high mistress'. In the case of the genuine creative artist this asocial way of life finds its justification in the completed work of art. The human worth of the singer is in the song.

However, at the age Rainer Maria Rilke had now reached, a quiet, sheltered life was indispensable to creative work. He had been doing his utmost to find a substitute for Castle Berg, where he had felt close to his work, but where he had not achieved complete concentration. He needed a new refuge, and he wanted to see the future before him 'in one piece': while still in Geneva he had been longing for *'un bloc d'avenir, soit-il même dur à travailler'*. How strongly he was to feel, when settling down inside the primitive, ancient walls of Muzot, the resistant hardness of which he had had so sure an intuition! Nevertheless, he set to work courageously with chisel and hammer, and the longed-for, long-delayed work was accomplished. The first thing he needed, Rilke wrote with despairing audacity, was 'to be alone for a long, long time, perhaps for ever'. The rivalry between social life and artistic work had at last to be decided in favour of the latter. The difficulties impeding concentration had to be overcome. No living being was to be allowed to distract the master on his way to the workshop, not even a dog – as had been well-meaningly suggested – let alone a human companion. He did not want ever again to feel compelled to give in to the claims of those about him. An irresistible urge towards the centre, towards concentration and preparedness, had drawn him into the mountains after the long time of exposure, to shelter behind the knightly bastion of an old fortress. To begin with the roof he himself had chosen was an oppressive burden – like 'heavy, rusty armour', he wrote to Lou Andreas-Salomé. The valley he had at first admired so much he now looked at 'through the hard visor', frightened by the 'challenging heroic landscape'. The sun, burning down on the vineyards, blazed also upon the walls of Muzot. In spite of these hardships the poet came to grips with his new life. He had to embark on an existence that was indeed 'knightly', and in spite of all assaults he remained true to his 'fief', with that immense patience which, he said, would hold out until all came right in the end. Until he was carried to his grave in the beloved valley where the song had been achieved.

Often before, when he was deciding on somewhere to live, the irresistible attractions of a landscape had determined Rilke's choice, and it was the landscape which led him to settle in the Upper Rhone Valley, the Valais or Wallis. The map of his life which he spoke of once in a letter from Berg – that map which made such a strange selection, mysteriously relating Moscow to the Spanish cliff village Ronda, the Dalmatian coast to Paris – was now enriched, thanks to a chance of his *voyages en zig-zags*, by an Alpine scene of very individual character. Having taken possession of it, he never tired of praising it as only he could praise, in conversations and letters, in poems and in prose, in

German and French – the bilingual Valais with its slopes and vineyards, its fortresses and its flowers. He had only to find an object worthy of his praise for the spontaneous side of his nature to appear – the inspired, devoted singer whose heart no suffering could embitter.

We have already mentioned that Rilke saw the Valais for the first time on a delightful, clear autumn day in 1920, before his winter at Berg. On that outing, which took him to Sion (or Sitten), Sierre and Raron, he was reminded both of Spain and Provence. It seemed to him that the severity of the one and the softness of the other were united here, mixed together in an unexpected way and to an unprecedented degree. He remembered longing before the war for a refuge in Spain or the South of France, and he believed that the Valais could offer him surroundings both hard and sweet, such as had once enchanted him in those countries. He admired the way the towers and ruins of Valères and Tourbillon soared up on their steep hills above the little town of Sion: he called the astonishing view 'a beautiful tarsia of stone work and landscape'.

The following detailed description shows how moved he was by his first encounter with that region[1]:

My idea of Switzerland has been considerably enlarged since I came to know *this* landscape: the spaciousness of this valley, which embraces whole plains, the restraint of its mountain slopes, which for all their strength and steepness have nothing remote about them, the lovely, picturesque gradations of colour on the hills below them, and the incomparably graceful way in which they lift their settlements towards the old castle towers – all this is part of an arrangement which never renounces the grand scale – beautiful as a pure talent and wonderfully, continually exercised everywhere. It was in the neighbourhood of Saxon, right behind St Maurice, that we first understood it: the embroidery of the vineyards, the dark-bright composition, already mentioned, of the inhabited middle distance, and behind, no more intrusive than tapestry, indeed like reflections of slopes, the mountains. Girls were standing on the platform in native costume, black, their pretty, calm faces under the flat hood of the *dix-huitième* – and I read in Baedeker that the mountain from the foot of which they came has a name that one of them might have given it: *La*

Pierre à voir! Is it due to Catholicism: that the *charme* of the eighteenth century is so often found preserved in these parts? We found it in the gardens, the steps still looked as if they were wreathed with it, and how many houses have not yet given themselves up. . . .

And further on, breaking into French: '. . . *c'est une Espagne un peu moins fanatique, un peu plus conciliante.* . . . Above, a sky of metallic blue, which also filled in the open gateway of the castle up at Tourbillon. . . .'

Nine months were to go by – spent at Berg and on Lake Geneva – before the poet left Etoy to return to the Valais, this time with the determination to find a home there. Accompanied by Mme Klossowska, he went at the end of June 1921 to Sierre, where he attended Mass on Peter and Paul's Day, visited the owner of the Goubin Tower and, after having a meal with him, went to look over a little house which, however, he did not fancy living in. But he was enthusiastic about his host's medieval tower, also about his large drawing-room and antique furniture: 'one felt as though bewitched'. On the following day Rilke was depressed, disappointed that the prospect of the little house had vanished, for he did not want to 'force' himself to like it. And yet the Valais seemed 'so wonderful, more wonderful than ever before'.

Still, that day was to be one of the most important in his life. A letter written in pencil in a Lausanne café on the return journey gives an account of it. Let us listen to him describing what happened in his own words – (as Rilke described everything, not really addressing Mme Wunderly-Volkart, but talking on paper to the sisterly human being to whom, in those years, he confided all the joys, miseries and happenings of his life with spontaneous honesty and boundless trust)[2]:

The day . . . looked as though it would have to be written off as a whole when, towards evening (now comes the miracle! . . .) we pulled ourselves together to go out again, for the sake of our own consciences – and discovered just think! in the window of the hairdresser, close close to Bellevue, which one passes everyday, the photograph of a tower or little castle '*du treizième siecle*', with – just think! –

with the notice *à 'vendre ou à louer'*: *Chère, et c'est peut-être mon château en Suisse, peut-être!*

The writer interrupts himself here to draw a rough sketch of the Château of Muzot.

Ce n'est que cela, bâtiment historique d'un caractère ravissant, vrai vieux manoir, entouré d'un petit jardin charmant, dans un site merveilleux; ten paces higher a little white church (chapel) *dediée à Ste Anne,* which seemed almost to belong to it, everything matched so perfectly. Inside, three rooms on each floor, some with very austere seventeenth-century furniture! (Besides some horrors that would have to be cleared out.) Linen and crockery can be had from the owner, the kitchen is almost completely furnished. . . . We were up there the whole morning, planning, furnishing, surprised, delighted, almost as if it were ours' already. . . .

Rilke's Muzot joys and Muzot tribulations had already begun during those first days. His friend Mme Klossowska gave him practical help in negotiating with the owners and afterwards with clearing and arranging his new home. Prosaic difficulties and worries of all kinds, including some very trivial ones, soon began to mingle with the pleasures of discovery and the plans for the future. Now it was the rent, which was beyond the poet's means, now the length of time for which he would have to bind himself (Rilke at first wanted to rent Muzot for three months only); then he was horrified by the old tower's extreme discomfort, for there was neither water nor electric light in the house. However, although he could have stayed on at Etoy, he did not want to forgo giving the château a trial:

the Valais outweighs everything else in my wishes. What, *what* this landscape says and means and does to me! Now just as in October. It is gloriously hard and grand, and in the neighbourhood of our château, where we have not only wine but also meadows, corn, fruit trees – at the heart of the garden almost tender. – The little *manoir* is called *Château de Muzot* or *Muzotte* (the 't' is sounded even with the first spelling), I already know a lot of its history, in the oldest time it belonged to a branch of the Blonays who had settled in the Valais, later to the de la Tour Châtillons, the de Chevrons, finally to the de Monthéis family. I shall tell you next time about the unfortunate Isabelle de Chevron, *femme de* Jean de Monthéis – the country people still know about her wedding at Muzot (about 1500) which lasted for three days, and I know the names of all the wedding guests and how they partnered each other. . . .

The writer in the Lausanne café wrote on, describing the little chapel near the castle, telling his friend about 'the swastika, the mysterious Indian crooked cross' carved in deep relief above its door. He told her how lovely the old walls were, not in the least 'gloomy and threatening'; about the two rose pergolas in the garden, and the 'wonderful poplar' at the roadside in front of the château: 'like a symbol again and an exclamation mark, as though it were saying, confirming: look, this is it!' From time to time Rilke made calculations – unpleasant ones, because the rent and living expenses for two people were going to come to 450 francs a month. However, he could forget his worries, and he wrote that he had lain for a whole Sunday morning in the meadow opposite 'his' château, quietly enjoying the magnificent summer morning in that landscape of 'indescribable relatedness and beauty'. He ends this letter, which is such a strange mixture of humour and distress, on a bantering note: '*Est-ce que, naturalisé, je m'appellerai Monsieur de Muzot? Ce serait parfait et si reposant!*'

After spending a few days in Geneva Rilke returned without delay to Sierre, where, staying at the Hotel Bellevue, he made arrangements to rent Muzot and to settle down there. But suddenly he found the decision a difficult one to make, partly because of his fear of being tied, partly because his longed-for home was so primitive and inconvenient: 'The other evening it seemed so cramped and difficult, and then again you see it standing there and it convinces you as though by a magic spell. What to do? What to do?'[3]

The continued devaluation of the German mark warned him relentlessly that he ought to leave Switzerland, and when a letter arrived from Carinthia suggesting a house on the Wörthersee, Rilke's dilemma became more agonising than ever. Nevertheless he believed that the Valais might well be 'the environment for an Elegy winter' and that 'Muzot's future may be to protect me'.[4] In spite of all his scruples, 'this valley inhabited by hills' had an irresistible attraction for the poet. When he grew weary, during 'those dreadfully untransparent days' of questioning himself and asking others for advice, a woodland walk in the Finges Forests – 'which are full of small lakes, some blue, some greenish, some almost black' – never failed to calm and comfort him. He admired, again, the way this region presented so many details in such a grand context; it looked to him like the world on the day after the creation, or the final movement of a Beethoven symphony.

At last the decision was taken. The prospect of being able to spend another winter in Switzerland helped him to overcome his hesitations and anxieties. Werner Reinhart of Winterthur had made up his mind to rent Muzot on Rilke's behalf. The latter used later on to tell his visitors that, by a remarkable coincidence, Werner Reinhart was already acquainted with Muzot through a picture. Four years before coming to the Valais Rilke had bought a picture postcard of Muzot in Sierre, without knowing the exact whereabouts of the striking old house. One of his friends, the painter Rüegg, liked the view so much that he wanted to paint the château and tried in vain to find it. Having failed in his search, Rüegg painted Muzot from the crude photograph on the card, and gave the painting to Werner Reinhart. When Rilke told his Winterthur friend about the 'tower' he had discovered above Sierre, and wanted to live in, both were astonished to find that it was identical with the elusive postcard castle: a coincidence, of course, in which Rilke saw a portent. Subsequently Werner Reinhart bought Muzot and gave it to Rilke to live in for the duration of his life. The poet used jokingly to call the castle's new owner his 'feudal lord'; he dedicated to him the German translation of Paul Valéry's poems, which he made at Muzot. Rilke's condition that he should be able to leave his new home whenever he felt like doing so was respected by his generous patron. That Rainer Maria Rilke always returned to his château may have been due in part to his consciousness that no one was trying to force him to remain there. He was never unfaithful to people or to houses provided that they did not try to put any sort of compulsion on him. The steep, stony hillside path, the light of paraffin lamps and candles, the well in front of the house, the rushing of the mountain stream under the windows, the simple old furniture in the rooms, the little bedroom next to his study, that looked like a monk's cell: of such things was it made up, the knightly but very simple dwelling-place which the poet called home during his last years.

The whole of July was taken up at Muzot with scrubbing, decorating, arranging, and making good the deficiencies in the furniture; and although feminine initiative and skill provided the new inmate with indispensable help, he was daily on the road between Sierre and the little mountain terrace where, as he rounded a bend in the path, the old tower appeared in its meadow setting with the poplar obliquely in front of it. Rilke drew plans of the two floors in his letters to Mme Wunderly; he described to her the state of the rooms and of the furniture he had taken over, noting everything that was missing and would be needed. There was a little covered porch in front of the house where meals could be taken in summer. The main room on the ground floor was the dining-room, with a beautiful old grey stone stove, a magnificent oak table and some seventeenth-century chairs. The little room next to it, which Rilke found 'quite charming', served as a '*boudoir*'. Those who visited the poet at Muzot will never forget the short time spent waiting, full of expectancy, in that room, looking at the huge picture of a saint which covered the whole of one wall, or turning over the pages of a little book lying on the table: '*Cités et Pays Suisses* by Gonzague de Reynold – before the slender, surprisingly young-looking lord of the manor suddenly stood before them, dressed in a dark blue jacket and light grey trousers, bidding the guest a cordial welcome with his urbane manners and in his warm, beautiful voice. . . .

Rilke allotted the third room on the ground floor to the house-keeper. Dark, polished beams, some of them dating from the eighteenth century, give these rooms their character. The doorways are so low that a man has to bend his head when passing through them (Rilke would hold his hand protectingly over you as you were about to go through, warning you to be careful). He had the old wallpapers distempered in lighter colours. Later he suspended from the dining-room ceiling a simple lamp bracket in which several candles would burn at dinner-time, and he hung the portrait of a Swiss officer on the wall. Lover of old portraits though he was, Rilke could derive no pleasure from the 'old Swiss warrior's' hard expression, and he used to turn his back on the portrait during his lonely meals in order to avoid looking at it. But when a guest was at the Muzot table, Rilke would give his usual place to him, seating himself opposite the guest and the picture, a graceful act of politeness which must have cost the host some effort, although few of his guests were aware of it.

The large room on the upper floor was the poet's study. There was certainly not much space to indulge his liking for walking up and down, but it was nicely square, with a table made in the year 1700 which could be extended on either side. A small sofa stood in the corner by the window. The furniture was completed later on by the addition of a small standing desk – an article which Rilke very much valued and used a great deal. He always had a standing desk made for him when he moved into a house for any length of time. The visitor who was fortunate enough to hear Rilke reading his poems at this desk would wait quietly in the sofa corner while his host, with movements careful to the point of solemnity, lit the candles in their candlesticks and placed them in front of him. Erect, with deep but controlled feeling, the poet would fill the nocturnal room with the rhythms and images of the poems, read with strong emphasis and in a virile voice. Unique experiences, for which the little mountain castle was a fit setting. Only the hurried plashing of the stream, which used to fill the pauses in the recital, can be heard today, through Muzot's low windows.[5]

During those first settling-in days candles already occupied an important place among Rilke's requirements. He needed a lot of them, he wrote: 'all those at Berg not quite burnt down, as well as the beautiful candlesticks if possible'. A door led from the study – for which a chest, bookshelves and coloured engravings had to be found – into the bedroom. This room, enlarged by a small stone balcony, overhung the garden, and contained the only mirror in the house: a little hand-mirror for shaving. Nothing was put into the chapel except a *prie-dieu*. Last of all Rilke, with childish pride, ordered some stamped notepaper – the same that, many years later, when its owner had long been lying in Raron churchyard, justified the title *Letters from Muzot* being given to a book.

> 'Château de Muzot
> sur Sierre
> Valais'

ran the heading. Underneath are the words:

> 'Magnificent, isn't it?
> Whoever would've thought it!?'[6]

Yet the fortress had to be conquered; it seemed hostile to the intruder, not responding at once to its audacious guest's advances, as had the more candid Berg. Originally, before discovering Muzot, Rilke had had in mind a château in the rococo style; and such a home would have seemed more appropriate than a medieval tower to this lover of the eighteenth century. For the time being he stuck to his plan of giving Muzot a three months' trial, during which time something else could perhaps be found. Already he welcomed a suggestion that he should take an old house in Kaiserstuhl (on the Rhine) from October 1st to May 1st, a house of which some very attractive photographs had been sent him: 'Since then I have been saying every day, almost longingly, that medieval houses are only possible for us when they have been well inhabited until the *dix-huitième*, and mollified through the influence of that period, and, as it were, broken in to life.'[7] The nearer the moving-in day came (he was still living in the Sierre hotel), the more Rilke wondered what sort of a house this Muzot might be. A house with two faces: the first attractive and cheerful, as it came into view with its poplar, 'but going into the house is always hard hard, like putting on heavy armour'.[8] And after he had laid claim to his unaccustomed knighthood, he was always astonished to find himself really inside the old walls again, and he would look out at the heroic summer, his eyes filling themselves with light and landscape from the windows' abundance.

A certain apprehension is noticeable in the letters written from Muzot during those agitated July days. Living there was difficult; he suffered from the primitive inadequacies of the place. The paraffin lamps dazzled his eyes, and when the first storms arrived he became anxious about the chimney which was in a poor condition. In such moments he was siezed with a longing for Berg and for his spacious study there which would always be irreplacable for him, with its reading corner, its fireplace and its many lighting possibilities. Even when, in the following November, Rilke could report to his publisher 'that preparation and possession taking have now been overcome, and it (Muzot) is more or less ready to be used', he added rather sadly: 'It is not Berg: much is lacking that there was taken for granted – above all the – irreplacable – Leni! As counterbalance, this is a land of pure creation, and this old strong house is just of a size that I can fill with the movements of my daily work.'[9] Then during those early Muzot days there was the burdensome summer heat of the Valais, full of promise for the grapes but oppressive and exhausting for human beings. It should be stressed here that in Rilke's diary letters of that period there are no complaints about health, such as we read in the Locarno and Schönenberg letters. But the light-heartedness of the May days in Etoy has gone from these lines; his mood has become stern and serious; the poet is beginning to concentrate on his coming work. There is no excuse now, not even the possibility of a disturbance or interruption.

Behind the achievement of moving into his new home we can sense the increasingly urgent claims being made upon him by his artist's conscience. In the last resort the story of the 'discovery' and 'conquest' of the little Muzot fortress was an allegory. All through his life, the way to the centre of his poetic workshop led through the concrete, objective rooms of the place he was living in at the time. Inversely, the struggle to get his surroundings into shape hinted at the coming creative effort. The furnishing of a house was, like letter writing, a necessary detour, or, to be more precise, a step in the direction of 'work'. As though to forestall the question: what was the use of making such a fuss about choosing and furnishing a home, he explained to me as he showed me over Muzot that a poet lacked the tangible raw material, offering resistance and allowing itself to be moulded, which was at the disposal of the sculptor and even of the painter. Poetry was a sublimated art form; it seemed – he said, with a gesture as though trying to draw water with his hands – to run through your fingers. For him environment and furniture replaced the missing raw material to some extent, giving him a chance to exercise his creative faculties. During the course of the same conversation he remarked also that the accomplishment of tidying up his living quarters and belongings was often a good omen for his future work. As he spoke he lifted the lid of a chest and let me have a glimpse of piles of letters in packets, manuscripts and books arranged in the most wonderful order. This orderliness, this precision with regard to the smallest and least important matters, was one of the most striking features about Rainer Maria's way of life. Speaking of the great effort it cost him to deal with his correspondence, he said once that the urge 'to do everything *well*' sprang 'a little . . . from an overflow of the sense of duty to my work: when we think', this very revealing observation continues,

that there is only one set of words really fitted to express any one situation that we want to describe – grace must come to our help in our work to make us so divinely exact, in life it's only effort that can make us human – alas – or almost so. But anyone who knows that blissful precision at the core of art is tormented at always remaining *à peu près* with regard to so many fields of accomplishment, or even bungling, making a mess of things. . . .[10]

It was, after all, an infallible instinct which led the poet to tackle the difficulties of hard Muzot at the moment when he was ready to take up the thread of the Elegies again and spin it further – that thread which had been broken so many years before. Berg had made everything easy for him – it had spoken to him, given its heart to him – but at Berg he had not been entirely successful in concentrating on his work. That was only to be made possible by his new home's sturdy resistance, and by his struggle to take possession of it. For what he was about to do in Muzot ought to have been done as long ago as 1914. After seven years of painful silence and with 'a heart diminished' by fate, he stood before what he considered to be his greatest task.

When she saw his 'armour' weighing so heavily upon him, his companion advised Rilke to leave the tower. But he protested: the little boy so skilfully and diligently doing the Muzot errands – wasn't his name *Essayez*? Try![11] Thus another omen came to the aid of this undecided yet obstinate man. Almost enviously, he would see the boy standing outside the door every morning at a quarter past seven 'with wonderful milk and butter', or watch him 'working away at the saw like a hero', engaged in a fervent struggle with the gigantic logs. 'If only I were half so efficient', sighed the new lord of the manor. 'Being there in the old tower has brought about a curious change: as though one did not see any longer the things one had admired before, or else; did not look at them any longer. . . . It should be given a serious trial, *quand même!* . . .'[12]

Rilke had been a little frightened by the transition from the 'Bellevue' in Sierre – an hotel which he found particularly congenial – to Muzot, when the latter was eventually ready for occupation. He felt that he had abandoned the rôle of comfortable spectator in order to move into the landscape and himself become part of it. '*Ce Muzotisme qui a failli devenir une espèce de maladie, sera au bout du compte quand-même une croyance, – espérons-le!*'[13] The decisive word had been spoken: in spite of everything that could be said against it Muzot was a faith – the 'Muzotism' which had almost made him ill was a code for belief in himself. These words conclude the elaborate reflections on his experiences with Muzot made by Rilke during that month of July. It was an adventure, the critical nature of which can be seen in every line of the poet's notes; but the crisis led to a real turning-point in his life. Already there was hope, and behind his slowly subsiding doubts fulfilment awaited him.

2

A STORM

THE enduring results of Rilke's first winter at Muzot – the birth of the *Duino Elegies* and the *Sonnets to Orpheus* – ought by rights to take precedence in this account over all accessory events and circumstances. So at least it would seem. Yet the slow, difficult descent into the mine – as he once described the process of preparing for work, using an image that was, like almost all his images, spatial – that slow, difficult descent abounds in references to his goal and hints as to its nature. How can we pass over these in silence? Everything that stood in his way, troubling, hindering, and disquieting him, as well as everything that was helpful to him, serving his ends and raising his spirits, deserves at least a mention here.

A letter to a young girl expresses in unwontedly solemn language the nature of the endeavour which was absorbing the poet at that time.

. . . In a little while I shall perhaps no longer comprehend all the circumstances that gave rise to these songs (the *Duino Elegies*), begun so long ago. . . . When I look into my conscience I see only one, inexorable law whose command is: to shut myself up inside myself and finish in one go this task that was dictated to me from the centre of my heart. I obey. For, as you know, when I was on my way here I wanted only that, and I have no right whatever to change the direction of my will before I have completed my act of sacrifice and obedience.[14]

At Muzot, as at Berg, Rilke regarded the overtaking of his immense arrears of correspondence as an indispensable preliminary to work. Counting his letters one morning, he found that he had written 115; none of them had fewer than four pages; some had eight, others even twelve in his neat handwriting. All gave an account of the new turn his life had taken and referred to the unexpected extension of his stay in Switzerland as a result of settling in the Valais. There were endless variations on the theme of the 'wonderful Rhone valley, restoring to me two landscapes

Photograph: H. Wyss

Muzot from the garden

R. M. Rilke and Paul Valéry at Anthy by Thonon, September 13th, 1926. In the background is the sculptor Henri Vallette.

which I had lost for a time: Spain and Provence'; and of the
'knightly dwelling' which, in spite of all its demands and the
weeks of heatwave, had remained victorious and still kept him
within its walls. To the friends in Austria, Czechoslovakia and
Germany who were always hoping that the poet would eventually
return, he apologised repeatedly, pleading 'this country's powers
of hospitality' which whenever he thought that he had finished
with Switzerland always drew him back by a surprise counter-
manoeuvre.[15]

Rilke's spirits improved, growing more stable and confident,
as winter came on, when he had finally put aside all other plans
(Carinthia, Lautschin, Kaiserstuhl) and had returned to his castle
after a few unavoidable journeys inside Switzerland. Of his
dwelling-place he was able to report that the 'armour' had turned
into an overcoat, rather stiff, but soft enough to be quite wearable.[16]

Muzot has a strange history and there are curious legends
attached to the place. Writing to the Princess Taxis, who was, he
knew, interested in such matters, he recounted at length the
story of the unhappy Isabelle de Chevron whose husband, Jean
de Montheys, was killed in the battle of Marignan. Afterwards
a couple of hot-blooded suitors fought a duel over the young
widow and killed each other. Rilke said that Isabelle used to
creep from Muzot Tower secretly at night with scarcely anything
on and walk to nearby Miège, to the grave of her two admirers,
and that, according to tradition, she was found one morning,
after a bitterly cold winter's night, frozen to death in the churchyard. 'One has to be somewhat prepared', Rilke felt, 'for this
Isabelle, or for the dead Montheys, everlastingly returning from
Marignan like a pendulum; and one ought not to be surprised
at anything.'[17] It is curious that Rilke should later on have
referred to these former inhabitants of Muzot in his will, leaving
instructions that he was not to be buried at Miège – the nearest
village to Muzot – for fear of disturbing poor Isabelle de Chevron
and starting her off again on her restless nocturnal wanderings.

I was reading about these legends in a book on the Valais
fortresses during one of my Muzot visits, when Rilke glanced at
the open book, saying drily and rather testily: 'That is stupid – it
would be better to give the facts about Muzot's past correctly
and honestly.' No more was said on the subject. The incident

bears out what Lou Andreas says about Rilke's intermittent preoccupation with psychic affairs, the influence of the dead, etc.: that in good times he would reject such things brusquely, even angrily. In spite of this we should not forget the warning to the living in the First Elegy:

> . . . . All of the living, though,
> make the mistake of drawing too sharp distinctions.
> Angels (it's said) would be often unable to tell
> whether they moved among living or dead. The eternal
> torrent whirls all the ages through either realm
> for ever, and sounds above their voices in both.
>
> . . . .

We have already mentioned how important good, tactful domestic service was to Rilke, his way of life being on the whole very simple and unassuming. Leni at Berg had performed this useful office so superlatively well that her name had come to be a synonym for the ideal housekeeper in Rilke's vocabulary. It was even more necessary to have someone of that sort at Muzot, as when Mme Klossowska left Rilke was wholly dependent on the services of a housekeeper. To find her, instruct her and attach her to him was one of the initial tasks of his Muzot life. The result was Frieda Baumgartner (so often mentioned in the *Letters from Muzot*) who looked after her master well and served him faithfully.

His precarious financial position worried the poet not a little; the deterioration of the German mark was making it more and more difficult for the Insel-Verlag to send money to Switzerland, and there were times when it was quite impossible to do so. That he was able to turn even this adverse circumstance to the benefit of his work is shown by a letter he wrote to his publisher, in which he says: 'At the moment I can manage, I must, it may even be a good thing for me to be without the means to leave the old tower even for a day, as this confinement would at present correspond exactly with my needs and my task.'[18]

Financial claims were made on Rilke at the beginning of that winter, when his daughter became engaged, and although he had been a permanent absentee from the family circle he did not try to evade his duty. He asked Kippenberg to make the necessary arrangements and to defray expenses from his account. The hermit was somewhat alarmed, however, because the announcement of the engagement at that time brought his mountain retreat to the notice of an unpleasantly wide circle of relatives and old acquaintances, just as he was beginning to feel hidden and secure; he wanted, he said, to be absolutely alone and undisturbed at Muzot until the spring. Being thus suddenly reminded of his distant relatives aroused in him once again the painful, ever-recurring sense of 'the rivalry between social life and work'.[19] In this context it should be noted that after coming to Switzerland, seven and a half years before his death, Rilke never saw his daughter again, or his old mother who was living in Prague. (His maternal grandmother also survived him.) He never met his daughter's husband and never saw his grandchild. (He did, of course, correspond with the young couple, and neither his mother nor his wife was left without news of him.) His wife, Frau Clara Rilke, visited him at Muzot in 1924. The plan to start divorce proceedings, which he had been thinking about before the war and again in Switzerland, was never carried through, chiefly for the reason that Kippenberg was very much against it. During these years he spoke oftenest of his long-dead father (Joseph Rilke died in 1906). His father really had tried to do what was best for him, Rilke would say in conversation, when his stories had made clear how little understanding the growing boy and youth had received from his solicitous but bourgeois-minded parent – and although he had then experienced the father-son conflict in all its painfulness. In the Fourth Elegy he invokes the spirit of his progenitor:

> Am I not right? You to whom life would taste
> so bitter, Father, when you tasted mine,
> that turbid first infusion of my Must,
> you kept on tasting as I kept on growing,
> and, still arrested by the after-taste
> of such queer future, tried my clouded gaze, –
> you who so often, since you died, my father,
> have been afraid within my inmost hope,
> surrendering realms of that serenity
> the dead are lords of for my bit of fate, –
> am I not right? . . .

This absentee from the family was in his later years not un-
moved by the tensions which those inner ties of relationship
produced in him. He often had to deal with family problems,
but he preferred to remain silent about them, so that some of his
acquaintances hardly realised that his relatives existed. Numerous
letters testify that Rilke could hardly warn people strongly
enough against interpreting his early work autobiographically;
and it depressed him and made him furious when, as often
happened, readers of his novel identified the fictitious Malte with
himself: he had no right whatever, Rilke maintained, to count
Malte's adventures as his own. Conversely, he was not describing
his own childhood experiences in the novel, putting them into
spiritual shape (a task he always kept postponing). Rilke has not
left us any book of self-revelation such as Gide wrote in the form
of an autobiography – although at an age which, unhappily,
Rilke never reached. The milieu described in the *Notebooks
of Malte Laurids Brigge* has nothing in common with that
in which Rilke grew up, nor should we identify the milieu
of his Prague stories with the one in which he passed his
childhood. The ideal mother so touchingly portrayed in the
figure of Malte's *Maman* is not his own mother; but the same
ideal appears again in the Elegies where, in the third, the
following lines occur:

Mother, you made him small, it was you that began him;
for you he was new, you arched over those new eyes
the friendly world, averting the one that was strange.
Where, oh, where, are the years when you barred the way
for him, with your slender form, to the surging abyss?
You hid so much from him then; made the nightly-suspected
    room
harmless, and out of your heart full of refuge
mingled more human space with that night-space of his.
Not in the darkness, no, but within your far nearer presence
you placed the light, and it shone as though out of friend-
    ship.
Nowhere a creak you could not explain with a smile,
as though you had long known *when* the floor would behave
    itself thus . . .

And he listened to you and was soothed. So much it availed,
gently, your rising: his tall cloaked destiny stepped
behind the wardrobe then, and his restless future,
that easily got out of place, conformed to the folds of the curtain.

When we set these wonderfully light, flowing lines beside a
Christmas letter that Rilke wrote to his old mother, Phia Rilke,
during his later years, we are struck by the tortuous effort which
the task of writing the letter has obviously cost him. Although he
speaks reverently of his dead father, although he sends his mother
living in Prague the precious filial gift of his recently published
books the *Duino Elegies* and the *Sonnets to Orpheus*, the joyful,
sympathetic heart is lacking. . . . No biographer has a right to
pass over this deep conflict in Rilke's life. He once confessed to
the Princess Taxis: 'I am not a lover, perhaps because I didn't
love my mother.' When he was a child Phia Rilke dressed the
little René in girls' clothes, so that he should remind her of his
little sister who died before he was born. He tells us of the strange
coddling to which he was subjected: how his parents used to look
at the thermometer before he went out, so that they could adjust
his clothing exactly to the temperature of the day. And then,
on top of all that, they exposed him suddenly, when he was still
a child, to the horrors of the Military Academy, far away from
home. Certainly we can hardly reproach Rilke's mother for still
thinking of her son when he was long since past his youth as an
adolescent and the writer of immature lyrics: she was incapable
of catching up with him on the steep path to his artistic maturity.
Quite early on he began to let a longer and longer interval elapse
between his meetings with her. He was just 28 when he wrote
from Rome to Lou Andreas-Salomé, on April 15th 1904,
describing one of those meetings:

My mother came to Rome and is still here. I see her only now and then
but – as you know – every meeting with her is a kind of relapse.
Whenever I am obliged to see this lost, unreal woman, who has no
connection with anything and who can never grow up, I feel how
even as a child I tried to break away from her, and deep down in
myself I am afraid that, after years of running and walking, I am
still not far enough away, that I still have somewhere inside me
movements which are the other halves of her abortive gestures,

fragments of memories whose shattered bits she carries around with her; then I am horrified by her scatter-brained piety, by her pig-headed faith, by all those distorted and disfigured things to which she has attached herself, she who is herself as empty as a dress, ghostlike and terrible. And that I am her child; that my entry into the world should have been through a scarcely perceptible, papered-over door in that washed-out, irrelevant wall – (if such an entrance can indeed lead into the world. . . .).[20]

This merciless statement was not the only one of its kind that Rilke made, for, as Lou says, the torment which gave rise to it followed him nearly all his life, engendering in him the idea that he had been 'stamped at birth with all the flaws that remained with him ever after' (Lou A-S.). Even in his later years he was tortured by the thought that his own inadequacies, passionately renounced yet still having dark repercussions in his soul, were obstinately holding their ground in the distant old woman. There was a connection between his attitude to his mother and his violent antipathy to the Christian Church (his 'rabid anti-Christianity' as he once called it) because these things reminded him forcefully of the old woman's rather foolish, scatter-brained bigotry (and the stuffy, spirit-deadening atmosphere of churchism in the old Austria). These links have to be ruthlessly exposed in order that we may recognise that the portrait of the ideal mother conjured up by the poet in *Malte* and in the Third Elegy was born of reaction to his own mother experience, or else of flight from it. Phia Rilke went to see her son several times when he was living in Munich during the war, but she never visited him in Switzerland. (She went there only after he was dead, when she wandered restlessly backwards and forwards between Muzot and the grave at Raron.) In a poem that is perhaps too raw because written immediately after one of her visits to Munich, the forty-year-old man reveals how much he suffered from these encounters:

Alas, my mother will demolish me!
Stone after stone upon myself I'd lay,
and stood already like a little house round which the day rolls
    boundlessly.
Now mother's coming to demolish me:

demolish me by simply being there.
That building's going on she's unaware.
Through my stone wall she passes heedlessly.
Alas, my mother will demolish me !

In lighter flight the birds encircle me.
The strange dogs know already: this is *he*.
It's hidden only from my mother's glance,
my gradually augmented countenance.

No warm wind ever blew from me to her.
She's not at home where breezes are astir.
In some heart-attic she is tucked away,
and Christ comes there to wash her every day. [21]

These lines are most revealing. (Rilke wrote them three or four years after the lines from the Third Elegy quoted above.) It is true that they were written during the war, when everything combined to exasperate the poet and make him conscious, to the point of despair, of the danger he was in. That this mother, so alien and yet so near, with her long face framed in its black drapery of veils and her belief that Jesus and Mary came to visit her every day at the hotel – that this mother should have had the power to 'demolish' him is a grave and terrible thought. The bond must have been a close one before such a woman's lack of understanding could hurt him. She did not see that he was building, did not notice that his face had been 'gradually augmented' – and it embittered him. Frau Albert-Lasard, who was Rilke's companion during the early part of the war, had first-hand experience of his mother's visits and describes them in her candid book. She says: 'The suffering caused him by her peculiarities was at the root of his revolt against everything conventional and artificial, in short against every kind of hypocrisy; it made him explore his conscience, going into all the corners most protected by pious lies.'[22] The long exploration of being and reality which is the essence of Rilke's spiritual and poetic life had developed in the most radical opposition to the prejudices and conventions of his social and family backgrounds, which seemed to him to be incarnate in his mother. His profound sincerity and love of truth made him continually fearful of not being honest and truthful enough, of being still entangled in a shred of the maternal veils. And so at the end of that poem born of revolt Christ appears, inseparably linked with the distasteful thought of his mother: Christ, with whom Rilke did not want to have anything to do; of whom he once said that nobody answers when you ring him up; for whom he found shrill and furious words such as he used in speaking of his mother; Christ, whose meditorial rôle he passionately rejected, having no use for a religion which inserted a mediator between God and man.

Because a great many sentimental, feeble things have been written about Rilke it is necessary to emphasise how ruthless and radical his way of thinking and expressing himself could be, in certain situations and about certain matters. The quality appearing as humour in the temperate climate of conversation appears as persiflage and irony in the somewhat severer air of the letters — as when he draws inimitable sketches of personalities like Romain Rolland and Franz Werfel; it becomes satire now and then, in parts of the *Duino Elegies* for example, and in the Young Workman's Letter, written at about the same time, even polemic. It is essential to see him in his true dimension, to correct the foolish attempts which have been made to overrefine this energetic spirit into a Rilke all delicacy and gentleness. During that Muzot winter of 1921-22 he was making ready: preparing fireworks which would one day be let off, hissing, into 'inner world space', to spread light in that great darkness with their magic powers of illumination, and to reveal immensity. Many traits came together in his rich and extremely fascinating personality. Rilke had a gentle, touching side: he could be child-like, spoilt and sometimes helpless; but there was also his great, consoling purity of character, his seductive personal charm, and all those accommodating qualities which made a woman who had written asking for his advice, and received an answer, say: 'I am wide open to the lucidity, scope and charity of your thoughts. . . . In them everything reaches a measure of reconciliation, so that misfortunes hardly seem unfortunate any longer.'[23] But as an eye-witness one can and should establish this fact: that Rilke's outward bearing gave the impression of firm self-control and inward discipline. Outbreaks of anger were rare, but they did occur and were very violent. Kind and considerate — yes; but anyone at all skilled in reading faces knew from the features of this man that there were demons lurking behind, storms waiting to be let loose. . . .

The self-communings of that first winter at Muzot took a strangely meandering course. For months on end Rilke lived in the old tower in unbroken solitude, alone with his housekeeper. As Christmas approached he even set strict limits to his correspondence. He had said all that he had to say about the difficulties of achieving complete concentration on his task. Saying it had in a sense been almost equivalent to overcoming them. As he recalled the 'indescribable obstacles' which had been 'put in his way throughout the years (and especially since 1914)' it became clear to him that all the words 'which I shall ever have to form now, . . . will be heavy and unwieldy by nature. I was never further from being able to produce easy, pleasing, occasional words. It seems to me that in my case speech can only be justified by the unique, the lastingly valid, the *one thing needful*.'[24]

Although the poet was living such a secluded life, forces from outside had a share in his approaching success. He was absorbed, enchanted and stimulated during those months by the poems and prose of Paul Valéry. All his life Rilke had had a capacity for admiring congenial painters and poets, and this admiration must be reckoned as one of the most powerful stimuli to his own work. Like every truly creative person he was a great receiver, a great adopter and adapter. As a beginner he was moved by Stefan George; he was introduced to him in Berlin, and the two met again in Italy at the end of the century. Tolstoy's novels exercised a strong influence on him, both before and after his visit to Yasnaya Polyana — although at the same time he completely rejected the religious prophet. Dostoevsky and the Dane Jens Peter Jacobsen inevitably come to mind in connection with the origin and atmosphere of *Malte Laurids Brigge*. Rodin and Cézanne and the French poets Baudelaire and Mallarmé, also Francis Jammes and Verhaeren were Rilke's mentors and companions on the upward path to artistic maturity. He felt a close personal link with Verhaeren, but his master Rodin and the visual arts had perhaps a larger share than any literary model in the conception and aesthetics of *New Poems*, which were written during Rilke's best years in Paris. In Spain Greco made an enduring impression on him: he stands unmistakably behind the towering images which occur here and there in the Elegies. Then, after *Malte* was finished, came the intense interest in Strindberg: the Strindbergian counter-current to Rilke's nature must be taken seriously, as a positive insight in his most far-reaching thoughts. Gerhart Hauptmann and Gabriele d'Annunzio were no more than passing, though highly important, acquaintances. Of great significance was his interest in Hölderlin during the first year of the war; he attended Hellingrath's Munich lectures on Hölderlin and the Germans and on Hölderlin's madness. Hellingrath's edition of Hölderlin's late hymns accompanied Rilke everywhere; he wrote his own *Hymn to Hölderlin* in the same volume.[25] After that it would seem that Rilke put Hölderlin aside, but the encounter with him appears to have had effects powerful enough to rank as one of the spiritual streams supplying the linguistic sources of the Elegies. Rilke did not read any of Nietzsche's work – he did not feel drawn to him. Sigmund Freud's psycho-analysis, which was brought to the poet's attention by Lou Andreas, left in Rilke's mind certain ideas which can easily be recognised in his work. (The cordial way in which he asks Lou from time to time to give his kind regards to Freud shows how simple and human his interest was.) Rilke was among Gide's, Proust's and Kafka's first readers. Their correspondence bears witness to his friendship with Gide. The fact that they both came from Prague was not his only link with Kafka; but it must be admitted that that name, still little known at the time, hardly appears in Rilke's letters. The discovery of Paul Valéry's poems early in the year 1921 had an effect on him which was both profound and enduring. He said once in Bern: 'I was alone, I was waiting, my whole work was waiting. One day I read Valéry; I knew that my waiting was at an end.'[26] At Muzot, before the Elegies and Sonnets were written, Rilke was able to translate Valéry's *Cimetière marin* 'with an equivalence . . . that I would not have thought attainable between the two languages'.[27] His success in rendering that difficult French

poem into German felt to the poet like an awakening of his own
creative powers, and he decided that, when he was 'a little more
secure' in his own work, he would translate the Frenchman's
prose pieces too, especially *Eupalinos*, which he called 'a glorious
dialogue'.

A stimulus of quite another sort came to him on New Year's
Day 1922, when he read a journal kept by a mother during her
daughter's fatal illness. Rilke was deeply moved by Frau Gertrud
Ouckama Knoop's touchingly simple account of her daughter
Wera's terrible suffering. Gerhard Ouckama Knoop, who had
died young, had been a friend of the poet's, and Rilke had
continued to keep in touch with his widow in Munich. He had
known the Knoop daughters as children during the war, and
now he heard that one of them had died two years previously –
the beautiful girl, scarcely yet adult, 'whose dark, strangely
concentrated charm was for me so utterly unforgettable and is so
extraordinarily easy to recall'. With all the intensity of his
sympathetic nature Rilke, as he read the mother's words, entered
into the incomprehensible horrors of physical suffering to which
that young, artistically gifted girl had succumbed. He encountered in the journal the strange, overwhelming lack of relatedness
between bodily suffering and its spiritual opposite, and he
could not refrain from trying to elucidate the mystery of physical
pain, to which we seem to succumb with our whole being. He
considered that physical pain was the result of a misunderstanding
between us and a Nature sympathetic to our desire for a happy
life. This simple document written by a heart-stricken mother
who had had the strength to be with her daughter during the
cruellest of her dying moments, 'because those moments had
now become her poor child's own, terrible possession', described
the conflict, Rilke said, as affectingly as Montaigne had done in
his account of the time spent at the bedside of his painfully dying,
disfigured friend. It seemed to him 'that something like a
privilege is involved when human beings are not spared such
monstrous torment, as if this ruthlessness were the expression
of a kind of initiation, a sign of election to the inordinate – as
though this desperate suffering could happen only to a being
from whom there were to be no secrets'.[28]

Rilke's whole work shows how deeply he was moved by the

thought of death, of physical suffering and of those who die young, and how he continually – with a kind of *credo quia absurdum* – tried to bring them into harmony with his reverent affirmation of life and nature. The last lines of the First Elegy, dedicated to the 'early dead', belong to that part of the Elegies which was written at Duino in 1912. The account sent by Wera's mother was directly responsible for the *Sonnets to Orpheus*; Rilke wrote the sonnet sequence as a 'memorial for Wera Ouckama Knoop'. The emotion aroused by the record of a young person's suffering and difficult death; the poet's inflexible determination to say 'yes' to life, even to the most terrible happenings it could bring forth, even to its annihilation and beyond; his 'affirmation of being that nowhere and nothing can restrain'[29]: here was the fertile polarity of pain and jubilation, praise and lament, which claimed his dammed-up creative powers when they were released by those songs of joy and mourning, the Elegies and Sonnets.

In the first days and weeks of the new year (1922) that state of readiness which for the poet was almost the same thing as 'work' announced itself. All else was grace. Rilke's mood was serene and, in the purest sense of the word, 'satisfied'. Every obstacle had been overcome; with the strength that springs only from patience and readiness for sacrifice he prepared himself for a victorious struggle. Nothing was allowed to disturb his concentration now. It was a kind of Lent. He did not permit himself any distraction, any social life; for many days he did not read a newspaper. Fewer and fewer letters left the Muzot study.

The work which was about to flower for the first time had to be given a chance to grow; and the one which had lain for so long as a torso in impenetrable winter sleep – it was about to reach fulfilment at last in the wintry stillness and seclusion of Muzot. Of this work, begun exactly ten years earlier, in the winter of 1911-12, in a cliff castle above the Adriatic, the following parts were already in existence: the complete First and Second Elegies, which had both been written at Duino; the whole of the Third, which is dated Duino 1912 and Paris 1913; the Fourth, also complete, which was the only one he succeeded in writing in Munich during the war (1915). Of the Sixth a fragment was composed in Ronda during 1912-13 and Paris in 1914,

while another fragment – apparently written in Toledo or
Ronda – was to take the ninth place in the completed Elegy
cycle. Since writing down the first lines of the Tenth at Duino
(he had added to it in Paris but not finished it) Rilke had always
thought of this Elegy as being the final one.[30] So of the ten poems
four were there complete, while beginnings and fragments
indicated that three more were to come.

Yet it happened that when the poet's creative powers burst
forth they rushed to begin with into another channel. As though
he had been given an unexpected surplus, he wrote down
between the 2nd and 5th of February a cycle of twenty-five
sonnets: 'as a memorial for Wera Ouckama Knoop! I realised little
by little when writing them that only one sonnett [*sic*] relates
to the dead girl, the XXIVth, last but one, and yet the whole is
like a temple built around that portrait. It is called "DIE SONETTE
AN ORPHEUS".'[31] In the final edition the poem relating to the
dying girl Wera, which is last but one in the first part of the
sequence, stands as number twenty-five in the glorious wreath.
He made a copy of the work, written in a few days, for Wera's
mother: 'You will see at a glance', he wrote on February 7th to
Frau Ouckama Knoop,

why you must be the first to have them. For, although the connection
is a loose one (only a single sonnet, the last but one, XXIVth, invokes
Wera's own figure in this excitement dedicated to her), it dominates
and influences the course of the whole, penetrating more and more
deeply – though so secretly that I only realised it bit by bit – into this
irresistible act of creation which has so convulsed me.[32]

After that, during 'a few days of tremendous obedience in the
spirit', Rilke completed his Elegies. In the afternoon of February
9th he sent a telegram to Mme Wunderly: 'Seven Elegies now
more or less finished – at any rate the most important ones – joy
and miracle!' While he was on his way back from the post office
'the Eighth and Ninth finished and formed themselves around
small and larger earlier fragments'.[33] Late in the evening of this
stormy day Rilke could report in a wonderful letter to his
publisher, Anton Kippenberg, in Leipzig: 'The "Elegies" are
there.' Although he was almost too tired to hold a pen, he wrote

141

these lines to his old friend (whom he thanked from a full heart for ten years of patience):

> I am over the summit.
> At last! The 'Elegies' are there! And could be published at once (or whenever suits you). . . .
>   So.
> Dear friend, now at last I can take a deep breath and, confidently, go on to easier things. For this was larger than life – and I have groaned in these days and nights like that time at Duino – but, even after the wrestling then, I had no idea that *such* a storm could assail one out of mind and heart! That one survives it! That one survives it!
> Enough, it is there.
> I went out in the cold moonlight and stroked little Muzot as if it were a great animal – the old walls which have granted it to me. And Duino, destroyed.
> The whole shall be called:
>   The Duino Elegies.
> People will get used to the name. I think. [34]

That same night – he repeated in French: '*Et je suis sorti pour caresser ce vieux Muzot, au clair de lune*' – he told his friend in Geneva what had happened, beginning his note with the cry: '*Merline, je suis sauvé!*' Beyond any doubt this companion of his first years in Switzerland played a great part not only in furnishing and organising Rilke's Valais home, but also in this success which he called a rescue. It says much for Rilke's clarity of mind in the midst of the tempest that he was able, in these hasty lines written 'after the divine storm', to say that the daily, peaceful, sunlit work now about to begin would seem to him 'like a great calm'.[35]

And next morning he wrote to Mme Wunderly, in a note which reads like an announcement of victory:

> . . . To think that I was permitted to experience this, experience what: *being*, being it, the prodigious! Not one day longer could I have held out (as at Duino that time – worse) everything that was tissue in me, ligature, cracked in the storm. . . . I must be well made to have been able to stand it.

May God now give me only peaceful, quiet, human tasks, no longer these that surpass all human, warrantable strength.

It is done, *done*!

The blood and myth cycle of ten (ten!) strange years has now been closed. I feel now that my heart was as though maimed by this thing not being there! This now existing.[36]

Rilke tells how on the very evening when he finished a postman brought white hyacinths – from an unknown giver. This significant coincidence touched him deeply. And then, on the 11th, the poet completed the last, Tenth Elegy, the one which, when he began it at Duino, he had thought would be the keystone of the wide-flung arch. Of the original fragment only the first twelve lines remain, all the rest having been added at Muzot.

Not until the Saturday evening, when the first lines:

> Someday, emerging at last from this fell insight,
> may I lift up jubilant praise to assenting angels . . .

of the magnificent long poem had been expanded and completed did Rilke communicate the event to the Princess Thurn und Taxis: the owner of Duino. And because, in the sublime courtesy of his heart, he felt that he could not dedicate to her what had belonged to her from the beginning, there was to be no dedication to the book, only:

'The property of . . .'[37]

Next day, in an unimposing little parchment book which dated from the time at Soglio, the poet sent a fair copy of the finished work to Mme Nanny Wunderly. It was '*mal habillé*', he said in the accompanying letter – but:

> Napoléon l'était aussi aux jours d'une de ses grandes victoires, dont il ne voulait pas amoindrir l'éclat par un vain concours de toilette! Mais vraiment, je le dis de grand cœur, c'est lui, le petit livre de Soglio, qui brille et qui est fier:
>> pas moi
>> jamais
> je n'était plus humble, plus à genoux:
>> oh
>> infiniment
>> R.[38]

With a touching humanity that was characteristic of him, Rilke did not forget to mention the ministrant, humble part played by his housekeeper:

Frida stood her ground bravely during those days when Muzot was riding the high seas of the spirit. Now she really has been the . . . 'little pixie' – hardly there and yet ministering and fearless, while I up here was uttering awful cries of command and receiving signals from universal space and booming out my tremendous salvos of welcome to them! – She is really brave, the little ghost. And cheerful and *infiniment de bonne volonté.*'[39]

When we learn that during those breathless days of 'elementary tumult' there was no time to think of food, no time to sleep for more than a late hour or two, we have to admit that great demands were made on the understanding of this conscientious, good-hearted girl.

It need hardly be said that Rilke's oldest friend, Lou Andreas-Salomé, was among the first to hear his news, on the evening of February 11th. For twenty-five years this remarkable woman, whom he had loved passionately in his youth and left later on, had been the steadfast gauge for everything that moved him; with her exceptional intellect and deep understanding of his nature she had continued to influence his spiritual development and his thinking to a greater extent than any other person. He told her everything without reserve, having the utmost confidence in her great intelligence and capacious heart; and her friendship remained always full of insight, sovereign, and at the same time loving. (For this reason Lou's books get closer to Rilke than any others.)[40] *The Lay of Cornet Christoph Rilke* and *The Book of Hours* were written under her eyes, and something of those early cadences, that youthful style, can always be heard in Rilke's letters to his Russian friend, even in those announcing the completion of his two late works, the Elegies and Sonnets. The joy it gave him to tell her of the sonnet – Number XX of Part I when published – in which he conjures up a memory of the Russian journey they took together in 1900 – shines out of these words:

And imagine, *once* more . . . I wrote, *made*, the horse, you know, the free happy white horse with the block tied to his hoof, who came galloping towards us one evening across a Volga meadow –

how
(I) have made him, as an 'ex-voto' for Orpheus! – What is time? –
When is present? With his entire happiness, he leapt over so many
years into my wide-open feeling.

So it was with one thing after another.

Now I know myself again.[41]

Next day and during the days that followed the completion of
the Tenth Elegy Rilke wrote a long prose work which was only
published after his death. The editor of the *Selected Works* says
of it: 'The same writing block which begins with the draft of the
Tenth Elegy and ends with that of the Fifth has on its intervening
pages the rough outline, passionately worded, of a "Recollection
of Verhaeren", out of which there grew directly an imaginary
letter from a working man to the Flemish poet (who died in
1916).'[42] The working man's letter occupies a central place among
Rilke's late work, being a paraphrase of everything expressed in
the Elegies and Sonnets. Like them it is included in the polarity
of praise and lament, but it is more intellectual – an exposition
of the thought and world view underlying the poetry. Rilke
demands the affirmation and justification of the 'this life',
of the world, of human earthly existence. The question '. . . oh
why / *have* to be human, and, shunning Destiny, / long for
Destiny?' gets this answer in the Ninth Elegy:

> Not because happiness really
> exists, that precipitate prophet of imminent loss.
> Not out of curiosity, not just to practise the heart,
> that could still be there in laurel. . . .
> But because being here is much, and because all this
> that's here, so fleeting, seems to require us and strangely
> concern us. Us the most fleeting of all. Just once,
> everything, only for once. Once and no more. And we, too,
>
> once. And never again. But this
> having been once, though only once,
> having been once on earth – can it ever be cancelled?

The Young Workman's Letter protests against what seems to
Rilke the wrong use of the Christian message, which has made
the world suspect and this life evil. For him Christ is one

who points the way, who hints at God – 'he is a gesture and not a resting place'; our world has not only changed outwardly – it has no entrance for him and the 'core of light' that was his originally, 'that made him seem so strong by day and by night, has long since been dissolved and otherwise distributed'. Rilke reproaches mankind for not having journeyed onwards 'in the direction of the cross's arms', instead of settling down in Christianity and making 'a *métier*' of it, 'a bourgeois occupation'. But Rilke's main objection to the Christian outlook, which he repeated again and again, is expressed in the following lines of the workman's letter:

They (mankind) fall over themselves in their eagerness to make this world, which we should trust and delight in, evil and worthless – and so they deliver the earth more and more into the hands of those who are prepared to wring at least a quick profit out of it – the earth which is no good for anything else, mismanaged and suspect. The increasing exploitation of life today, is it not due to a continuous disparagement of this world, begun centuries ago? What madness to divert our thoughts to a beyond, when we are surrounded here by tasks and expectations and futures! What a swindle to steal pictures of earthly bliss in order to sell them to heaven behind our backs! Oh, it is high time that the impoverished earth got back all those loans from its happiness with which men have endowed the hereafter. Is death really any more transparent because of all those pilfered sources of light which have been placed behind it? And, there being no such thing as a vacuum, is not the place of everything removed from here taken by a counterfeit – is that why our cities are so full of ugly artificial light and noise, because we have surrendered the true brightness and song to a Jerusalem which we hope to move into presently?

The writer holds that it is an offence against God not to see in 'all that is granted to us here the wherewithal to make us perfectly happy, to the very limits of our senses, if only we would use it rightly: *The right use, that's the thing*' – Rilke's accusation culminates in these words, which he underlines, and in advice to the living about how life should be used.

In the MS. this imaginary letter to the dead Verhaeren comes immediately after the Tenth Elegy, and their close relationship is made evident by the great poem, which depicts, as it were, the 'bad use' of this world, with satirical pathos:

> Strange, though, alas! are the streets of the City of Pain,
> where, in the pseudo-silence of drowned commotion,
> loudly swaggers the casting cast from vacuity's
> mould: the begilded ado, the bursting memorial.
> How an Angel would trample it down beyond trace, their market
>   of comfort,
> with the church alongside, bought ready for use: as clean
> and disenchanted and shut as the Post on a Sunday!
> Outside, though, there's always the billowing edge of the fair.
> Swings of Freedom! Divers and Jugglers of Zeal!
> and the figured shooting range of bedizened Happiness: targets
> tumbling in tinny contortions whenever some better shot
> happens to hit one. Cheer-struck, on he goes reeling
> after his luck. For booths that can please
> the most curious tastes are drumming and bawling. . . .

But the Recollections of Verhaeren, from which the idea of the workman's letter eventually sprang, was still only an unfinished draft when, two days later – on Tuesday, February 14th – Rilke was given what he called in a letter written next day 'a shining afterstorm'. It was as unlooked for and miraculous as ever, and in its throes an Eleventh Elegy was born, which he called *Saltimbanques*.[43] This poem came so unexpectedly that the little Soglio book with the copy of the ten Elegies had already been sent off to Nanny Wunderly. In any case Rilke still definitely wanted the Tenth to be last in the cycle. He subsequently discarded the poem which had been the Fifth, and of which he had once said that it was a beautiful poem but not really suited to the Elegy cycle because of its different construction. (Under the title *Antistrophes*, this poem is included in later editions of Rilke's work, the *Saltimbanques* taking its place as the Fifth Elegy.) 'And so', Rilke writes to Lou Andreas, 'the *Saltimbanques* are there too, they who have so much concerned me since my earliest time in Paris, and who have been set me as a task ever since.'[44] We now know from one of Rilke's Paris letters, written on the 14th July national holiday, 1907, that on the previous day he had watched a family of acrobats – old '*Père Rollin*' and his

family – making their preparations outside the Luxembourg
Gardens, near the Panthéon. Everything was the same, he wrote,
as in the previous year: '. . . the same carpet is lying there, the
same threadbare coats, thick winter coats, are piled on a chair,
leaving just enough room for the little boy, the old man's
grandson, to sit down a little bit on the edge, with his long
serious face. . .'.[45] But it is not only the members of this troupe,
each one of them so wonderfully described, who are resurrected
in the Fifth Elegy; a painting by Picasso, dealing with the same
subject, is also brought to life there. Rilke loved this picture,
which he had once prevailed upon some Munich friends to buy –
friends in whose flat he had lived for a time during the summer
of 1915. He wrote in a letter then: 'I'm living meantime in a flat
belonging to friends (who have gone into the country) with the
most beautiful Picasso (the "*Saltimbanques*"), which has so much
of Paris in it that for moments on end I forget.'[46]

The Fifth Elegy is one of the grandest and most profound of
Rilke's descriptive poems. Its connection with the themes of the
work written during those incredibly productive February days
is obvious. 'But tell me, who *are* they, these travellers, even a
little more fleeting than we ourselves. . . .' The great poem begins
with this question, and already we are in the midst of their
acrobatic performance:

> . . . . as though from an oily,
> smoother air they come down on the threadbare
> carpet, thinned by their everlasting
> upspringing, this carpet forlornly
> lost in the cosmos.
> Laid on like a plaster, as though the suburban sky
> had injured the earth there.

After giving an elaborate description of the different figures
making up this itinerant artist troupe, the poet enquires for the
place where man is to be found, for the true place of man in the
world – man for whom the acrobat with his vertiginous leaps
and empty oscillations is so uncanny and impressive a symbol:

> Where, oh, where in the world is that place in my heart
> where they still were far from being *able*, still fell away
> from each other like mounting animals not yet

ready for pairing; –
where weights are still heavy,
and hoops still stagger
away from their vainly
twirling sticks. . . .

And then, in this wearisome nowhere, all of a sudden,
the ineffable spot where the pure too-little
incomprehensibly changes, veering
into that empty too-much?
Where the many-digited sum
solves into zero?

This is followed immediately by lines which, employing a gruesome metaphor, conjure up 'fate's fashion workroom, which is the fashion workroom of death':[47]

Squares, O square in Paris, infinite show-place
where the modiste Madame Lamort
winds and binds the restless ways of the world,
those endless ribbons, to ever-new
creations of bow, frill, flower, cockade and fruit,
all falsely coloured, to deck
the cheap winter-hats of Fate.

But the end of the poem? Where is the 'ineffable spot'? Where the place carried in our hearts, a never attained perfection which is not a 'pure too-little' nor yet an 'empty too-much'? The poet says:

Angel: suppose there's a place we know nothing about, and there,
on some indescribable carpet, lovers showed all that here
they're forever unable to manage – their daring
lofty figures of heart-flight,
their towers of pleasure, their ladders,
long since, where ground never was, just quiveringly
propped by each other, – were able to manage it there,
before the ringed onlookers there, countless unmurmuring dead:
would not those then fling their last, their for ever reserved,
ever-concealed, unknown to us, ever valid

coins of happiness down before the at last
truthfully-smiling pair on the quietened
carpet?

So, once again, the poem ends with a question. Rilke puts the
place 'we know nothing about' under the guardianship of the
Angel, who in the Elegies symbolises everything that has not
been granted to confused, inadequate mankind (whose destiny he
satirically evokes in the startling image of 'the cheap winter-
hats of Fate'). Throughout all his work there sounds the
lament that human beings are not *capable* of love, that, beginners
and bunglers, they loiter far behind the demands which love
makes on them. Now they, the lovers capable at last, are the
artists and acrobats on some 'indescribable carpet'; their onlookers
are the 'countless unmurmuring dead' – and these – perhaps! –
throw to the 'at last truthfully smiling pair' the 'coins of happiness', eternally valid, 'unknown to us'. But the question about
the 'clearly defined metaphysical place of man' remains unanswered. It is a place – as a sensitive interpretation of the
Saltimbanques Elegy puts it – 'on the far side of feeling or in the
realm of the dead, . . . where everything which on earth here
must remain unreal, abortive, disfigured by fate, achieves its
fulfilment, and all feeling activity enters a state of perfection'.[48]

This long poem of one hundred and six lines, which fell so
unexpectedly into Rilke's 'wide-open feeling' from the remembered past and the urgent present, was written down and completed by him in *one day*. (When the Elegies were published he
dedicated it to the owner of the Picasso picture, Frau Hertha
König.)

But the after-storm in which it took shape brought him new
images and rhythms: in those same days he began to write
twenty-nine sonnets which he finished in a few days – the whole
second part of the *Sonnets to Orpheus*. The amount of sheer
penmanship that Rilke got through during those days and nights
almost baffles the imagination. In addition to the copy of the
first twenty-five sonnets which he had sent to Wera's mother
in Munich, he sent another copy to his Zürich friend, Professor
Jean Strohl, a remarkable man, congenially sensitive and with a
most versatile mind, with whom, during the years in Switzerland,

Rilke found many links, chief among which was their mutual friendship with André Gide. But Strohl had hardly returned the little book with the twenty-five sonnets when this thread, as Rilke wrote from his hermitage, was being woven into a new fabric. By Saturday, February 18th, there were fifteen or more new sonnets, though not all of them came up to his standard. So, even in these moments of heightened productivity and supreme self-confidence, self-criticism and artistic discipline held their own, eliminating everything which could not stand up to his own judgment: '. . . I am so rich at present that I can allow myself to *choose*. What a world of grace we live in! What powers are waiting to fill us, us the continually shaken vessels.' At the end of this letter to Mme Wunderly there is a characteristic remark: ' "*Offrande*" and "*verger*", and the word "*absence*" in the great *positive* sense in which Valéry has used it – these were the very painful spots which often made me realise while I was doing this work how desirable it would be to collect all the *advantagen* of all the different languages into ONE and *then* to write: *then* to write!! But even so it was glorious!'[49] During Sunday and Monday the stream continued to flow: sonnet after sonnet came pouring from the tireless pen.

3

FULFILMENT

IT had been like that from the 2nd to the 20th of February inclusive: nineteen days. From the 2nd to the 5th he was writing the first part of the *Sonnets to Orpheus*. Between the 7th and 11th three whole Elegies were written (including the subsequently discarded 'Anti-Strophes'), also the greater part of three others which had some lines already in existence. From February 12th to 15th Rilke wrote in a hurried script the *Recollection of Verhaeren*, from which the *Young Workman's Letter* grew. The 14th was the day of the after-storm, in whose blast the 'Saltimbanques' was written. Finally, between February 11th and 20th the twenty-nine sonnets of the second part of the Orpheus cycle came into being. But these are just the works which Rilke chose for publication. He had originally thought of publishing some of the Elegies' satellite poems as a second part, under the title 'Fragments'. That was never done. The poems were published posthumously, but they, and the sonnets which the poet discarded, belong to the body of work done during this short month. Rilke reports that the last Sunday of this month, February 26th,

was from early until late a real namesake of the sun (and already it was shining with summer heat over this landscape which, right down into the soil, it knows so well). And when I came into the study, early, roses were there – and downstairs, on the breakfast table – for no special reason – a dough-cake and a little bowl with the first cowslips from our meadows, still soft and very short in the stem but already quite happy. . . .[50]

We see and feel: Rilke had 'caught up' with himself, as he expressed it in his happiness at this fulfilment. It was in keeping with his more relaxed, more genial mood, after the Elegy storm had passed – his childlike delight in a sunlit Sunday morning, in roses, dough-cake and wild flowers – that he should give a privileged place to the sonnet which he calls 'a little spring song for children' – number 21 of the first part. That poem too was the offspring of a memory, not this time of Russia or Paris but of Spain. In Ronda many years before he had attended Mass in a convent and heard the convent children sing it, to a curiously gay, dancing rhythm, accompanied by tambourine and triangle; the sonnet seemed to Rilke like the 'interpretation' of that music:

Spring has come again. Earth's a-bubble
with all those poems she knows by heart, –
oh, so many . . . With prize for the trouble
of such long learning, her holidays start.

Stern was her teacher, he'd over-task her
from time to time; but we liked the snows
in the old man's beard; and now we can ask her
what green, what blue are: she knows, she knows.

Eager to catch you, Earth, happy creature,
play with the children now outpouring !
Conqueringly foremost the happiest springs.
All she has ever been taught by her teacher,
all that's implanted in roots and soaring
difficult stems, – she sings, she sings!

Here the poet has succeeded in catching the truth about spring and its transformation in a remarkable poem, in which the distance between the describing subject and the described object seems to be eliminated, the metaphor itself, as feeling, acting, stating subject, taking the place of the statement. Statement and metaphor are here one and the same thing; the metaphor is no longer a decorative addition, filling in a space between descriptive words: everything is included in the space of the metaphor, as direct sense impression, which itself produces the association. From the simple image: '. . . Earth's a-bubble / with all those poems she knows by heart' everything else springs and sparkles, to the cheerful, dancing rhythm of the song he heard the Ronda children sing, accompanied by tambourine and triangle. The earth gets a reward from her strict teacher for learning so many poems. And then we are told of the children's liking for the old white-bearded man. Colour – the green, the blue – is no longer a decorative addition to the picture of spring: no, the earth has learned it and: 'she knows, she knows!' Now the awakened, gleeful earth is a schoolchild who has been given a day off, and she is asked to play with the children: 'eager to catch you, earth, happy creature'. Finally, all that the teacher has taught her, all that was 'implanted in roots and soaring / difficult stems', all those earthly school exercises – 'she sings, she sings', exultantly. 'This one poem,' says Hans Egon Holthusen,

representing countless others, can be taken as witness that the spirit of the German language, using an individual whose capacity for feeling was far above the ordinary, has taken an epoch-making step across a frontier. . . . The feeling activity leaves the place where it was attached to a subject and goes over to the object, or to a whole cosmos of objects. These poems are not 'anthropomorphic' but, as we said at the beginning of our study of Rilke philology, 'cosmomorphic'. The world is a magical physiognomical entity, which becomes easier to apprehend as we approach it from the standpoint of a reality penetrated by one universal feeling. The world is 'inner world space'.[51]

We must, however, stress – even if we are to some extent opposing the learned commentaries of the pundits – that Rilke's lyric poetry was spontaneous, unforeseen, unintellectual; that he was not a practised thinker. His poems sprang from a unique mixture of visual image and association, of instinct, intellect and feeling, all of which elements were for him indistinguishable from one another. The old distinction between 'naïve' and 'sentimental' poetry simply does not apply here. Only close biographical study can throw a little light on the creative event which took place during those nineteen days, at a standing desk between two candlesticks in a tiny room inside an old tower. The event must be followed from day to day: from its beginning with the two dozen sonnets which even the poet himself did not expect, through its hurricane change into the primitive chaos from which the Elegies were born, its lull for the clarification of thought in a piece of prose, its renewed outburst as an Elegy after-storm and its gradual ebb in a long series of thirty-three sonnets.

No precise thinking, no planning, not even an act of will, was at work here. Rational, logical thought was never Rilke's strong point; his mind was not 'schooled', his way of expressing himself remained imprecise. The construction of his poems, which in an earlier period, that of the *New Poems*, had been more or less a conscious process, became half-conscious in the later work, because of his mastery of the medium. Reducing it to the simplest possible formula, one might say of him during this creative period, as of the earth in spring, he 'knows it' and he 'sings it'. That is why, after the completion of these great works, he returned so effortlessly to ordinary life, accepting everyday impressions with childlike gratitude, taking pleasure at his Sunday breakfast in dough-cake, early wild flowers and late winter sunshine on the fields. For now it was done; it had been accomplished in the heightened awareness of a creative ecstasy, and the poet, a human being once more, did not rack his brains to find out the real meaning of that luxuriant wealth of images, those imposing questions. He had caught up with himself, he knew himself again, he was, in his own words, his own contemporary once more. That was all. Ten years earlier a remark of Kassner's had impressed him deeply: the remark that the way from feeling to greatness lies through sacrifice. He knew all about feeling – he possessed a superabundance of it – but the thought of the necessity of sacrifice had been troubling him for a long time. But where was Rilke's sacrifice? It may well have been in his humble, confident pursuit of the *inner* way, his refusal to allow anyone or anything to divert him from his journey to the centre, the single task that had been imposed on him, and to make any concessions to those purely transient affairs by which most people, busy and harassed, are completely enclosed. During the difficult war years and his post-war wanderings Rilke had yielded to many distractions, but he had never taken his eyes from the goal; he had always kept open the way leading to that goal, to 'the one thing needful'. Only immense self-control and an unwavering faith in his vocation had made it possible: the price of it had been a sacrifice. The way was a terribly difficult one for him, but it did lead from feeling to the greatness achieved in the great hymns written at Muzot.

It is clear, however, that with the completion of this work he had not ceased to be in peril from his own nature. On the contrary. The release of the force which had been accumulating during many lean, silent years and had now, in less than three weeks, gushed out in overwhelming abundance, was bound to be followed by a time of slackness and, in the end, by exhaustion. Lou Andreas, vigilant though distant, had seen this coming with her inexorable eye, and had warned her friend, after his jubilant victory letter of February 11th, of the reaction which would follow the hypertension.

On the day he finished his work, February 11th, Rilke replied to Lou:

I know quite well that there may be a 'reaction', that one must fall somewhere after being thrown like this; but after all I'm falling into the spring, already quite close here, and besides: as I have had the patience, the long patience, to get as far as this which has now been achieved, why shouldn't I be able to manage some side patience through more difficult days; and gratitude (of which I never had so much) ought ultimately to outweigh everything in them that is tiresome and confusing![52]

Two years later, when sickness was knocking more and more threateningly at his door, Rilke reminded his great friend of her warning:

You wrote me at the time when the Elegies had just come into existence, been rescued – I was not to get frightened if one day reaction set in and I had to go through a bad time, and I remember that I answered courageously, but now I really am frightened, you see I have been living for two years more and more in the midst of a horror. . . .[53]

However, that time had not yet come. Rilke was still full of the magic of his poetry, which had enabled him to find what the human race in its stupidity is always seeking, and to express it in verbal imagery, shape it into song. Rainer Maria Rilke thought of himself in his poetic vocation as being completely under the orders of mysterious powers and voices, whose humble tool he was. For that reason 'all that his conscience required of him was to be ready. He realised this in the productive hour, which would never come to order but which had to be obeyed.'[54] He was reassured by the thought that everything which had for so long distracted and diverted him had at last given way to this state of preparedness, making conception possible. He was able to be quite easy, too, about what one might call the artistic quality of his work. All his life he had revered 'pure mastery'; he had admired it in the studios of great sculptors and painters, and even in the work of craftsmen, watching carefully and applying what he learned to his own creations – and now, at the zenith of his life's work, this helped him to express himself with incomparable lightness and dexterity. For long he had been strict with himself, obedient as an artist, spiritually disciplined; and finally grace came to his help and he became like a child knowing poems by heart.

'Song is existence', he says in the third Sonnet to Orpheus. In these three words he coined the shortest, most concise definition possible of the art he practised, *as* he practised it. After his great poems were written Rilke the artist was once more one of the 'favourites of fond creation', as he called the angels in the Elegies. But 'song is existence' meant also that his creative work depended on his state of spirit, mind and body being natural, free and light. Having found his way back to himself after such long detours he was borne along by the current; it seemed to him like breathing – or:

> An aimless breath. A stirring in the god. A breeze.

So he puts it in the third sonnet of Part I. Rilke expressed perfectly what he felt on completing the Elegies and Sonnets when he wrote the following dedicatory poem for his Zürich friend in her copy of the Duino Elegies:

> All that rushed in the river,
> all that dripped in the cave,
> give I with arms that quiver
> back to the god who gave,
>
> and the Feast of the Circle starts.
>
> Frightened or onward smiled
> every wind that shifted;
> every latch uplifted
> made me again a child,—
>
> and I knew in my heart of hearts.

Oh, I know them indeed,
names and their metamorphoses:
still the original seed
deep in the ripeness reposes,

out of which it has bloomed.

Bonds for a god the word,
rising in bold conjurance,
weaves till it, undeterred,
stands in the glow of assurance

singing and unconsumed.[55]

The Magic Tower

Sickness was near. In grip of the shadows already,
darklier thrusted the blood, though defiantly ready
to surge to its natural spring-tide just as before.

Time and again out of darkness emerged with a mocking
earthly effulgence. Then, after terrible knocking,
entered the hopelessly open door.

R. M. RILKE,
Sonnets to Orpheus, Part I, XXV

1

SIDE - HOURS

FEBRUARY 1922 was Rilke's great time. He himself thought and spoke of it as such. The 'storm' in whose tremendous blast the Elegies and Sonnets were achieved had subsided. There followed for the poet a tired winged return to earth again. It is the fate of the creative artist never to encounter until it is really too late those who can share his work by being receptive to it. By the time his book appears the poet is no longer the man he was when he was writing it. The state he was in while his poems were ripening and when the ripened harvest was granted him—that state is over and far away. His spirit has been liberated, his heart is light. But the artist who has finished a work is already living in another reality. In a reality which he must fill with new images and new goals if he is not to fall back into a void.

We have seen how in the moment of his success Rainer Maria Rilke told his news to the people nearest him while he was actually working and during pauses in the work. He sent fair copies and copies to privileged friends, sometimes even before the cycle of poems had been quite completed. Rilke's habit of reading his poems aloud to a small circle – preferably to a single listener – was another way of trying to bridge the gulf between the creative hour and the participating other person. At the same time these readings gave him the opportunity to find his way back into himself. After such hours of winged communication he often felt as though he had received a gift. The significance of the *Sonnets to Orpheus*, whose obvious family likeness to the Elegies their own creator had not at first realised, became quite clear to him for the first time on just such an informal occasion. It was in June 1922, when the Princess Taxis visited the poet at Muzot. As befitted the lord of the manor, he allowed himself the luxury of meeting the old lady in Sierre in a fly. They drove together up the steep road to his tower, where he read all ten Elegies to her at one sitting. Next day he recited to her the entire sonnet cycle 'whose inner unity and whose connection with the Elegies, to which they form a glorious parallel, I first realised as I listened. I feel that neither of these works is mine (because by their very nature they are *more* than "by" me) but that both now have really been given. . . .'[1]

Rainer Maria Rilke often gave himself such hours of pure joy. For his love of life remained strong and abundant to the end, and his creed was a limitless affirmation of being. His rich nature had wealth over and to spare, which he poured out on fresh poems, on translations, on his correspondence – but no less on things, people, flowers, landscapes, books, works of art. The hours spent in this way were side-hours, to use his own expression, compared to the creative month February 1922. But side-hours 'in which, nevertheless, a main feeling was active'.[2] Although Rilke spent 'eternal winters long in excessive intimacy with silence' (as Paul Valéry put it, not without a slight shudder), his hermitage faced entirely towards the world. Life in the tower was not an evasion – it never had been. It had enabled him to concentrate and had bestowed success on him. Afterwards it continued to provide him with security, but he tended more and more to interrupt his time there with travel, with visits to other parts of Switzerland and to Paris, and with the comings and goings of numerous visitors, whom he received and entertained at Muzot.

Before long the shadow of doom was to fall across his path. Rilke was to need cures and nursing-home treatment, for in spite of his brave resistance he was not going to be able in the long run to avoid what he had always thought of as a humiliation: the mediation of a doctor between him and his suffering body. The state of affairs described in the great sonnet about a dying girl (*Sonnets to Orpheus*, XXV, Part I) was soon to arise for the poet himself:

> Sickness was near. In grip of the shadows already
> darklier thrusted the blood, though defiantly ready
> to surge to its natural spring-tide just as before.
>
> Time and again out of darkness emerged with a mocking
> earthly effulgence. Then, after terrible knocking
> entered the hopelessly open door.

Almost five years were to pass before Raron church bell would toll across Rainer Maria Rilke's open grave. Those five years

were not lacking in events, but whoever looks over them with a
sense of biographical order must be struck by the absence of any
consistent purpose. Until then the poet had lived for the one
great task which had now been accomplished. And no matter
what turmoils, vicissitudes and difficulties were bound up with
his pursuit of it throughout the years, that achievement was
always present as goal in the poet's mind and will. Had he not
read the existing fragments of the Elegies to his hosts at Sils,
soon after his arrival in Switzerland? During the happy time in
the Soglio library was he not, even then, seeing the room as a
suitable place to work in? Was not the stay in Locarno a failure
because it removed him again from those favourable conditions,
and the winter in Berg so happy because he had the feeling there
that 'Work' was near? The old walls of Muzot had at last granted
it to him.

Now a calm had set in and he must carry on with ordinary
life again; from the moment he finished the Elegies Rilke
decided to attempt in future only 'more manageable' things, no
longer tasks 'larger than life'. It was easier, however, to make
such a decision than to put it into practice, for even though Rodin
had given the young poet the parting advice: '*il faut toujours
travailler*', Rilke had never made writing an everyday, routine
occupation. He was too conscious of his poetic calling as a divine
gift to take up literature as a profession. For this reason he
refused to use his pen in the capacity of man of letters or journalist. He would not expose himself to the dangers of those
professions, which lay so close to his spirit-claimed creative hour.
Well-meant offers of book reviewing Rilke never accepted, nor
would he consider invitations to write articles on poets or
novelists. Yet we know from his letters and conversations how
lively an interest he took in contemporary literature; his approvals
and disapprovals reveal an almost unerring judgment. But he did
not feel called to be a critic, and anyone who knew him must
agree with the Paris journalist who summed up his impressions
after an interview in these words: 'I have indeed met few people
who gave poetry the importance due to it. I might even say
that until I met Rainer Maria Rilke I had never been in the
company of a man who lived like a poet.'[3] This poet's life is so
tremendously important for our understanding of genuine

poets and artists just because there was no pedagogic intention concealed in it.

However, it was this consistent basic attitude which gave rise to the problems connected with Rilke's way of living. Whenever he finished a piece of work he had to face a time of painful readjustment. This reaction could be very confusing for the poet, and was often so intense that it made him feel 'redundant'; he suffered most from this state of mind after finishing *Malte*. Rilke often bemoaned the fact that he had no secondary occupation, no *métier* or profession with which to fill the uncreative periods of his life. He did not disapprove of Mallarmé teaching English, he envied Hans Carossa his medical career, he praised Paul Valéry for being able to do mathematical research, and spoke with warm sympathy of Joseph Conrad's adventurous seagoing life, which Valéry told him about when he visited Muzot. He himself intended to occupy the time after the completion of the Elegies in translating Paul Valéry's work – but he also asked his friend Strohl to draw up a plan of mathematical study for him. Yet in spite of these good intentions and the regular work it soon became obvious that the balance between soul and body was in danger.

To begin with Rilke remained in his tower. Spring melted the snow on the meadows and mountain slopes. The valley wind hurled itself in powerful gusts against the walls of Muzot. The harebells, out before Easter, softened the green meadows with mauve-grey patches. The little garden began to make claims on the lord of the manor's attention. The pergolas expected to be freed from protecting fir branches. The vegetable beds were dug. Soon the whole landscape would be transformed into a fertile, blossoming tree-filled garden. (The poet kept thinking about the French word *verger*, which seemed to him untranslatable and which he had missed so painfully during the previous February. . . .) One evening when he was returning from Bellevue to the tower he heard singing in Sierre church. It was school-children, practising hymns for Easter under the baton of the village clergyman. The walker sat down quietly in a pew and listened attentively to the children's voices. Such were his beliefs that listening to the bright voices of children gave him a deeper religious experience than formal church services conducted by the clergy. He loved those simple hymns and he also loved the children and the valley people, because their faith was simple and naïve, close, it seemed to him, to the sources of religion, to the powers of nature, to paganism. A little above Muzot, yet looking as if it belonged to it, stood the disused, dilapidated chapel of St Anne, in which no Mass had been said for ages. Of it also Rilke was fond. He liked to think that it was dedicated to all the gods. He brought the first flowers from his garden to this chapel, adorning the neglected altar with their freshness.

As the sun became warmer and the days longer Rilke liked to make a detour on his way home from Bellevue after tea. He would start off in a westerly direction, taking the road which led up the valley past the small, square, pink-washed vineyard house close to the railway line – the little house that he would look at appreciatively, saying that it was a graceful *chinoiserie* in that heroic land. After bending sharply, the road led uphill to Muraz, a little village where the people soon got used to the strange gentleman who answered their '*Bonsoir*' in such a friendly way. The only inhabitant who now and then gave him some trouble was the postman, who was rather too fond of the delicious local wine, and who had been known when in his cups to put the mail for which the poet was impatiently waiting into the village letter-box, instead of delivering it at Muzot. But next day, after scolding the good man severely for his crime, 'Monsieur Rilke' stopped in Muraz on his way home and chatted to him for quite a while. Rilke called this 'the feast of reconciliation with the postman', and afterwards he would laugh heartily at the comical, very nearly mysterious, circular journey taken by his letters.

At the end of May Rilke had to move into the Hotel Bellevue, Sierre, as workmen were in Muzot. His concern for the old house, and the worry of supervising the necessary repairs, about which he was most particular, seemed to have upset him a little. That same month Werner Reinhart decided to buy Muzot, and Rilke undertook to see to the purchase formalities on behalf of his absent friend. In the summer his garden gave him great joy with its roses, phlox, tobacco and vegetables. At the same time it had to be watered, a job that Rilke and Frieda did together from 6 in the evening until 8.45. Sometimes he even did it alone, when it took him between three and four hours. When Frieda went on holiday and he himself began to long for a change, Rilke looked for a boy to do the watering during his absence. He did not intend to go away unless he found one, for the thought that the garden might suffer would have spoilt every step of the outward journey for him.

Rilke stayed on in the country, however. The Princess Thurn und Taxis's visit took place early in June, and the Prince and Princess of Battenburg (brother-in-law and sister of the King of Italy) came to stay in the Bellevue as well. So there were opportunities for conversation and for readings of the (still unpublished) new work. But when, after this sociable interlude, Rilke was left alone in the hotel, in the midst of the summer valley, that spacious valley which a year before had enchanted him and made him its captive, he admitted for the first time that he had grown weary of it: '. . . I see with horror', he wrote at the end of June, 'that one can grow dulled to even the most beautiful sights if one is surrounded by them all the time; how many things here (because I imagine that I know them) fail to move me as much as they did a year ago.'[4] He found it difficult to return to the tower at the beginning of July: 'something quite different ought to come now', it seemed to him; and yet long journeys (Vienna? Bohemia? Italy? Paris?) were perhaps not worth the trouble. Rilke felt unwell: he was suffering from indigestion and needed a tremendous amount of sleep. He went to bed early and slept for ten, even twelve hours. During those July days news came from Berlin of the murder of Walter Rathenau, the Foreign Minister, whom Rilke had known and esteemed. '. . . Rathenau's death', he wrote from Muzot, 'both as loss and as sign of the times fills me with horror and haunts me continually, as you can imagine.'[5]

He spent some cheerful weeks during the second half of August and early part of September on the Beatenberg by Lake Thun. It was a holiday, like the time in Etoy, but now the feeling that his work had been accomplished could add to his enjoyment. Rilke was able to devote himself again to his gifted little friend Baltusz Klossowski, who, with his mother, was keeping the poet company. Rilke had intended going to Vienna to see to some personal business connected with a legacy. But the tormented, unsettled state of afflicted post-war Europe and the bad news coming again from abroad made him give up this plan.

The inflation in Germany had now reduced the purchasing power of the mark almost to zero, so that for a long time economy was among the reasons for Rilke's Muzot seclusion. He returned there with Mme Klossowska and her younger son, intending to spend the winter of 1922-23 in his tower. As his friend's financial position was precarious also, and a livelihood and home had to be found for her and her two sons, Rilke was 'extraordinarily concerned about her and about the boys Baltusz and Pierre'.[6] Incidentally one learns from these circumstances how conscientious Rilke was about taking on the duties resulting from a close personal tie, and with what affectionate sympathy he followed the development of the two growing boys during those years. What he found difficult at all times, in maturity as in youth, was to settle down to domestic life with a woman: indeed as a permanent arrangement he found it quite impossible. Concerning the latest experiment, tried for many weeks, of living with 'Merline' who had been his occasional companion for three years, Rilke wrote to Mme Wunderly:

Alone I can manage everything, and when I've a chance to be so again you will find me as content and circumspect as ever. Only I simply have to be *alone* . . . anything else can only be exceptional, for single hours, days – never again so constantly and permanently; so many things get spoilt by that – by doing things together in the wrong way, for no other reason than that you are living together, while the right sort of in-common hour becomes rarer, shier, more anxious. . . .[7]

Rilke reported that Mme Klossowska left precipitatedly for Berlin on December 1st, with Baltusz.[8]

Rilke discusses politics a great deal in his letters of 1922 and 1923. At the turn of that year he wrote about the threat of disaster overhanging the world, in the form, as he realised even then, of new wars; he said that he blessed the years he had been able to spend in Switzerland, those good years saved from dark times, which had meant indestructible gain for him. As Christmas drew near he began to long for the past and to curse the century he lived in. '*Sommes-nous dans un temps fou*', he wrote,

how we should have enjoyed living in a snugger time, when one drove out for a walk as though sitting on a sofa, and the good trees along the avenue moved a little, so that it should look as if they were really walking, the beautiful, well cared for rocking-horses harnessed to the driving-sofa. And in the houses the friendly, trustworthy solidity, the residency of everything, then sometimes, suddenly, destiny was in the midst of it all, but only destiny was allowed to behave in that way, it played the storm now and again, but existence itself was the calm, was the peaceful landscape, where nothing made horizontal rushes, but everything just rose vertically and sank back into itself, enriched by experience, like the sap in the trees. And one had time to listen to the melody in oneself, not just to three beats but to the whole. Only the mornings were brief and rapid, and one thought, shaking off an even more rapid dream. But then the days, how long and long-suffering, and each evening like all the others. Christmas then was allowed to be. Like a village, a pealing church towards which one went, which one had always seen, but which was still far away, and suddenly even hidden by the backs of the hills. . . .[9]

When he wrote like this he was thinking of his distant, lost Berg by the Irschel – he seemed to be sitting there in his sofa corner, the firelight flickering in front of him among the room's background shadows: 'Where certain situations are concerned I always have to start from Berg in order to see things clearly.'[10] Yet at that Christmas season Rilke's heart found its way back to his Muzot, where he celebrated the festival alone, enjoying the restored silence and solitude. The Insel-Verlag had just sent him the proofs of the Elegy volume (the difficulties that German publishers were struggling against at the time had prevented Rilke's new work from being published in 1922). The days between Christmas and the New Year found the poet at his standing desk, his head bent over this task.

It had now become clear that Rilke would not stay in Switzerland only for as long as he needed a secure refuge in order to fulfil his poetic task – the completion of the Elegies – but that he would remain a lifelong exile. He put up with the drawback of financial insecurity until at last, in 1924, the mark was stabilised and the Insel-Verlag could send him larger sums again. It is impossible to weigh up retrospectively the advantages and dis-advantages of Rilke's life in his adopted country; although at first he found much there that was difficult to put up with, he had acclimatised himself, and the atmosphere of intimacy and order appealed to him. He encountered, too, a great deal of hospitality and help, so much so that he was sometimes weighed down by the thought of the 'pre-preposterous', as he once called it, amount of help that he had received from his fellow human beings. What sensitive person would not, in times of depression, have felt weary of such hospitable treatment, even though offered in the most considerate of generous spirits? Rainer Maria Rilke was in certain respects a stranger upon earth: he was a guest here below, always a guest – he lived as a guest in adopted countries, he stayed in houses as a guest, he found hospitable friends; hospitality was indispensible to him since he was in no way cut out for a settled life.

There were, however, other very definite and obvious reasons for his exiled life in Switzerland after the Great War. Nothing would induce him to return to Germany. Like Hermann Hesse before him and Thomas Mann after him, who turned their backs on Germany in order to save their spiritual independence and their literary work (and even like Stefan George, who left the Third Reich so that he could die in Switzerland), Rilke, after his experiences during the war and the 1918 Revolution, left the country to which he was bound neither by citizenship nor by any deep accord but only by language. He was keenly sensitive to the discrepancy between spiritual and political life which since Goethe's day has been characteristic of German development; he makes mention of it, not without acrimony, in letters and diaries. He had little sympathy to spare for literary men who put themselves at the service of nationalistic ideas and feelings. Even at the time when he was staying in Locarno, a few months after leaving Munich, he had written about Count Hermann Keyserling: 'Keyserling has been coming more and more into the public eye since that Darmstadt foundation . . . unfortunately he has fallen increasingly into the mistake of ascribing an "extraordinary rôle" to the Germans, when it would be so much better if they could achieve a simple, honest self-control.'[11] From Etoy, too, came utterances which showed Rilke's opinion of the *Reich* of Bismark and Wilhelm II. Those men had been 'tamers' rather than representatives of a lawful social order. Nor, for all its ideals, had the revolution of 1918 brought any turn for the better. Early in 1923 Rilke wrote the following lines to Lou Andreas from Muzot, lines in which there is no lack of shrewd insight:

I often worry a lot about *you*, dear Lou, about *all of you*, when I hear and imagine how everything in Germany is growing more and more absurd, life and the cost of living almost impossible. It would seem – and that was my impression in the year 1919 – that the unique moment when agreement could have been prepared by all has been missed on all sides, now the divergences are growing bigger, it is no longer possible to read the sum of mistakes, so many figures has it gone into; perplexity, despair, dishonesty, and the wish, so characteristic of the time, to profit at any price from this disaster, even from this. These evil powers are driving the world before them.[12]

A month later Rilke admits in a letter to Frau Nölke that he is suffering 'to the point of insomnia' because of the general situation, growing so much worse 'out there in the world', and

because of these cruel conflicts, their hopelessness, and even more because hatred is at work once again, because hatred is once more the decisive and driving force in a world which can only be healed in the long run by a superfluity of love, mercy and goodwill! – The newspapers too have taken on the tone of the war years again, their pages rustle incitingly when you turn them . . . Where will this lead?[13]

Rilke's attitude was by no means as esoteric and a-political as has sometimes been said, and although he was by temperament averse to any publicity, that does not mean that his judgment with regard to public affairs was lacking in clear-sightedness. The years that followed proved him to have been right when he said in 1923 that his own life and the lives of people of his generation would be 'exposed indefinitely to these chaotic conditions'; and when he wrote about perhaps being 'allowed to discover even the smallest rift in the clouds destined to open out into the pure firmament under which those now growing up will live'[14] he was not so much expressing a belief as a fervent wish. 'Remote and far away from it all as my old Muzot seems', its isolation did not prevent him from suffering on account of the disastrous times, while the evil 'interruptions of life' often dismayed him profoundly. 'If things go on like this', he said in January 1923, 'they will deprive those of us who are no longer young, for the remainder of our lives, of the spiritual guilelessness with which we used to move about the world – and with it, of how much joy, how much satisfaction, the rest of our future.'[15] After some lines in which he expresses his dislike of political Germany and his violent opposition to the *Reich* founded by Prussia, Rilke goes on to say that his 'Austrian nationality, with its distinctly different inner composition', has never been more precious, and he ends: 'May Switzerland protect me long enough for me to find a far, far distant refuge somewhere, or until I disappear in Paris as a private individual, as a Czech citizen strolling along the quays and comporting himself in the Luxembourg without ringing any political bells.'[16]

The last thing he thought of doing was of returning to his native city, Prague. News had come from there of the death of his cousin, Paula von Rilke-Rüliken, with whom he had not been on good terms, but whose family portraits and papers he would have liked. The news aroused memories of the 'decline of the family' and of the 'narrow Prague conditions'. 'It is all so sad,' he wrote, 'sad as things only could be in ancient Austria and in narrow Prague. *De la province engourdi.* Those family affairs, as I look back on them now, are simply grotesque from every point of view. . . .'[17] Of course, we are listening again to the old tone of irritable disgust, how queer things were on the maternal side, at the aged grandmother's and the rapidly ageing mother's – and perhaps one would not be very far wrong in supposing that Rilke's visit to his Thurn and Taxis friends in Bohemia, which he kept putting off for a hundred reasons, also his journey to Vienna to settle the legacy affair, were postponed partly in order to avoid having to go and see the two old women in Prague.

On top of this, Prague as a childhood memory was bound up with so many horrors – a theme he would touch on now and then in intimate conversation – that he wanted to steer clear of his native city. As regards his attitude to Czechoslovakia, which has at times been the occasion of misunderstanding, if not of spiteful comment, Rilke said in a letter written a year before he died:

To President Masaryk I have offered, not on this but on an earlier occasion, my veneration, through his representative in Bern at that time. This feeling existed long ago, even before the rising of the year '18 lifted him into that conspicuous place. How should I not have felt that my applause was called for, when a man of world-wide importance was given the highest place in the country of my birth, from which I am distant enough to be faithful, in an aloof way, to its particular fate?[18]

Nothing could have been further from Rilke than to look down upon the Slavonic races and cultures; his experience of Russia in his youth had left far too deep and abiding an impression for that. He seemed to have no link with modern Czech literature, but he remembered the Czech language well enough from his childhood and youth in Prague to be able to reproduce, when writing from Geneva to the Princess Taxis, a conversation in that tongue heard between strangers passing in the street. '. . . more than I can say, my own feeling confirms the supposition', he wrote to his Polish translator, Witold Hulewiez, 'that the Slavonic stream is not the least of those mingling in the multiplicity of my blood.'[19] Rilke was not free from a vague 'blood mysticism'; the word 'blood' occurs often in his writings, although the meaning that he attached to it was never clear. The investigations of Carl Sieber and other genealogists have shown that none of his ancestors were Slavs, but that he was descended from German-Bohemians and Alsatians; so spiritual affinity must have played a larger part than biological inheritance in his feeling of kinship to the Slav people (unless there had been some undiscoverable connection further back).

Politics, family memories, physical discomfort, indigestion, shortage of money: these and other things formed the turbid circle at the centre of which Rilke was reading and working towards the end of his second Muzot winter. One has only to go down, he wrote to Lou Andreas, a single layer below politics,

to find everything beginning to look different already, and one thinks that a most secret growth and its pure will must be using that chaos simply in order to be able to hide under it, hale and sound, from the curiosity that is busy with other things. (Just now in France, among the people taking no part in politics, those concerned with the inner life, how many turnings, renewals, hesitations – what new orientation of a spirit drawn to reflect further, even against its will. . . .)[20]

And immediately there follows the clue 'Proust', whose influence, he said, was enormous, and whose name he mentions oftener than any other at that time (with the exception of Paul Valéry's). Rilke's great contemporary had recently died in Paris – and if we listen carefully enough we may think we hear an echo of Proust's *Du Côté de Chez Swann* in the passage quoted above from one of Rilke's letters, in which he speaks of the 'pealing church towards which one went, which one had always seen, but which was still far away, and suddenly even hidden by the backs of the hills'. Does not this picture involuntarily recall the famous description of the Méseglise way in Proust's novel? The January number of the *Nouvelle Revue française*, dedicated to the French novelist's memory, only further increased Rilke's sympathetic feeling for Proust's personality. He marvelled at that 'freedom', that 'confidence in the personal', that 'indifference to success'. And he praised

that devotion to society, so narrowly escaping snobbishness, rescued by that search for something in everything, something pure and forceful, which more and more took over the leadership of that life, dominating everything in a sense, even the illness. Finally, that death, refusing medicine, but even in the midst of the agony correcting the description of an agony! . . ., after the word

Fin

. . . had been written at the end of the last page of the XXth notebook![21]

Who could deny that Proust's personality, as Rilke describes it here, had much in common with the poet's own? Even Rilke's bearing during his illness and when he lay dying was not very different from Proust's. When the translation of the *Notebooks of Malte Laurids Brigge* appeared in Paris during the last year of Rilke's life the French critics continually drew attention to the relationship between that work and Proust's novel. Before Rilke's great poem-cycles had appeared in good French translations – long after his death – French Rilke criticism seized eagerly upon *Malte*, which explains why Edmond Jaloux and other French critics judged the German poet mainly by his great prose work, and why they gave so much space to the question of his spiritual relationship to Proust.

2

PAUL VALERY AND ANDRÉ GIDE

FROM the moment that the name of Paul Valéry entered Rilke's literary universe it outshone with its brilliance even the more nearly related Proust. These influences had a close spiritual and temporal connection: Rilke translated Valéry's book of poems *Charmes* into German barely a month after reading the special Proust number of the *N.R.F.* which we have just mentioned – in February 1923, a year after the Elegies were written at Muzot.

Rilke's accord with Valéry is much more surprising than his affinity with Proust. For when we compare Valéry's personality with Rilke's we get the impression that the two men were as unlike as possible, a complete contrast to one another. On the first occasion (1924) when he made personal contact with his German translator, Valéry was obviously very much aware of this unlikeness. It cost him time and an expenditure of his own different kind of sensitiveness to become aware of the 'strange bond' that he had with Rilke, and to recognise its value. He found it doubly hard to understand his congenial admirer and translator because he did not know any German, and also seemed hardly able to penetrate Rilke's secret, intimate language. After the latter's death Valéry frankly admitted these difficulties. Statements he made at the time to the Swiss essayist Max Rychner are very revealing: 'I loved Rilke', he said:

and through him came to love many things which I could not love directly: that dark and almost unexplored deep space of the soul which we have described with vague words like mysticism and, more bluntly, occultism, knowledge of portents, presentiments, inner religious voices, intimate communications from things afar off – which at times have the character of womanly intimacies. All that side of existence which I knew nothing about, or which I had decided to ridicule, Rilke presented to me in a charming way. . . .[22]

This utterance made by Valéry in his later years gives us a clear idea of the relationship between the two poets; its source was Rilke's spontaneous, enthusiastic, wholly one-sided admiration for the French poet's work, which, as he told me in conversation, he came across by chance while reading a copy of the *Nouvelle Revue française* (it happened to be the number for June 1st 1920, in which Valéry's *Le cimetière marin* appeared, but Rilke came upon it only in the spring of 1921). His encounter with these new poems gave him the spiritual jolt he needed, enabling him to find his way back to the centre of his own creative powers. Their author was one of those virile personalities, dominated by will, intellect and passionate concern for truth, by whom Rilke's receptive, open mind was fertilised more than once during his life. Proust, perhaps, confirmed him in his own chosen way, but Rilke never had it in mind to translate the novelist's prose. Valéry, Rilke's temperamental opposite, could supply stimulus, impetus, even leadership. That is why Rilke had such an unqualified, almost extravagant devotion to the other's poetry. It is not for us to discuss here the place of Valéry's work in the body of modern French literature, or whether there is not something academic about it, which would explain the curious fact that his books had more influence abroad than on young French writers. For us it is sufficient to know that the introduction to Valéry's poetry and prose made 1921 an important date in Rilke's life. From then on he directed towards Valéry's work his capacity for enthusiasm and his subtle powers of understanding, as well as his need to adopt a foreign masterpiece by translating it into the imagery and sound of his own German poetry. He was turning towards a man distinguished by a lucid and subtle intellect, and by an exceptional mastery of literary expression born of long experience, a man with an intimate knowledge of art, who had renounced rhetoric and who practised an extraordinary freedom of thought and image association. Beyond any doubt these qualities encountered Rilke's own at the ripest period of the latter's creative life. They were able, at all events, to confirm and fortify him in the path he had taken after the war, and which he had chosen more from an obscure urge than as the result of any clear plan. An intellectual dam had been set up against the flood peril from Rilke's feeling, so often in a melting state. Valéry, in the remarks on his relations with Rilke which we have just quoted, summed up the things which separated them. What it was that united them had been sensed by Rilke from the day when (at Berg by the Irschel) his eyes had first fallen on one of the Frenchman's poems. The part that Rilke's acquaintance with Valéry played in bringing the *Duino Elegies*, and, even more, the *Sonnets to Orpheus* into existence cannot be denied.

It is impossible to exaggerate the importance that Paul Valéry had for Rilke during the last five or six years of his life. His letters and conversations are full of the impressions which he had received from Valéry. What struck him most, because it touched him at his most vulnerable spot, was that the French poet only came into the open with his poetry after a silence lasting many years. How he approved, how he praised, such a silence, in which the work of art could grow and ripen slowly, imperceptibly, hidden from the world! And how that silence justified his own silence, before he was able to break it at Muzot.

Looking at this experience non-personally, we find that it agrees with what we know of the development of other important German poets and artists. Since Goethe's time every German poet has made an 'Italian journey' of one sort or another. For – we have heard it said often enough – the German is by nature amorphous, excessive, a creature of dreams and visions. He has need, in order to discover his boundaries and so his form, of contact with the Mediterranean tradition and culture – in any one of its manifestations: antiquity, Renaissance, Italian art, French language. In his struggle with himself the German summons to his aid the free virility of the Romance people, which is elastic, clear and hard (not brittle, confused and sentimental like the Germans). Rudolf Kassner thought it necessary to warn people against 'seeing in Rilke's love for France anything more than the German love for the foreign'. He rightly observes that Rilke always found the thought of England unattractive: it was impossible to persuade him to visit London. The Americans seemed to him 'monstrous', 'the Italians basically not quite transparent and on that account not quite important'. Kassner distinguishes between style and character and in this connection says of Rilke: 'He loved France because he saw in her a superior style. . . . Character with him could not make up for the absence of style. Style there came before character.'[23]

Assuming that what Kassner says is correct, are we quite wrong in maintaining that the German (and perhaps the Slav) in Rilke had need of the Mediterranean element, especially as manifested in the French way of life? We know from a note written in French at Etoy (May 1921) that he was engaged in a struggle with the German language, and in the last resort with its deeper aspect as the means of self-expression used by a very complex race which had never been capable of thinking quite clearly. He admired the French language, which, carefully tended as a vineyard, had been ripening for centuries, and he lamented that the language he himself used was far from having attained such clarity and confidence. Half of the poetry written in Germany, he said, lived on the vagueness of the German language and added to it. All sorts of arbitrary expressions were simply the result of exploiting its weaknesses, while some of its 'audacities' would have been simply incorrect and impermissible in French. Germany had always lacked an academy, which would have had the duty of bestowing its incontrovertible majesty on a language left lying about the street: the only German academy that had ever existed was the works of Goethe and Stefan George. Academies could always be destroyed when they had served their purpose, for it was well to revolt against senile, somnolent authorities; but that was not to say that we could do without their yoke to begin with. On the whole the deplorable spectacle offered by the German language entirely corresponded to that presented by the *Reich*, whose dispersed forces had never been set in order, and where there had never been any true government; for the obedience to Bismarck and Wilhelm II had really been government's antithesis, those two autocratic men never having represented a true legal order.

Before we can speak of the translation of Valéry's poems, it is pertinent to remark that translating works of art from the French was nothing new for Rilke; he had already translated some poems by Verlaine (1914), by the Comtesse de Noailles (1915), Verhaeren (1919), Baudelaire (1921), and by Moréas and Mallarmé. But even before the world war he had been deeply engrossed in the work of André Gide, with whom, from his thirty-fifth year until his death, he enjoyed an unclouded friendship: a friendship which, unlike the new one with Valéry, was based on mutual understanding. (A volume of the letters exchanged by Gide and Rilke between 1910 and 1926 will soon be appearing, to illumine this history of a literary friendship.) Rilke was living in Paris, with long and short breaks, from 1902 until 1914. The first years were passed under the sign of the pupil-master relationship with Rodin; 1907 was dominated by the impression made on him by the painting of Cézanne. The *New Poems* and the *Notebooks of Malte Laurids Brigge* were written during those Paris years. Verhaeren, whom he got to know in 1906 at the latest, was the first French poet with whom he entered into a personal relationship. He mentions André Gide for the first time in 1908, in a letter to Hofmannsthal; and in a letter written a year later to the Danish critic George Brandes he gives at length his reasons for admiring Gide's story *La porte etroite*. He wrote that

The impression may depend on a certain kinship of mind (because of which a near acquaintance brought the book to my house). Gide's resources, which I was able to admire here for the first time, are strangely in control of the world he describes; they fulfil (it seems to me) his purposes completely, and from this there results a finely branched security, which nourishes the book tranquilly, like a sap, right to its incommensurable margins.[24]

There can be little doubt that Gide's early work had an influence on the work Rilke was doing in Paris before the war, and one can take it as certain that right until the end of his life Rilke stood in a close spiritual relationship to Gide's literary universe. When they translated each other's work, not shrinking from the labour and trouble involved, it meant for them both a form of close communion and a mutual recognition of achievement. *Malte* had hardly appeared when Gide plunged into it and wrote to Rilke about it (in October 1910): 'For a fortnight now I have been living with you and dwelling in the deeps of your book. How grateful I am to it for teaching me to know you better, so that I can love you more.'[25] In the *Nouvelle Revue française* for July 1911 long extracts from *Malte* appeared in French for the first time, translated in masterly fashion by Gide. Among them was the passage with the horrifying description of the ruined house in Paris, which stuck in Gide's mind to such an extent that he mentions it in his journal for 1929 (three years after Rilke's death). There Gide speaks about his plan to write a description of the outskirts of Paris, which he says he would do '. . . in my own fashion, and that would not be in the least like Huysmans'; more like Rilke's. . .'.

All his days Rilke remained grateful to André Gide for this literary act of friendship; he owed his entry into French literature to Gide's translation. As to the Rilke-Gide relationship, the cause of their mutual attraction was chiefly and undoubtedly something other than the harmony of their natures; it was also the deep-seated differences between them. Their bond was, among other things, that state of individual isolation involving a break with society to which the word 'deracination' has sometimes been given. Both had rebelled against conventional family life and the bourgeois moral code and had made their emancipation the basis of their work. Common to both was their 'availability', i.e. their almost unlimited openness to spiritual and sensuous impressions; and both were thorough-going nonconformists, ready to explore all the rarest phenomena of nature and the human psyche, and to incorporate these into their own lives when they found them sufficiently attractive. Finally a meeting-ground was provided by their common belief in the goodness of all life, for by this each justified his assent to the passions from which he derived a wealth of intellectually sublimated enjoyment, and which helped him in his intensely personal exploration of reality. At the same time, nothing could have been further from Gides' pursuit of intellectual clarification and love of order than Rilke's torrent of metaphorically expressed, ardent feeling; nothing more remote from Gide's firm grasp of objects, his almost graphic delineation of their perspectives and outline, than the mysterious, fantastic, morbid atmosphere pervading *Malte* as a whole, and the existential *Angst* which pursued its creator all through his life, from one terror to another. Above all, Rilke differed from Gide in his powerful sense of vocation, a vocation which had no use for lines and planes, but where all was hovering, dynamic, transformed into pure relation, detached from geometry and perspective; which manifested itself as an energy generating images and associations.[26] Altogether Rilke's mental bearing was unswervingly subjective, a fact which enabled him to take statement and metaphor, impression and description, knowledge and vision, and weld them together into convincing images, parts of a moving whole which seem to owe their existence rather to supernatural communication than to an act of the artist's will. These subjective processes were in complete contrast to the disciplined, methodical work being done by a Gide, a Proust, a Valéry, each in his different way. With these Frenchmen the graphic and analytical predominated, with Rilke the visionary and synthetic.

It must be remembered too that Rilke never accepted or 'learned' the French, or rather cartesian, attitude of mind; he had had no training in logic or philosophy and nothing could have been more unlike him than the intellectual curiosity and rational desire for knowledge of a Valéry, who regarded all and everything simply as a means to the clearer perception of natural phenomena and the human intellect's complete grasp of the visible world. Making poems, said Valéry, who often talked in paradoxes, was of no immediate interest to him except in so far as it gave him food for thought about the poet; and he did not want to be thought of as a *poeta* but as an *artifex* – in the same sense as Leonardo, in whose method Valéry saw a means to disenchant the world and acquire it and its 'mechanism' for the intellect. For Rilke, on the other hand, everything turned to enchantment, even mathematics, and when, in February 1924, after translating most of the poems in the volume *Charmes*, he wrote a poem called *The Magician*, he was probably, though not quite certainly, thinking of Valéry. For with Rilke the clear was always becoming obscure, the bright mysterious, the rational magical; and whenever he encountered life's nocturnal side he was surrounded by demons. His occupation with Valéry's poems did not in any way alter his basic attitude, for he wrote from Muzot in the summer of 1924 (in a different connection):

By and large it is an inborn tendency of mine to deal with the secret as such, not as something to be unmasked but as the mystery which remains mystery right to its core, the secret which is all secret just as a lump of sugar is sugar through and through. Possibly, thought of like that, it solves itself in the circumstances of our life or of our love, when otherwise we should only achieve a mechanical diminution of the immensely secret without really transforming it into ourselves.[27]

Rilke's awkwardness when it came to thinking logically and making methodical distinctions was often astounding and explains much that is obscure and vague in his writing, especially in his letters.

All this means that the French influence could change nothing in Rilke's deeper nature. He exposed himself to important influences and examples as a plant exposes itself to rain or sun; or he was like a stone in a brook which after a long, long time is worn smooth by the incessant flow of the water. Rilke learned much from those influences and models but he scarcely ever imitated anything – with him there was no imitation, no mere literary form. He was a learner all his life, a humble learner who never hesitated to acknowledge the greatness and merit of others, especially when those others were French painters, sculptors and writers. But he also remained throughout his life unmistakably and unchangeably himself, true to the central core of his genius. His skill in the art of translation, which he tried out in the year before the war on Gide's *Return of the Prodigal Son*, shows his linguistic double nature: in his admiration for the assurance and precision of the French tongue, and his innate gift for adapting a foreign text to the German language, or rather, to his own spontaneous way of expressing himself. Mme Renée Lang, the greatest authority on the friendship between Gide and Rilke, is quite right when she says of Rilke's version of the *Retour de l'enfant prodigue* that it is, in spite of certain imperfections, 'beautiful and melodious. But perhaps this beauty is a little too close to Rilke's own poems. . . . Under his pen the prodigal son turns into a bodiless pilgrim, a metaphysical dreamer.'[28] A Rilkean German version is never a word for word translation: it is always at the same time a poem by Rainer Maria Rilke – he cannot do otherwise than make what he has received from another into something of his own. This is the light in which we must see the translations of Valéry's poems which he did during his last years, and in which the original is given a different shade of meaning.

The state of belligerency with his own language in which Rilke had been living since his early Paris years was nothing more than a strenuous and irritating concomitant of his effort to create his own poetic expression out of the frequently resistant

181

material of words. The thoughts on this subject which he wrote down in 1921 had already been confided to André Gide in 1914, when Gide wrote in his journal: 'Once more I have been able to observe the so instructive irritation of a German writer with his own language; an irritation which I have noticed before on other occasions, and which I doubt if any other writer from any other country has experienced.'[29] One day when he was translating Michelangelo's sonnets, Rilke had gone to Gide's house to consult the Grimm dictionary. He had told his French friend then how much it astonished him that there should be a German word for the back of the hand but none for the inside, which in Italian is *palma* and in French *paume*. 'At best one can say the *plain of the hand*. The inside of the hand a plain!' exclaimed Rilke. 'And yet they speak quite often about the back of the hand. What they look at then is the back, that unimportant, impersonal, unsensuous, untender surface, that surface which opposes itself, and they prefer that to the warm, fondling, soft inside, the *paume*, which tells the whole history of mankind!' Rilke also found in Grimm's dictionary the expression *Handteller* (hand plate). 'But this', he said to Gide, 'is the *paume* of the hand as one uses it to collect alms, to stretch out when begging, and which serves as a bowl! What an admission of the inadequacy of our language!'[30] The quick, thumbnail sketch of Rilke that Gide gives us here has an overwhelming authenticity. The thoughts and images in Rilke's later poems are often traceable to their source, and the entry in Gide's journal is confirmed by Rilke's French poem *Paume* (from the 1926 volume *Vergers*, published in Paris):

> Paume, doux lit froissé
> où des étoiles dormantes
> avaient laissé des plis
> en se levant vers le ciel.
> etc. etc.

With his translation of *Return of the Prodigal Son*, published by the Insel-Verlag in 1914, Rilke introduced Gide to a wider circle of German readers. At the beginning of the same year Gide spoke of his wish to translate the *Lay of Cornet Christoph Rilke* into French, but by July he was explaining to Rilke why he had to give up this plan. It is evident that Gide's path as an artist had taken a direction leading him away from the musical, romantic, charming but rather nerveless little production of Rilke's youth. Rilke's own development had led him away from it also, in an aesthetic direction where, for all the individuality of his work, he kept in touch with the artistic feeling of the time, which leant so much towards the unromantic; and perhaps with his intuitive mentality he was more of a pioneer than Gide was in his strangely limited world. It is not surprising that Rilke, too, answered his friend in the negative, though with a heavy heart, when Gide wrote to him in December 1921 asking whether he would be prepared to translate his *Nourritures terrestres* into German. After the war Rilke was no longer standing where Gide had seen him during the earlier days in Paris. His recollections of the younger Rilke led Gide to suppose that he would be extremely well suited to translate the most lyrical of his works into German. He could not know that Rilke's inner music had changed and was seeking for new forms of expression. Besides, it was the time when Rilke was putting his endeavour to complete the *Duino Elegies* before everything else, and when their completion was imminent. Gide's question reached him at Muzot a few weeks before the 'storm' in which the Sonnets and Elegies were written, but after he had translated Valéry's *Cimetière marin* into German. He told Gide in his answering letter that he belonged with his whole being to a couple of tasks, one of them a translation; and we know from other things written by Rilke during that same month that he was planning to translate more of Valéry's work as soon as he felt secure in his own. His friendship with Gide remained unaltered, but thereafter the full intensity of his admiration belonged to Valéry, from whom he had just received his first letter.

'No one making a survey of France's spiritual assets after the war would have thought even of mentioning Valéry', Gide wrote in a periodical in the year 1922.

Hardly a memory survived of his youthful poems. . . . Then, suddenly, came the famous, extraordinary blossoming. One after another, in less than two years, the *Jeune Parque*, the *Cimetière marin* and the *Serpent* were published – surely the most wonderful poems that our time can boast of – together with many pages of the richest, most perfect, most sonorous prose that we had had the chance of reading for a long time.[31]

It speaks well once more for Rilke's highly developed sagacity and sense of quality that he should have recognised the work and the new name at once, without having his attention called to them by anyone else (just as he recognised Hermann Hesse in 1899, Thomas Mann in 1902, Proust in 1913 and Kafka in 1914). For Valéry to enter the first place in his estimation he had only to learn that that poet, who was the same age as Gide and himself, had been silent until he came into the open in full maturity with technically perfect literary works: he seemed to be justification and stimulus for Rilke's own creative work. As we look for the clue to the astonishing, almost enigmatic bond between Rilke's cosmos and the very different one of Valéry we are enlightened by a sonnet (the tenth of Part I, *Sonnets to Orpheus*), connected with Valéry's native district in the South of France where Rilke, many years before, had seen the avenue with the Roman sarcophagi at Arles:

> Welcome, whose meaning in me so long
> coffins of stone, has been quietly growing,
> you the Romans' gladdening water's flowing
> through today as a wandering song;
>
> you also, as open to all delight
> as a wakening shepherd's eyes,
> full of stillness and flowering nettle and flight
> of delirious butterflies;
>
> welcome to all we have snatched like this
> from doubt, the mouths re-endowed with power
> of speech, after knowing what silence is.
>
> Knowing or not, friends – which is our case? –
> Both alike has the lingering hour
> graved in the human face.

Here the experience of a poet wakening from deathlike silence has been translated into Rilkean imagery, rendered into the medium of his own music and feeling: from the entirely southern picture of Roman sarcophagi, to which the comparison with an awakening shepherd's eyes adds a note of the idyllic and bucolic, springs the association of 'the mouths re-endowed with power / of speech, after knowing what silence is'. 'The lingering hour / graved in the human face' means a compliance, a slight pallor, contrasting with the uncompromising tint of that which has gone before.

In the last but one verse of his poem *Palme* – which is a counterpart of the sonnet, although the imagery is different – Valéry praises the patience necessary for the silent, steady ripening of fruit. Here is the original, with Rilke's translation:

Patience, patience,	Gedulden, Gedulden, Gedulden
Patience dans l'azure!	Gedulden unter dem Blau!
Chaque atom de silence.	Was wir dem Schweigen verschul-
Est la chance d'un fruit mûr!	den
Viendra l'heureuse surprise:	macht uns das Reifen genau.
Une colombe, la brise,	Auf einmal lohnt sich der Glaube:
L'ébranlement le plus doux	ein Windhauch kommt, eine Taube,
Une femme qui s'appuie,	ein leisester Anstoss geschieht,
Feront tomber cette pluie	eine Frau neigt leicht sich entgegen
Ou l'on se jette à genoux!	und bringt ihn zum Fall, diesen
	Regen,
	in dem ein Gesegneter kniet!

Rilke spoke often of his luck in hitting upon the exact equivalents for Valéry's poems, and of how he had never even found it necessary to change the sequence of the lines. One certainly can say that these German renderings are the equals in value of the original French poems, but he has often transformed the values – in the sense of 'valeurs' – in the freest, most astonishing way. Here the rhythm and whole spirit are different in the German version. The four times repeated *Gedulden* creates a different tone, and the longer lines give more scope than those of the original. Valéry says (translating word for word) 'every atom of silence the chance of a ripe fruit' – and Rilke is not just taking a liberty but giving the original a new, subjective, metaphysical twist when he renders this as: 'What we owe to the silence makes our ripening exact!' That is beautiful, dark and deep, but not in the least what Valéry said. In *Viendra l'heureuse surprise* the original is speaking, clearly and lucidly, of a coming 'happy surprise', four words which in the German become 'a faith which was worth while'. Rilke has certainly been following a different train of thought up to this point, after which he reproduces closely the purely descriptive lines of the original, until the last, 'where one falls on his knees' (Valéry) and 'in which a blessed one kneels' (Rilke). This example picked from many, sometimes long, poems by Paul Valéry which Rilke translated into German, throws light on the strange spiritual and artistic transformation which took place in the interval between the absorption of the foreign text and its reproduction in the translator's own language. It helps us to understand how it was that Rilke could make apparently contradictory statements: saying at one time that these translations had made him as happy as his own creative work, and at another that he had been able to translate Valéry's poems with an equivalence which he would not have thought possible between the two languages. There is, of course, no question of 'translator's errors' here, arising from an imperfect knowledge of the language – errors such as Rilke did make now and then when translating Gide's *Return of the Prodigal Son* ten years previously: his knowledge of French had progressed so much during the interval that he was now capable of understanding the utmost obscurities and subtleties. It was simply that, half intentionally, half unconsciously, he immersed the French lyric in his own lyrical river bed, so that it was borne along by his own waves while at the same time undergoing a strange metamorphosis. It was like those deities of ancient times who never lost their identity when changed into animals or plants, although they appeared as animal or plant and not in their original form. . . . They are incredibly close to the originals, Rilke's translations of Valéry's poems, while at the same time incredibly far from the original tone, metre, rhyme, mode of expression. Rilke was never an imitator, he was too deeply rooted in his own personality to be able to imitate and the – very numerous – translations which he made during his life from English, Russian, Italian, Danish, Swedish, but above all from the French, form an extension to his own work which he permitted himself whenever the tide of ideas and subject-matter ebbed, when the foreign material would stimulate his desire for productive-reproductive work. He was never a copier, but he often made use of subjects borrowed from other people. So when we carefully compare Valéry's text with Rilke's translation, we encounter ever new variations of the experience of hearing the French original adapt itself miraculously to the cadence of Rilke's verse. It was the same with all the impressions to which Rilke threw himself upon, whether of things, people, works of art, books or nature: when he reproduced them, 'sang' them, they all assumed the unmistakable tone, the strange, sublimated style which was the fruit of his personality.

Valéry's verse, like everything French, appeared to Rilke not only as the related opposite, but as something of a higher order, which he never, until the end of his life, grew weary of admiring and learning from. When we compare Rilke's different creative periods we can say that this work on himself bore good fruit. His translation of Valéry's poetry made him uncommonly happy because he was able to get so close to the original: for he was honestly convinced that 'his language expressed the original more closely and appropriately than any other'.[32] Anyone familiar with both languages will have no difficulty in hearing the lyrical note introduced by Rilke's stream of rhythm and music into Valéry's much more conscious, calculated and elaborate poems — as though an organ were playing a piece of music written for the clavichord. Or: 'as though in the translation the crystalline form had melted into a liquid, the soulish had become mixed with the intellectual, the place of vehement thought been taken by a dynamic, lively comprehension'.[33] The question whether Rilke himself realised the difference is somewhat irrelevant: in view of his enthusiastic acceptance of Valéry and of his own work, and his lack of interest in (and perhaps aptitude for) critical analysis, one would be inclined to think that he did not.

But let us look at another example (the last) of the strange metamorphosis undergone by Valéry's poetry in the process of being recast by Rilke. In the second stanza of the *Cantiques des Colonnes* (The Song of the Columns) Valéry writes:

Douces colonnes, ô
L'orchestre de fuseaux!
Chacun immole son
Silence a l'unisson.

Rilke's version runs:

> Selige Säulen, wie
> Spindeln der Melodie!
> Jede singt, da sie steigt,
> Schweigen, das einig schweigt.

The Frenchman hails the sweet (blessed) columns: 'O the orchestra of spindles!' In the German this becomes: 'like / spindles of melody!' With Valéry each of these spindles, which unite to form a dumb orchestra, makes a sacrifice of its own silence. Admittedly this presents a difficult problem for the translator; Rilke could not make the image fit into his verse, so it becomes 'Each one sings as it climbs / Silence, in unison' – a nuance only, yet forming a narrow gulf between the original and the translation. What pleased Rilke was his translation's faithfulness to the original, what delights his readers is that they have to do, not with a philologically exact copy, a cast, but with a creative transcription, whose warmer life, hazier tone, more tuneful pulsation, would arouse a mild astonishment, if one did not concede to a great poet the liberty to transpose foreign poems into his own key and adapt them to his own instrument. As a final example of Rilke's extraordinary gift of entering into another's feeling and of his art as a translator, we will give here, with the original, four verses of his translation of the *Song of the Columns*, which show how astonishingly faithful he could be:

Si froides et dorées	Meissel aus unseren Wiegen
Nous fumes de nos lits	holten uns, golden und kalt,
Par le ciseau tirées	wie die Lilien stiegen
Pour devenir ces lys!	wir in diese Gestalt!
De nos lits de cristal	Plötzlich erweckte man
Nous fumes eveillées	uns in dem Bett von Kristallen,
Des griffes de métal	und metallene Krallen
Nous ont appareillées.	fassten uns formend an.
Pour affronter la lune,	Dass wir den Mond bestehn,
La lune et le soleil,	Sonnen- und Mondglanz hatten,
On nous polit chacune	hiess es jegliche glätten
Comme ongle de l'orteil!	so wie Nägel der Zeh'n!

Servantes sans genoux,	Mägde wir, ohne Knie,
Sourires sans figures,	Lächeln ohne Gesichter,
La belle devant nous	vor uns die Schöne: die
Se sent les jambes pures.	Schenkel werden ihr lichter.*

* A literal translation of the German would be: Chisels out of our cradles collected us, golden and cold, like lilies we climbed into this shape! Suddenly we were awakened in our bed of crystal, and metal claws touched us, forming us. That we might bear the moon, have the radiance of sun and moon, all had to be smooth as toe-nails. Servants without knees, smiles without faces, before us the beautiful (woman): her limbs become lighter.

FIRST ILLNESS

THE translation of Valéry's poems which Rilke completed early in 1923 concludes the third great cycle of his later work, equal in importance to the *Duino Elegies* and the *Sonnets to Orpheus*. He had gathered it from a foreign shore of language, but although he had been the active partner in that enterprise the opposite seemed to him to have been the case: he felt that the French poet had been his pilot through the shallows of a not so good, not so productive time, and that he was, anyway, 'the nearest to me of the poets of my generation, as I have always felt'.[34]

After finishing this work:

I should like so much to breathe freely for a bit; Muzot is becoming more and more one thing only, nothing but 'cell', made to measure for work and solitude. It has become this to such an extent that it suffers the guest only as seasoning, as a little addition, a drop which dissolves immediately. And sometimes I ask myself whether, after getting so acclimatized to this place and having so much practice in it, I shall ever again, on any evening of my life, be able to endure not being alone?[35]

In spite of feeling unwell, Rilke remained in the Valais; he was able to celebrate Easter in good spirits, as joyfully as a child; he turned the visit of this host Werner Reinhart and the violinist Alma Moody, who gave Muzot its 'baptism of music', into a little festivity for himself and for them, but he is still plagued by 'every kind of malaise', his stomach troubles him, and he even begins to think of getting medical advice in the summer, because he can no longer manage his bodily infirmities on his own. 'Muzot is bound up with so much that is hard and difficult', he writes in May, 'and only in the fire of work does it burn itself out, purely and without any residue.'[36]

None of the many people who saw Rilke driving about the country in the early summer, or turning up here and there: in Zürich, at his Meilen friends' house, on the idyllic shore of the

Greifensee, even on the Thun racecourse for the *Concours hippique*, in a friend's car on the mountain roads, then again in the Valais at the head of Lake Geneva, in Gruyères, in the midst of his circle of friends at Bern – none of those who saw him could have guessed how many troubles were oppressing this man. For he seemed to enjoy chatting and going for sociable walks, accepting invitations, telling stories in the evening for the benefit of young ladies – looking a little strange as he settled himself in an armchair in the corner of a drawing-room, wearing his dinner-jacket and resting, characteristically, his hand on his knee. After returning to Sierre and Muzot on July 5th, he could not stand the summer heat for long. A change was essential, and his ailing body cried out more and more urgently for care. At the end of August Rilke went to a nursing-home on the Lake of Lucerne. Reluctantly he had to give in and allow himself to be massaged by a doctor – 'and so the grotesque thing happens: an old gentleman walks pensively over my body every morning on his hands. A circus number.' Rilke could find no charm in Goethe's and Schiller's classical Lake of Lucerne: *'quel lac en lambeaux que ce malheureux lac des Quatre Cantons'*, he wrote, 'like four handkerchiefs waving goodbye in different directions . . .'[37] More pleasant than the unsuccessful cure were short visits to Lucerne, where he could enjoy the comforts of a big hotel: *'C'est délicieux ici'*, he reports, *'toute la maison sent comme une belle fille qui sort du bain. Enfin, un hôtel volupteux.'*[38] In this town Rilke met some German acquaintances, including a young poet, Xaver von Moos, of whom he thought highly.

From Lucerne his way led to the Grisons – not into the mountains, but to the pleasant dominion watered by the Rhine, where he was often to return during the last years of his life: to those old, well lived in houses of the local families, which appealed to his feeling for style and tradition: to Malans, to Maienfeld, to Zizers. But he did not feel well enough to stay there until the grape harvest. He returned (October) to spend a long time at the Wunderly's home at Meilen on Lake Zürich, where he recovered from the illness which had attacked him again in the Grisons. From there he went for some days to Bern, the town he visited more often than any other in Switzerland after settling at Muzot:

where he used to visit a wide circle of acquaintances, do his
shopping and pay repeated visits to the dentist.

At length, as autumn draws on to winter, we find the poet
again at Muzot. And we are not surprised that, looking back
from his snow-covered tower, he should see the months which
have just passed as 'a lost summer'. His complaints about health,
the falling off in the number of letters he writes, the more
subdued voice, the blunting of his feeling for the landscape, the
restless journeying hither and thither – all these have prepared us
for it. The man who took soundings of unexplored depths has
come up to life's surface again, to remain there until, presently,
his deep doom closes over him; that doom from which there is
no return to the world and to the company of human beings.

At Christmas Rilke sent his 'friend and host' Werner Reinhart
a small copybook containing poems in his own handwriting and
bearing the title: '*Seven Sketches from the Valais*, or *The Little
Wine-year* – as a little Christmas yield of his castle estate of
Muzot. (1923).' In these poems he sings for the first time the
praises of the landscape which has become a new home for him.
The verses have a clear, light ring as though they had altogether
escaped the shadow lying upon Rilke's spirits. Two quatrains of
this produce of his wine press may be given here:

> Vine terraces: manuals, where unremitting
> sunlight is preluding.
> Then into the bowl the serenely transmitting
> vine's more resonant ring.
>
> Till at last in perceptive mouths a perceiving
> of pure grape-sound has begun.
> With what was the lightened landscape heaving?
> Am I feeling its daughter? Discerning its son?[39]

Yet, alas, the winter was going to be 'almost bad'. So that
Rilke had to report sadly: 'It seems that I have come to a few
not so good chapters in my nature; no help for it! They must be
read and understood.'[40] Feeling ill, he went between Christmas
and New Year to the clinic at Valmont above Montreux – three
hours from Muzot – for medical treatment. He stayed there
three weeks, and it was a godsend to him and a great source of

confidence to have found in Dr T. Haemmerli-Schindler just the medical adviser he had wished to have during the coming years. In fact, Rilke would be obliged to accept the advice and treatment of this doctor very often. In spite of the medical verdict of continuous objective improvement, he was still feeling very tired when he returned to Muzot on January 20th.

At this point we touch the fracture, the incurable fracture, which broke the poet's life. Rilke felt it, knew it – although Dr Haemmerli tried to persuade him to take another, more hopeful, view. The fissure went through the very centre of his being. The convulsion which had shaken his health in December had been terrible, he said, penetrating him as no illness had ever done before. It had filled him with fear and anxiety: 'I was as though lifted to another level of being, perhaps to that where the incurables are.' At Valmont he understood that he would never learn to be ill. The illness would change him into a different person, just as being forced to put on uniform had done, eight years previously. 'Exactly as at that time, nature, sky, trees, no longer existed for me, when I looked at them from my bed; I could not reach them any more, I was somewhere else. When I got your flowers I experienced it: I was separated from them as by a window pane, . . . they stood in front of me like a distant past, a past almost disowned by my hemmed-in, hidden, reluctant being.' He was not complaining, Rilke asserted, only stating a fact. His body had played too big a part in his spiritual joys, it had been too closely bound up with the ecstasies and '*élancements*' of his being, it had served him too efficiently, for him to continue to be himself if the 'wonderful instrument' should suddenly start to rebel and contradict.

I shall never be one of those who can use a physical breakdown for the enlargement of the spirit; my whole work was nothing but an increasingly intimate union between my bodily and spiritual faculties; and this body of mine has contributed too fervently to my soul's riches for me to have any right to exploit them when it no longer has a part in them. All this I have felt with the intensity of complete certitude.

The doctor, however, told him that he was quite wrong to look at things in that way. And he, the patient, was unwilling to accept the change in orientation that illness would bring: he wanted to remain the person he had been until a few months before – remain so at any rate until he was fifty; anything else would be an 'abdication'. But would he be able to recover his equilibrium and to work again? He had been his normal self even during and after his cure by Lake Lucerne the previous summer; but not in Valmont and not afterwards.[41]

Rainer Maria Rilke, who concealed his illness with the utmost shyness from all but those nearest to him, made that terrible confession in a letter to Mme Wunderly. He returned to it in another letter written to the same correspondent in February – to the distress which from then on was never to leave him completely:

My body has been too much my companion and fellow-worker for me to decide in my forty-ninth year(!) to practice a mental attitude that would extort from it something beyond its comprehension or *opposed* to it. In that I am very different from most intellectuals. At least since I was twenty-four or twenty-five, *all* the elements of my being have contributed to everything I have been enabled to produce, working together in indescribable harmony: mind, body, soul – it was as if no one of them were superior or inferior, but each precious in its own way, each at once familiar and divine – and the achievement always came at the mysterious culminating point of their harmony. This experience and attitude ought to be taken into account by anyone who wants to understand exactly what has been upsetting and worrying me since the middle of December.[42]

Other letters that Rilke wrote at this time also contain – not exactly complaints, for nothing in these sick reports suggests the self-pitier or the weakling, but numerous hints at the 'not so good chapters' in his nature which he was making such a great effort to read and understand. He produced theories about the origin and associations of this upheaval; perhaps it was caused by a sudden change in the relations of his inner secretions, or perhaps it was the repercussion of two deaths and a birth 'which followed each other quickly in the realm of my blood and resulted in changes in my blood pressure, vascillations and uncertainties'. (Rilke became a grandfather on November 2nd 1923.) 'But above them both,' he reflects, 'however they may be, stands authoratitively *what I never forget*, the single miracle of life and death!'[43]

(When Rilke speaks here of the 'realm of my blood', he is not using the words in a scientific-medical sense; but he did in fact die from a blood disorder.)

When he was feeling better Rilke regarded his illness from the point of view of a detached observer. Yet he would never again be able to enjoy quite freely that wonderful balance of body and soul. Body and soul would, however, still often be capable of those 'surpluses' which could help him to pleasurable days and small victories over the lurking malady. As in the two previous years, the month of February (1924) brought him the gift of the creative spirit, albeit only on a small scale: it was at this time that he wrote his first French poems (*'quelques lignes de poésie qui me sont venues en français'*).[44] When Paul Valéry came to see him at Muzot soon afterwards, the French poet's appreciation of these original French poems delighted Rilke so much that he was encouraged to further efforts in the same line. If Valéry had not asked him to do so, he would never have thought of publishing his French poems. In the autumn of 1924 the Paris periodical *Commerce*, edited by Valéry and Leon-Paul Fargue, brought Rilke's first attempt at French lyric poetry before the public.[45]

Unfortunately we do not yet know the correspondence between Valéry and Rilke,* but some years afterwards Valéry preserved the memory of his visit to Muzot in the form of a letter to his dead translator. 'Do you remember', he says there,

how surprised I was at the utter solitude in which I found you when I made your acquaintance? I was passing through: you stopped me on my way to Italy and kept me by you for some moments. A terribly lonely, very small château in a vast, sad mountain region; old-fashioned, serious rooms with dark furniture, narrow windows: it constricted my heart. My imagination could not restrain itself in your rooms from eavesdropping on the endless monologue of a completely isolated soul with nothing to distract it from itself and from the consciousness of its uniqueness. A life so withdrawn seemed hardly possible to me, eternal winters long in such excessive intimacy with silence, so much space for dreams, so much freedom for the quintessential, the all too concentrated spirits which inhabit books, for the writer's fluctuating

* See translator's note. p. 14.

powers, for the forces of memory. Dear Rilke, you seemed to me locked up in pure time, and I feared for you the transparence of the too monotonous life which through the line of eternally similar days gives a clear view of death.[46]

In the final paragraph of this imaginary letter to his dead friend Valéry corrects his first impression: it had been foolish of him to pity Rilke when 'his spirit achieved a miracle in that emptiness and made a mother of time'. Now 'that awful peace, that excessive calm', appeared to him as 'glorious conditions' – and he called the 'low tower' 'an enviable abode', the 'magic tower of Muzot'. And yet Valéry's first feeling had not been so far wrong. Rilke's life at Muzot, his poetic life as a whole, perhaps asked more of human nature than it could bear.

During his third Valaisian spring (1924) the visits to which Valéry's appearance at Muzot had been a happy prelude followed each other at close intervals: Werner Reinhart and Alma Moody again for Easter, then Anton Kippenberg and others. This coming and going of friends stimulated Rilke and he became more cheerful and talkative. Afterwards he felt somewhat dazed, but he began once more to delight in the charm and advantages of his home. How he would praise it to his guests, how show them the old corners of Sierre, the neighbouring villages, the small churches and all the paths through the great 'hill-inhabited valley'! How, returning from such walks, he would stop as the poplar came into view at the roadside, the square-built, strong walls with their obtuse-angled saddle roof obliquely behind it. 'You must look from here, they belong together', he would say, coming to a halt and inviting his companion to see old Muzot through his, Rilke's, eyes.

After Easter Rilke left Muzot again and stayed away for some weeks. A motor tour with his Zürich friends gave him the opportunity of seeing French Switzerland in comfort and at leisure. In memory of this drive they took together Rilke composed for Mme Nanny Wunderly a poem about the four lace cushions which they saw in Valangin Castle (Canton Neuenburg): the cushions were lit by a curious lighting arrangement, so that they could all receive an equal amount of illumination. This was the subject of the following filigree like poem[47]:

Valangin

1

Die vier Lichter der vier Glasglocken
waren kreuzweis dicht zusammengeschoben
an die kleine Röhre mit dem Globen;
hinter den vier Wasserkugeln, innen,
stand das Licht.

2

Licht, für immer uns dahingeflossen ...
Daß es manchmal einer von den Knaben,
wie es ihn verklärte? – Mag es ihnen
jenes Handwerk unwirklich haben
und das zugeneigte Angesicht.

3

Wer da einsah, meint er nicht, unter
lauter nicht mehr Wirklichen zu sein?
draußen war sogar das Dunkel bunter, –
hier war nichts als Schein und Widerschein
von dem reinen Unterwasser-Licht

197

4

Ach, wie ging es in die Spitzen über,
dieser Schimmer, der sich einbezog.
Wenn sich nur der Mädchen vorwärtsbog,
war er manchmal so bewegt, als hüb an
selbst ein namenloses Angesicht.

5

Wie der Wasserball ein Licht aufging
und so unbeschreiblich so verteilte,
daß man nicht mehr wußte, ob es weilte
oder abschiednehmender verging —,
dieses beinah innerliche Licht.

6

Faßt wie Licht in einem lichten Leben,
faßt wie schon vom Glück verbrauchtes Licht,
so verschenkt, so sinnlos hingegeben
und so nah schon wieder am Verzicht:
Licht für Spitzen. Blößeslicht.

FIRST ILLNESS

VALANGIN

Four work-cushions for the four inclining
bobbiners stemmed cross-wise on the floor
from the little daïs bearing four
water-globes, in midst of which, through-shining,
stood the light.

Light now shone for evermore away . . .
Was some lad there now and then perceiving
how it quite transfigured them? – It may
well have made of this their weaving
and bent faces an unreal sight.

Must it not have seemed to an instrayer
that he'd entered an unreal sphere?
Even the surrounding dark was gayer, –
only shine and counter-shine was here
from that candid under-water light.

How it found its way into the lace,
that incorporative shimmer!
Sometimes, when a girl bent near, a face
of its own would seem to glimmer
into momentary sight.

As the water-globe received its ray
and so indescribably divided,
there was no more telling if it bided,
or was going farewellinger away, –
that almost interior light.

Light within some luminous existence,
through sheer happiness suspended light,
scattered with such prodigal persistence,
then once more so nearly taking flight:
light for lace-work. Bobbin-light.

Via Bern, the poet returned to the Valais. In May his letters are once more dated from Muzot. They tell of a visit from Frau Clara Rilke and her brother. (Rilke had not seen his wife since 1919, when he had said goodbye to her in Munich; this was to be their last meeting.)

In the early summer Rilke spent a few weeks at the spa of Ragaz, where his aristocratic friend Marie Thurn und Taxis was also taking the cure. The poet grew so fond of this place, its snug atmosphere, its good, wholesome (if rather humdrum) social life, and the whole neighbourhood near and remote, that he was to return there for longer visits during the next two years (the last years of his life). The hours spent in the old lady's circle, the charm of the little Windischgraetz princesses; Mme Wunderly's visit, an excursion to the Tamina Gorge (which he described at length in a delightful letter to the two young girls); some visits to acquaintances in the 'dominion', at the castles Salenegg, Bothmar and Zizers; pleasant drives in the two-horse landaus which were still used there; the invigorating baths: these, briefly, were the things he enjoyed most during those weeks dedicated to recovery, when he really did recover.

Jokingly, but with the vivid detail characteristic of his imaginings, Rilke talked of opening a bookshop in Ragaz, where he could give people advice about their purchases and praise and explain the books he himself loved. . . . A charming example of his humour, but also a witness to his lifelong passion for beautiful books. Even without a bookshop: how often and how incomparably Rilke would tell stories that he had read in books; he awakened to new life the spirits slumbering in their pages; they became present in his words; one listened spellbound as they emerged from Rilke's descriptions with their destinies, their adventures, their ideas. How vividly the poet brought the imaginary to life, so that one became breathless as one listened and was led, enchanted, through the terrors and marvels of this immaterial world. These were among the unforgettable moments of the small sociable gatherings with which Rilke would interrupt his solitude. I shall never forget how, sitting under the luxuriant foliage of the chestnut trees on the cathedral terrace at Bern, he told us stories from the Princess Bibesco's *Perroquet vert*. . . .

After staying for a little at familiar Meilen, which always did

him good, it was once more to the Valais that the poet returned
(in August). Again he is spending 'Muzot-days, *tout simplement*,
which is to say, good ones'. Rilke writes letters, 'but a lot of
abundances too, French poems and, think of it, *dédiés au Valais,
de véritables, "Quatrains Valaisans" dont je me servirai pour
appuyer ma future demande de nationalité suisse; je ne peux pas
prouver mieux que j'ai ce pays dans le sang, et j'espère que ce sera
parfaitement convaincant pour les autorités qui décideront de ma
demande*'. (' "Valais Quatrains", which I shall use to back the
application I am going to make for Swiss nationality; there is no
better way of proving that I have this country in my blood, and I
hope that it will entirely convince the authorities who have to
deal with my application.') This cycle of French poems written in
the vernacular of his home valley and dedicated to it brought
Rilke a renewed delight in his unexhausted creative powers. A
postscript to the same letter confirms his cheerful news with these
words: 'The Valais Quatrains have themselves been such a surprise and largess, such a corroboration too, in that the country to
which I am so greatly indebted has become speech in me.'[48]

However, from this time onward every new attempt at flight
was followed by a sudden, cruel fall. Those propitious, productive
Muzot days lasted five weeks at most. Harassed, restless, ashamed
and humiliated at being so much at odds with himself, Rilke
turned for comfort in September to his Vienna friends the
Weiningers, who had invited him to Ouchy. Then once again
he had news to give of 'excellent hours', spent at Lausanne with
Edmond Jaloux (who by his sympathetic interpretations of Rilke's
work did more to further it than any other French critic of the
time). At the outlet of the lake, 'shining, glistening Geneva . . .
(and so many memories one was all but overwhelmed)'.[49]

The return to Muzot was very melancholy: Rilke felt imprisoned in his 'doom', as though he were breathing under a
rubbish heap. No human being, he believed, could help him:
'help must come from the same source as the grace for a great
poem'. There had been an unusual amount of rain in the Valais,
the weather was cool, the grape harvest, one of his joys there in
former years, was wretched. He gives a moving account of this
failure even of the seasons: 'This year summer and autumn are
like gigantic mirrors cracked right across: and now one cannot tell

whether this crack is distorting the reflection of the universe, or whether a strangely disfigured universe is in fact bending over it.'[50]

How willing and how fertile the spirit was in spite of such distorted conditions is shown by the fact that Rilke had no sooner returned to Muzot than he began dictating a translation of Paul Valéry's prose work *Eupalinos* to a secretary he had engaged to type out his translations of Valéry's poems. Eighty-nine large book pages were dictated in a few days! So once again – not yet for the last time – the poet was granted a success which made him happy.[51]

But the motive of suffering was now dominant in this life. In its grip, as he says in the poem about Wera's death, the blood 'darklier thrusted' until 'after terrible knocking' it 'entered the hopelessly open door'. As we read the notes Rilke made about his illness, we see clearly that he never, through weakness or morbid acquiescence, gave his permission for the disease to enter: he did not take the part of his malady by complying with it, or even long for death as a deliverer. His assent to being, his affirmation of life, remained whole-hearted until the end. Sickness had come upon him as an intruder and a destroyer, and the last two, almost three, years of his life, were nothing but a continuous, courageous struggle against a terrible fate, endured in gallant silence. A shame born of extreme sensitiveness made him try to hide his illness from everyone. But with his infallible powers of intuition he recognised it before any doctor and said: 'Something has forced its way into me.'

A few days after Rilke had dictated his impromptu translation of Valéry's *Eupalinos*, something happened which alarmed him profoundly, more profoundly perhaps than he admitted. Early in the morning of October 15th, while he was still asleep, peasants from Muraz, who owned the piece of land on which it stood, felled the poplar! That magnificent poplar which had called to him on the day he discovered Muzot: 'Look, this is it!' The tall, upright tree which stood at the turn of the road like a symbol, obliquely in front of the low tower and pointing towards it. One morning the poplar was nothing but a heap of sawn-up, splintered wood.

Rilke's brief account of the event makes a sad contrast to the letter in which, with a heart full of joy and confidence, he told of the discovery of his castle. 'By the time I understood,' he wrote,

what had happened, and reached the spot, it was too late to save it. And the worst is, it looks as though I really *could* have saved it. '*Si j'avais su que cela vous fait plaisir! . . .*' the peasant said, an unknown pale man wearing dark glasses, who looked as though death itself had ordered him to do this work. . . . You wouldn't believe how different the landscape is since it lost that great measuring unit of the vertical, it's as though it had fallen down onto the level. . . . Only with averted face can I pass those ruins of a tree. (That anything which has entered so deeply into one's imagination should be removed from sight between one day and the next!)[52]

Rilke has written the sad date in the visitors' book at Muzot.

The winter and spring of 1924-25 were the first for three years that he did not spend in his castle. The secret inner discord brought about by the constantly recurring malaise and the difficult living conditions, endurance of which only seemed justified when he was concentrating – as now he could not – on literary work, combined to keep him away from the familiar valley for almost a year. After some dental treatment in Bern and a short visit to Montreux, Rilke went again at the end of November to the Valmont clinic, to be in the care of his understanding doctor. An abscess under a tooth had made him very run down again. Outside his sick-room window there was a dense fog which 'hid Paris' from him. 'For', he writes from Valmont, 'I play fondly with the possibility of not letting the summer pass without seeing Paris again, the avenues of the Luxembourg and the beautiful curves of the Seine near Sèvres.'[53] And he tells a Paris friend that his heart beats faster at the thought that it could one day be granted to him again to walk along the rue de Seine, to step into the rhythmic landscape of the Luxembourg Gardens and to lean on the little balustrade above the Medici fountain, as though on his standing-desk, there where he often used to work under the flowering hawthorns. . . .

That December Spitteler's *Prometheus the Sufferer* was published. Rilke read it immediately – read it, as his custom was, aloud – so that his experience of the first Prometheus should be 'enlivened and modified by taking a part in the old man's moving work, which bids so profound a farewell to the figure he over-toweringly raised up in earlier days'.[54] On December 29th, a few days after reading it, he heard, and was moved by, the news of Carl Spitteler's death. Rilke had never in his life met that lonelier, proud, misunderstood poet, whom he admired as one of the greatest; but two years later death was to summon him on December 29th, the anniversary of the very day when he had mentally taken leave of Spitteler.

Six weeks went by in Valmont without any perceptible allevi-ation either of his intense physical discomfort or of the troubled state of mind associated with it. Everything seemed to suggest that a long period of rest and care was advisable. For all those about him his sudden decision to go to Paris came as a complete surprise. On January 6th 1925, he left. It happened, as he said in a letter from Paris to his Bern friends, 'in a moment of weariness and revolt'. He had decided that his illness, which for weeks had been receiving so much attention, must now be given the opposite treatment. It was a bold act of evasion, a flight: an attempt to escape his destiny.

LAST HARVEST

RAINER MARIA RILKE'S final creative period is less easily surveyed and summed up in a phrase than some of his earlier ones, and than the important late period which, with the Elegies, the Sonnets, and many of their satellite poems, stands large and clear under the date February 1922. The year 1923 was so dominated by the experience of translating Valéry, it is not surprising that his output of original work should have been scanty during that time, apart from some occasional poems. True, he wrote, on a summer journey, a longish poem, *The Traveller*, which he dedicated to Anton Kippenberg, and contributed to a booklet published in Kippenberg's honour; true also that he wrote a poem called *Imaginary Career*, which relates the story of his own past in a highly condensed form; and that he composed the *Little Wine-Year* cycle for Werner Reinhart, which a newspaper published years after the poet's death: but all these works were the products of 'side-hours', albeit 'side-hours' into which the 'main feeling' kept on breaking. We must not forget that during his lifetime Rilke wrote countless numbers of these poems of dedication and friendship, which he scattered to the four winds: lover of order though he was, he did not for the most part go to the trouble of making copies to keep by him.* For the Rilke expert such *opera minora* mean always enrichment and enlightenment; the poet himself was hardly ever satisfied with anything that was not part of a 'work' – an expression which, he said, he used only sparingly (whether of his own achievements or of others').

The year 1924 was more productive. Strangely enough, it was once again in the month of February that poems came (for the third time now at Muzot), although they were also written in

---

* The second volume of Rilke's *Sämtliche Werke*, edited by Ernst Zinn and published by the Insel-Verlag in 1957 contains all the uncollected poems and fragments (known till then) from the last twenty years of Rilke's life. A complete English translation by J. B. Leishman, *Poems 1906-26*, was also published in 1957, by the Hogarth Press. Translator.

March, in the early spring and in June. Rilke had now recovered from the first menacing attack of his illness, and was already able to look back in a more relaxed mood at the distasteful episode of his stay in the Valmont clinic. As in the *Little Wine-Year* some of these verses sprang from direct experience of the landscape around Muzot: Rilke began, at first in German, to write poems about the Valais. The one which follows has the title *Early Spring*:

> Harshness gone. And sudden mitigation
> laid upon the field's uncovered grey.
> Little runnels change their intonation.
> Tentative caresses stray
>
> round the still earth from immensity.
> Roads run far into the land, foretelling.
> Unexpectedly you find it, welling
> upwards in the empty tree.

Of wider scope were the drafts of poems (written during two winter evenings in February), the 134 lines of which he dedicated to Kippenberg on the occasion of his fiftieth birthday; and the significant poem called *The Magician*, in which Rilke deals searchingly with the life of the poet – as it appears to him. And in the same month he was already writing his first French verses. After returning to Muzot from his cure in Ragaz and the calming, reviving summer weeks spent among people in the outer world, Rilke employed himself during the month of August in writing French poems. They developed into a sequence, and at last a cycle of poems lay before him again: the *Valais Quatrains*. What had been begun in German, as the straight description, explanation, celebration of a landscape, became a blossoming wreath of Valais poems only when he wrote in the 'borrowed language', the language of the valley he felt to be his home. But the *Valais Quatrains* form only one of several sequences written in French. He added it to his little book *Vergers* as an appendix or second part; the first part, to which he gave the title, consists of about fifty-nine poems dealing with a variety of motives, themes and subjects, while there are only thirty-six in the *Valais Quatrains*.

The title of the whole, *Vergers*, may be a hint that the poet feels this French work to be under the sign of a bucolic inspiration. But it would be straining Rilke's intention to see in his French poems a new and decisive phase of development, as O. F. Bollnow does. Bollnow believes that in the French poems, and also in the German written at the same time, 'there is a quite definite, consistent view of the meaning of world and existence', which is as much as to say that the poet ended by denying, certainly by triumphing over, the view expressed in the Elegies.[55] Rilke no more had to 'triumph over' himself when he created those lighter, more genial images, than a composer has when he inserts a charming scherzo between two tragic movements. Even in the *Sonnets to Orpheus* there is often just such a note of cheerful affirmation, a delight in praising, in creating music full of reverence for the world, full of childlike affection for the earth and all that comes out of it. On the other hand, the French poems are not lacking in more sombre, elegiac tones. We cannot agree with Bollnow's interpretation when he tries to show that behind the 'late Rilke', writer of the great 1922 cycle, there is an even later one, hitherto unnoticed, whom he calls 'the mature Rilke' and whose view of the world has changed. Gabriel Marcel has said, rightly in our opinion, 'we must at all costs guard against a method of interpretation which is in the last resort rational', which is just the method that Bollnow suggests we should apply to Rilke's thought.[56] Bollnow is undoubtedly right when he finds between the lines of the *Duino Elegies* 'the distressing experience of man's forlorn condition in the midst of a world which has grown sinister and is collapsing upon him' and in which man is seized by a feeling of desperate loneliness. It is also true that the Valais poems are uplifted into 'a quite different, free and happy atmosphere, where human feelings grow lighter and more genial in the ripe summer landscape'. But in certain of Rilke's basic conceptions there had been no change during that short period. He had breathed more freely when the Elegies, the vision of which had burdened him for ten years, were finished, and had planned from then on to attempt only manageable, leisurely works. The first of these works were the Orpheus sonnets, written before and after the Elegies. They were followed by the Valéry translations, by numerous German poems and an even greater number of poems in French. Of the Elegies Rilke had said, even before they were finished, that their words were 'heavy and unwieldy by nature'. He said of the word *verger*, which he had fallen in love with and chosen as the title of his French poems, that it sounded 'light, bright and sappy'. The French poems lack the tragic greatness of the *Duino Elegies* and even the deep, thoughtful and formal, annealed lustre of the *Sonnets to Orpheus*. Nor yet do they have the immense vitality and power of the *Charmes* versions. But they take their place — intimate, sweet and a little diffident — beside the great master-pieces, together with charming miniatures, sketches, landscapes and pieces of thought play; and the unmistakable tone of Rilke's unique, original voice sounds even through the medium of the foreign language.

The attempt — new for him, and yet not quite new — to write poems in a foreign tongue occupied him intensively and unceasingly during the last years of his life, interrupted as these already were by his illness and by the distracting states of depression which it caused. The discovery that the poetic gift had been granted to him in another language was among his last great joys. It was, however, marred when his first French poems appeared in the Paris review *Commerce* and *Nouvelle Revue française*, by attacks made on him by misguided, foolish chauvinists, attempting to cast suspicion on his innocent enterprise. This truly European poet, who had exchanged a homeland for the treasures of several countries, for various languages and cultures, was in his guilelessness quite unprepared for the attacks and the censure with which his attempts to write French poetry were received in Germany. Kippenberg's reproaches upset him most of all. The German publisher feared for his author's reputation — but he was to put his groundless anxiety aside in later years when his Insel-Verlag published in a luxury edition a volume of Rilke's poetry which included the French poems. For Rilke's biographer and readers there simply exists the fact that three little books of French poems appeared under the poet's name: the first, *Vergers suivis des Quatrains valaisans* in his lifetime (1926); two others, *Les Roses* and *Les Fenêtres*, shortly after his death, but in accordance with his wishes (1927); a fourth, a kind of gleaning and supplement called *Carnet de poche*, published (1929) by French friends, reverently but also perhaps a little arbitrarily – at all events without the rigorous scrutiny that the author would have given it (1929).[57]

Attempts at writing, even at composing poems, in foreign languages had been made by Rilke in his youth. Lou Andreas-Salomé tells us how he tried his hand at writing Russian verses. Rilke composed them during the long journey they took together across Russia, 'out of a deep desire, and although their grammar was bad they were somehow incredibly poetic'.[58] Several years later, in Paris, he tells Rodin that some French verses have come into his head. We know that during his second winter in Switzerland, at Berg by the Irschel, 'Count C. W.' wanted to dictate Italian verses to him, which he refused to take down.

Rilke's intense practical interest in other languages is more clearly demonstrated by his German renderings of foreign poets than by his diffident attempts at writing poems of his own. We need not say any more about his translations from the French. From Italian he translated Michaelangelo's sonnets; while his advice to Marie Thurn und Taxis about alterations to her Italian versions of the Elegies show how very familiar he was with the finer shades of that language. He also translated Leopardi and d'Annunzio, and, from Russian, Lermontov and others. Rilke knew enough Danish to read Kierkegaard and to translate Jens Peter Jacobsen; for a long time he read Georges Brandes's weekly essay in the Copenhagen newspaper *Politiken* (as he himself told Brandes in the letter he wrote to him in 1909). English books he could only read in translation, as he did not know the language well enough. In spite of that he ventured to translate Elizabeth Barrett Browning's sonnets; his imagination was fired one day by this poetess, and by dint of intuition and a kind of guesswork, he very soon acquired enough English to be able to translate her *Sonnets from the Portuguese* with the help of a collaborator. After that he did not bother any more with the English language. That he never quite forgot it is shown by an incident recounted by one of his friends. Once when the conversation turned to questions of English usage, Rilke suddenly threw in the sought-for expression, or the correct grammatical construction, with a malicious smile. Similarly, in Egypt and Tunis, he learned just enough Arabic to give him a better understanding of the parts of North Africa he visited, and of the Islamic world, and to enable him to read Arabic poetry and the Koran. During his last stay in Paris (1925) it was a great joy and encouragement to him to meet in Dr Mardrus the man who, after publishing a critical edition of the *Thousand and One Nights* in the original Arabic, published the whole work again in a translation by himself. Rilke did not translate anything from Spanish, but we know from Gebser's book on Rilke and Spain what sort of impression that country made on him when he visited it immediately before the world war, and how important the experience was for him. Between the years 1902 and 1906 he was already corresponding with the Spanish painter Don Ignacio Zuloaga.[59]

With his international or rather universal outlook, Rilke was wonderfully free from patriotic reservations and prejudices, a true cosmopolitan – and if he found fault with the Germans of his day it was mainly because they were 'insular'. He did not, in fact, recognise any intermediate steps, any barriers, between man and the world, but only a boundless wealth of interchanging relationships, which he experienced as vibrations. In the deepest sense, there was no limit to his gift for languages, and whenever he encountered any congenial thing or being he responded with the most sympathetic, sensitive insight, losing not a whit of his own individuality through this identification of himself with others. Living poised between two cultures had always been deeply satisfying to him. He had started to cultivate the habit in his youth, in his native Bohemia, where his sympathy for the Czechs had given offence to the German colony in Prague, to which his family belonged. His study of the Czech language during those early years was the first step he took towards fulfilling his urge for linguistic expansion. Not the least of his reasons for feeling comfortable and at home in Switzerland, and thinking of taking Swiss nationality, was that he could use two languages there quite freely, without any danger of being misunderstood or arousing suspicion. I have heard him speak French as often as German. His French conversation was fluent and very charming, a little foreign sounding like that of a Russian who speaks the language well and is familiar with its finest nuances.

In his letters written in French Rilke is rather unsure of his syntax; he uses some astonishing turns of phrase, while his grammar, always inclined to be a little odd, sometimes breaks down altogether owing to his lack of an elementary grounding in the language. Before publishing his poems he got his knowledgeable French friends to look them over and make a selection.

As we have heard several times already, Rilke found the German language unsatisfactory and inadequate in certain respects. There is, however, no lack of evidence that he was as full of this his native tongue as a vessel 'heaped up and shaken together', and that he was familiar with it right to its innermost recesses of mystery and possibility. The by no means uncritical Kassner says that in Rilke's poetry there is 'perhaps a certain amount of decoration, flourish, ornament and conceit, but never, never a cliché. Hence its precious, wonderful unity . . . the quality in his art which many might call aestheticism did not mean lack of greatness, but rather the absence of the cliché of greatness. Or: his real greatness lay in unity of form and content.[60] What was Rilke's idea in wanting to get more out of the German language than it was able to give? He answered the question once in the following sentences:

(I think always in terms of *le soleil* and *la lune* and the reversal in our language goes against the grain for me so that I always want to make 'the great sun' masculine . . . and the little moon feminine!) Jacobsen once wrote that it now seemed wrong to him to call that curious short story of his with the Salzach setting *Two Worlds*, he always felt impelled to say *Two World*, and it often happens that one does not agree with the outward behaviour of a language and longs for its innermost core, for an innermost language, without endings possibly, a language made up of word kernels, a language not plucked from stalks, up above, but gathered as speech seed – would not the perfect hymn to the sun be composed in this language, and is not the pure silence of love like heart soil around such speech kernels?[61]

Here he is speaking of a metaphysical deficiency of human speech in general, 'surmising what talk may be like *there*, where the silence is' – and not discussing the defects and clumsiness of any particular language. It was the latter with which his imagination was concerned when he lamented after finishing the Elegies that he had missed certain words like '*verger*', '*offrande*', and '*absence*' in the positive sense which Valéry gives it.

Rilke loved the word *'verger'* so much that he said it had given him the courage to write in the 'borrowed language'. What he meant by it he explained in a letter: '. . . A meadow planted with fruit trees, neither garden nor field but perhaps a combination of both – the trees, the hum of bees, the sweet scent of wild flowers, the freshness of grass, all expressed in this word, which is light, bright and sappy as a poem by Francis Jammes – how should I not have been tempted to write in this language?'[62]

The poem *Verger* runs:

> Peut-être que si j'ai osé t'écrire,
> langue prêtée, c'était pour employer
> ce nom rustique dont l'unique empire
> me tournmentait depuis toujours: Verger.
>
> Pauvre poète qui doit élire
> pour dire tout ce que ce nom comprend,
> un à peu près trop vague qui chavire,
> ou pire: la clôture qui défend.
>
> Verger: ô privilège d'une lyre
> de pouvoir te nommer simplement;
> nom sans pareil qui les abeilles attire,
> nom qui respire et attend. . . .
>
> Nom clair qui cache le printemps antique,
> tout aussi plein que transparent,
> et qui dans ses syllabes symétriques
> redouble tout et devient abondant.

Rilke could not emphasise enough that his French poems were not 'translated' from German but were really thought out and shaped in the spirit of the language in which he was trying to write. Apropos of this he once told us in Bern of a remarkable occurrence. It was his habit to write in his notebook everything that came into his head, even when the sense and connection of the ideas were not immediately obvious. The fragmentary jottings would then sometimes turn out, later on, to have the most unlikely connections. Wanting to write a poem for Hugo von Hofmannsthal's fiftieth birthday, he was looking through the notebook one day when the words *corne d'abondance* arrested him; and he chose this as the theme of his good wishes and sent the Austrian poet some German verses entitled *Cornucopia*. Later it seemed to him not without significance that his entry had been made in French: *corne d'abondance*, and he felt that he must treat the same theme again in French verse. He let his intuitions have their way, for it was his practice never to compose anything according to plan, but docilely to allow poems to form themselves in his imagination and under his pen. How surprised he was when the work now forming itself took a different direction to the German *Cornucopia* and there came into being a French poem quite unlike the German![63]

This event, Rilke concluded, was significant in showing just how different are the demands and secret laws of the two languages. If he also remarked now and then how wonderful it was to be able 'to say everything over again' on the instrument of the other language, that is only a further proof of how closely, at least as to theme, his French poems resemble the German. Short, plain and thinly orchestrated, they are in form identical with, or very similar to, the German poems of 1923-24, poems entirely stripped of the solemn and the exalted, in which Rilke shows a preference for the four-line stanza (and which, from this artistic and formal point of view, undoubtedly constituted a new creative period). In trying to place Rilke's French poems in a historic literary setting, one looks in vain for a model among the more recent French lyric poets; they do not stem from Rimbaud, Moréas, Mallarmé or Valéry – not even from Valéry, which shows again how strangely certain of his direction Rilke was, even at a time when he seemed to have surrendered himself to an influence. These French poems stand quite alone in French literature, strange and foreign. As once with his Russian poems, Rilke had composed them 'out of a deep desire', and of these too one could say that they are 'somehow unbelievably poetic'. Edmond Jaloux, who judged him both as a friend and an expert, says of them: 'Rainer Maria Rilke's verse is extremely fluid: if it recalls anything it is Gide's *Nourritures terrestres*.' (Gide had not been far wrong in thinking that Rilke would be the ideal German translator for that work, the translator spiritually closest to the original.) 'But how fleeting such an impression is!' Jaloux continues.

As always, Rilke is completely himself here. His poetry makes the impression – at least in French – of a great humility, a trembling submissiveness to the object, a question which sounds half anxious, half tender. Nowhere a sharp edge; everything is in process of becoming; the eye has no sooner observed a thing than it grows aware of the change in it; a touching fragrance hovers about each image; a desire to be fleetingly united can be sensed in each poem, but it almost evaporates into the air, so free and light it is. What a wonderful delicacy reveals itself in such poetry![64]

The Paris of the past and the Valais of the present both had a share in the creation of Rilke's French poems. Let us remember his remark that the word *verger* 'sounds like a poem by Francis Jammes' – which perhaps brings us near to his own poetic tone. Francis Jammes is the poet Rilke is thinking of when he makes his Malte Laurids Brigge write:

You don't know what that is, a poet? – Verlaine. . . . Nothing? No memory? No. He didn't seem to you any different from those you knew? You aren't aware of a difference, I can see. But it is another poet I'm reading, one who doesn't live in Paris, quite a different one. One who has a quiet house in the mountains. Who sounds like a bell in the pure air. A happy poet, who talks about his window and about the glass doors of his bookcase which thoughtfully mirror a beloved, lonely world. This is the very poet I'd have liked to become, for he knows so much about girls, and I too would have known a lot about them. He knows about girls who lived hundreds of years ago; it doesn't matter that they are dead for he knows everything. And that is what matters. . . .[65]

The question here too is Rilke's: 'when is present? what is time?' It looked as though after many years Malte's wishful dream had been fulfilled in Rilke's life. True, he had become a different poet from Francis Jammes, but he too had a quiet house in the mountains. The windows looking out on to the countryside, the fruit trees and roses in his garden, the surrounding vineyards and the grape harvest which he celebrated with the valley people, the old fortress towers on the hills and the sound of church bells, the roads leading far into the country and pointing it out, the gurgle of streams careering into the valley, and, above all, the blazing sun of these southern summers, the great noon on the heroic landscape: this round of daily, familiar dealings with an environment he had grown to love provided Rilke with the subject-matter and imagery of his Valais poems. In them this countryside becomes language and song; it was Rilke's closeness to nature and existence which made a festival of the days when, in bucolic harmony with the world around him, he was writing his *Quatrains valaisans*. The following poem, representing many others, is given as an example of these carefree, tender songs in praise of the landscape (though unlike the majority of his *quatrains* it runs to more than a single four-line stanza):

> Pays, arrêté à mi-chemin
> entre la terre et les cieux
> aux voix d'eau et d'airain,
> doux et dur, jeune et vieux
>
> comme une offrande levée
> vers d'accueillantes mains:
> beau pays achevé,
> chaud comme le pain!

Rilke dedicated the thirty-six *Quatrains valaisans* to one of his Valais friends, Mme Jeanne de Sépibus-de-Preux of Sierre.[66] The writer Robert de Traz, who was at that time editor of the *Revue de Genève*, published some examples of them in his periodical, before the little book *Vergers* appeared.

To share this production of his muse with others was so characteristic of Rilke at that time that we should like to quote here a passage from a short memoir: 'In the following autumn', it says,

we again joined Rilke in Sierre for the occasion of the grape harvest. We collected him at Muzot, he received us with his usual cordiality. He was so cheerful, no one would have suspected that his health had been seriously threatened. We had planned to have a meal in our vineyard with some friends. Rilke accepted the invitation gladly, the prospect of the outing seemed to delight him. . . . We arrived at the vineyard on the little hill and there, with the colourful landscape spread out below us in all the richness of its autumn finery, high above the golden yellow valley with the silvery Rhone meandering through it, Rilke at our request read his Valais poems to us. . . .[67]

Had this homeless man turned into a singer of the homely? Had this master of the German lyric been won over by the Gallic word? Had Rilke at the height of his artistic maturity become a creative poet in the French language? His own modest opinion is probably the right one: that his French poems were a 'side achievement' compared with the totality of his work in German; yet the excessive modesty with which he repeatedly refers to this poetry in his letters from Muzot should not always be taken as a yardstick for the critic. These charming miniatures, strains of pastoral chamber music, which Paul Valéry at his own request had taken in hand to scrutinise and publish, are not unworthy to stand alongside Rilke's great masterpieces. The gift of proclaiming, praising, singing, in both tongues had been bestowed on this poet living in that border country of two languages, the Valais – in the low tower which through him has become a cairn to commemorate the happy meeting of two great cultures. And on the foreign lyre, too, although he does not handle it as confidently and expertly as his own, there is always to be heard Rilke's personal, incomparable melody.

The works written during his time in Switzerland form a bilingual unity. Whether German or French, Rilke's poems could always be picked out from hundreds of others. They are spoken by the same voice, they spring from the same consistent world of thoughts and feelings which transform themselves directly and spontaneously into images from the same workshop – and yet they differ from one another. They differ as much as the two instruments of language to which the poet alternately entrusted himself. The Valais poems did not come into being in a 'storm'. They were 'abundance'. For the organ thunder of the Elegies he had received 'signals from space'. A valley wind had brought him the poems, ripe sounding as a chime of musical bells, written in the language of his chosen home. Rilke had now succeeded in realising his wish of that victorious 11th of February 1922, when the little Soglio manuscript book had lain before him on his standing desk with the *Duino Elegies* written in it at last: he had been occupied with the 'peaceful, leisurely human tasks, no longer these that surpass all common, warrantable strength'. The numerous French and German poems, satellites of the more important works, which Rilke wrote during his later years, have a fraternal proximity to the masterpieces. To divide them into 'late' and 'mature' would be forced and artificial; all have a share in the maturity of the late period. Incidentally, the French poems are not lacking in echoes of the *Sonnets to Orpheus*. In the following pair of quatrains we recognise familiar themes:

> Vues des anges, les cîmes des arbres peut-être
> sont des racines, buvant les cieux;
> et dans le sol, les profondes racines d'un hêtre
> leur semblent des faîtes silencieux.

> Pour eux, la terre, n'est-elle point transparente
> en face d'un ciel, plein comme un corps?
> cette terre ardente, où se lamente
> auprès des sources l'oubli des morts.

The vision of heaven and earth as seen by the angels; the earth of the dead and of the water springs; the mystery of the trees with their crowns and roots: we find these themes of an unearthly-underearthly world repeated everywhere in the German sonnets (as in the Elegies). That they seem at one moment ominous and oppressive, at another to shine with the transparency of a carefree, consenting heart, is not entirely due to the difference of language; nor is it the result of one view of the world being replaced in course of time by another: such an evolutionary interpretation would run counter altogether to Rilke's feeling about time, which in place of the temporal sequence of past, present and future experiences only presents – even the presence of the not-present: '*la présence absente*'. The varying tones, dark and light, in which the image often appears, may also be connected with the ups and downs of the poet's moods. Yet it was, so to speak, Rilke's 'message', expressed in his letters with every conceivable variation, that the difficult and evil calls for acceptance, so that at last, assimilated and understood, it may be dissolved and changed into a positive attitude towards life, the attitude which enabled him to sing 'jubilant praise to assenting angels' (which explains why Rilke urges his readers again and again to read *Malte* 'against the current'). The polarity of such a world view, which is at the same time an ambiguity, cannot be denied. It finds expression in the alternating record of joy and lament in the Elegies. Current and countercurrent flowed in rich succession through the channels of this uncommonly sensitive nature, in which inspiration far outweighed intellect and sensibility reason. This it was that gave rise to the tension apparent in all Rilke's literary work. One may suppose that the artist was continually drawing his creative power from that tremendous tension in the man. In a 'philosophical' poem about 'the sacred law of contrast' Rilke – not setting out an ingenious theory but groping and demonstrating – speaks of this 'moving equipoise' and of 'play and counterplay'. This poem too is found in the little book *Vergers*:

> Combien le pape au fond de son faste,
> sans être moins vénérables,
> par la sainte loi de contraste
> doit attirer le diable.
>
> Peut-être qu'on compte trop peu
> avec se mouvant equilibre;
> il y a des courants dans le Tibre,
> tout jeu veut son contre-jeu.
>
> Je me rapelle Rodin
> qui me dit un jour d'un air mâle
> (nous prenions, à Chartres, le train)
> que, trop pure, la cathédrale
> provoque un vent de dédain.

The man who all his life had been in search of the exalted, the pure, the absolute, was deeply conscious of the peril involved in his daring enterprise. When Rilke tried to see the world through the eyes of the angels, those 'spoilt darlings of creation' free from all the imperfections of human nature, the devils and their horrors were lurking just around the corner. But every earthly thing too that Rilke loved, everything that uplifted his heart and inspired him (a beloved woman, an admired city or landscape, even a bunch of roses) was liable, with astonishing suddenness, to weary him, to seem stale and unattractive, if not downright unendurable or uncanny. The beautiful letters and poems which Rilke wrote in praise of the Valais and the mountain home which grew so dear to him must not hide from us the ambiguity of his attitude to the Valais landscape and everything connected with Muzot – right from the days when he was moving into the 'hard little house'. We have already heard how, soon after writing the *Quatrains valaisans,* he remarked in a letter from Muzot that summer and autumn that year were like 'gigantic mirrors cracked right across', and now one could not tell 'whether this crack is distorting the reflection of the universe, or whether a strangely disfigured universe is in fact bending over it'. The landscape motive – round which, that same summer and autumn, he had woven the French Valais poems – has undergone this rather sudden reversal from cheerful to tragic not only on account of the wet weather and the bad grape harvest, which Rilke gives as the reason in his letter, but doubtless also because of a fresh disturbance to his health and the pain being caused him at the time by a personal relationship. The mirror is an attribute of the magical, the break in it a crack running through the picture which the poet magician has conjured up. Security and threat: he experienced both with the same intensity, at the same place, from the same object, in the same circumstances. His work speaks of both.

Having a brave and guileless heart and being a man of good will, Rilke refused to take a pessimistic view of the world, or to rebel against the inscrutable laws of creation. On the contrary, he held that assent to this world, not from philosophic conviction but from an intense attachment to life, was the true human task. He read to me at Muzot (in the year the French poems were published) an entry from his notebook, the gist of which I remember very vividly, although I cannot recall his exact words. It was a short note for an address on God's love for man. The essence of it was: the real task of the God seeker is 'the great Yes' to the entirety of things and appearances. To this entirety, however, the works of God must belong also, without any distinction. God must be included somewhere in 'the great Yes'. Yet the seeking, wrestling man could only find God when God's love acted and came towards him. (Two years earlier he had said in the *Young Workman's Letter*: 'If I say God I mean by that an immense conviction in me which I have never learned. All creatures, it seems to me, say that word, without reflection, though often also out of deep thoughtfulness.'). Rilke, who employs the word 'God' very sparingly in his late work, and would have preferred not to write or speak it at all, uses it in a French quatrain which he dedicated to Lamartine's great-granddaughter (it is one of the things published posthumously in *Carnet de poche*) :

> Pour trouver Dieu il faut être heureux
> car ceux qui par détresse l'inventent
> vont trop vite et cherchent trop peu
> l'intimité de son absence ardente.

'To find God we must be happy; those who invent him in their distress go too fast and search too little for the intimacy of his ardent absence.' Metrical epigrams of this sort occur here and there in Rilke's late work, especially in the French poems. In the above quatrain there appears, not without a certain formal lucidity, the desire expressed with so many variations during the Muzot days – to follow the road to God over 'the great Yes', over the happy acceptance of all the works of cosmos and earth; but he who grasps at him in distress, pain or sorrow, like a drowning man at a straw, fails by his too quick grasp to enter the intimacy of the absent God. There would seem to be a development here of the strange conception of the 'neighbour God' which we find in the *Book of Hours*: that God also is ardent and tender, absent and intimately near; he too is present and not present, dark and there in his secret darkness only as the 'never learned conviction'; all created things utter the word 'God' (and for Rilke what all created things utter must be right). But this God who, Rilke feels, is not a fact set over against man and creation, can never be the subject of a theology, can never have walls of dogma built round about him and moral codes derived from him. Morality seemed to Rilke remote from God, if not actually hostile to religion. God must come to meet human beings with his love – it was Malte's tragedy that he never found God's love – and Rilke confessed that he himself as a child was capable 'of lying on stones that God might turn to me sooner'. It is impossible to tell here whether he is thinking of God as a subjective idea, or as a being active, knowable, and so objectively present.

Rilke said all these things in a very positive tone, as he said everything in his poetry of 1922; he attached images to them, but for these he found only inadequate words or, as Lou Andreas says, speaking of the esoteric in Rilke's later poetry: 'as he dealt more and more with material drawn from the inner life, which could not be translated into the language of the senses' Rilke's words in fact became 'audible only to those who carried around with them, unredeemed and waiting, experiences of a like magnitude and depth. To the others', says Lou, 'the poet must often have seemed like Moses coming down from the mountain, so transported by his revelation that he had forgotten to write it down in full on the ten tablets.'[68] Gabriel Marcel implies something of the sort when he remarks that there is often a gap between what Rilke says and what he wants to say, his way of expressing himself being often 'disappointing and close to rhetoric'; but, the French philosopher goes on, 'perhaps Rilke's secret greatness lies in this interval between the positive way he utters a thing and the always inadequate terms he uses to express it'. This seems strange to Marcel and, from the point of view of a trained philosopher, absurd.[69]

Taking, so to speak, a naïve view of the poems written during Rilke's last years – particularly the French, for the German are not all known yet* – we recognise a blossoming wreath of variations on constantly recurring themes: angel, rose, window, fountain, fruit, tree, and so on – also a very curious attempt to conceive of poetry as the simultaneous 'use' of all the five senses. The changes rung on these themes are indescribably various. We find them again in his letters and prose writings. For example, *La Fontaine* in the book *Vergers* recalls a letter written from Berg Castle in which Rilke describes the fountain in front of his window, at first the variations in its sound, and then the way it changes its shape as he watches. How surprised I was to discover, as I grew more familiar with his poetry, that the most unforgettable things he said in conversation were nothing but rich paraphrases of his poems. For with him everything flowed from the same source and returned to the same centre: source and

* See translator's note, p. 60.

centre were himself, the self out of which he had all his life been building a full, completely individual world. The laws this world obeyed were the poet's secret.

We have already mentioned how in 1920 when on a visit to Freiburg Rilke conceived the idea of writing a series of window poems; his companion, Mme Baladine Klossowska, was to do the illustrations. Seven years later – a few months after the poet's death – this joint work by Rilke and Baladine was published in Paris, in an edition de luxe, under the title *Les Fenêtres*. The ten poems in the book are grouped around a single theme: the window. Not a very promising subject, but it was all that Rilke needed as a pivot for his meditations on essential things:

> N'es-tu pas notre géometrie,
> fenêtre, très simple form
> qui sans effort circonscris
> notre vie énorme?

> Celle qu'on aime n'est jamais plus belle
> que lorsqu'on la voit apparaître
> encadrée de toi; c'est, ô fenêtre,
> que tu la rends presque éternelle.

> Tous les hasards sont abolis. L'être
> se tient au milieu de l'amour,
> avec ce peu d'espace autour
> dont on est maître.

Or the same motive gives him occasion to make an unexpected comparison: the window, he says in the seventh poem, fastens our wide outlook like a buckle:

> Boucle qui ferme
> la vast ceinture de notre vue.

Conceit? Ornament? Perhaps. But it becomes full of meaning when touched by this poet. It is never spoilt by mere aestheticism. He put his heart into all that he did, even the most trivial things, and for that reason everything he wrote is genuine. Even in the writing of a graceful flourish Rilke expressed his personality. When he opened a window he gave his whole heart to the window.

It was all quite natural and unassuming. And suddenly we realise that this handful of magic words about a few windows is teaching us to see. Or a window stands open and empty and we hear someone quietly sobbing:

> Sanglot, sanglot, pur sanglot!
> Fenêtre, où nul ne s'appuie!

To the cycles *Vergers*, *Quatrains valaisans* and *Les Fenêtres* was added a fourth: *Les Roses*. There was a rosebed in the Muzot garden. Rilke cared for the roses like a gardener, watering and pruning them with his own hands. Like everything he did, it was done with love. The garden, the roses, returned this love. For their sake he kept going back to Muzot. When he was out of tune with himself, suffering and ill, and nothing else could help him, he found consolation in his roses:

> Amie des heures où aucun être ne reste,
> où tout se refuse au coeur amer;
> consolatrice dont la présence atteste
> tant de caresses qui flottent dans l'air.
>
> Si l'on renonce à vivre, si l'on renie
> ce qui était et ce qui peut arriver,
> pense-t-on jamais assez à l'insistante amie
> qui à côté de nous fait son œuvre de fée?

Rilke himself sent the MS. of his twenty-four rose poems to the Dutch publisher A. A. M. Stols, who published it in a bibliophile's edition shortly after the poet's death. A foreword by Paul Valéry – in the form of an imaginary letter to the dead Rilke – describes in wonderful words the quietness and solitude, so uncanny to him, in which he found the poet when they met at Muzot.

All his life Rilke made it a rule never to read any published articles about himself or his work. If friends had not drawn his attention to them he would never have known about the attacks on him in German periodicals and newspapers after the publication of his French poems in two Paris literary reviews. Some of his younger friends offered to take up arms in his defence, but he decided to 'plead his own cause'. He was all the more anxious to refute the unexpected misunderstandings with regard to his French poems, as reproaches had already reached him in letters from German friends, causing him a great deal of worry and annoyance. Rilke decided to take the course of sending a letter to the literary critic of the *Neue Zürcher Zeitung*, Dr Eduard Korrodi, explaining how his French poems came to be written. As the imminent publication of the little book *Vergers* led him to expect a renewal of the attack, he wanted to have in the Zürich critic someone who knew the whole story, 'because', as he wrote from his sick-bed in Valmont (on March 20th 1926), 'for sooner or later, the measuring-rod should be preserved somewhere, to enable those who love order to fit the *Vergers* episode into its proper place in my life. With those who are offended by the little book I have no concern; to those who are astonished at it I feel related by my own joyful astonishment.'[70]

In the following passage from this detailed apology the last years of Rilke's life and work are concisely recalled. He writes:

Finally, no one is obliged to understand (don't you agree?) the importance the great Swiss hospitality came to have, more and more, for the continuance of my life and work, after those terribly disturbed and interrupted years; and I ask myself whether it is my duty to speak out about these providential dispensations. I supposed it was enough gradually to present the results. To these, after the *Sonnets to Orpheus* and the Elegy volume, belongs also this collection of French poems, which I might fittingly have called *Side-hours* (the title chosen by Christina of Sweden for certain notes). Side-hours: in which, however, a main feeling finds expression. The feeling for the pure, immense landscape from which, during years of solitude and concentration, there accrued to me a continuous, inexhaustible aid. Apart from those former attempts of my youth, in which the influence of my native place, Prague, tried to appear, I had never felt the urge to praise an experienced landscape directly in a poem, to sing it; then in the third year of my residence here a Valais voice rose up and issued from me, so loudly and urgently that the involuntary word pattern took shape before I had given it the smallest encouragement. It had nothing of the planned work about it, it was a marvel, a compliance, a subjugation. There was the joy of being given this unexpected credential by a landscape I was getting to know better and better; the discovery that I was allowed to associate with it in the sphere of its own sounds and accents. And, quite finally, if everything is to be mentioned, there was the happy experience of being younger, almost young, in the use of a second language which hitherto one had used only for receiving or for practical ends, and the mounting abundance of which (as in youth with one's own language) started to carry one into the space of the unutterable life. . . .

Here again he says that *Vergers* is above all a Swiss book, whose publication (in a selection made by Paris friends) was as unplanned as its genesis. But the wish to show the Valais Canton his gratitude for its gifts, and 'the other wish to be visibly linked, as a modest pupil under an immodest obligation, to France and to the unforgettable Paris which meant a whole world to my development and memory', had brought him round to agree to the venture of publishing his French poems.

Rilke's expression was one of astonished happiness when at last, in June 1926, he held a first copy of the small, paper-backed olive green book *Vergers* in his hand.

5

THE MAN RILKE

RILKE'S outward behaviour was always, from inclination and conviction, that of a private individual. Nothing could have been more remote from him than the busy self-advertising which had become widespread in the literary world of his time. The wish to be a representative figure was also alien to him. Well-meant offers to arrange ceremonies in his honour were without exception refused. One could meet him in private houses and in hotels, encounter him shopping in the town, see him – surprising as it may sound – looking over factories or business houses, but he never, never visited a literary café. And when he chanced to land in a salon among literary snobs he was always, because on the defensive, exquisitely polite. He was too young to be awarded the Nobel Prize for Literature, and when he thought of it it was only to dream a little of financial independence. But official recognition was not withheld during his lifetime. In 1925 Edinburgh University expressed its admiration, and a year later the sick man was cheered by the publication in Paris of *Reconnaissance à Rilke*, a volume compiled by French writers and to which German, Danish, Spanish, Dutch, Czech, Hungarian, Italian, Polish, Swedish and Swiss voices also contributed.[71] The poet was already the subject of essays, theses and lectures. Although he did not read these publications his courtesy prevented him from leaving unanswered questions addressed to him by literary historians, translators of his works and others with a practical interest in his writings. The explanations he gave his Polish translator Hulewicz, his French translator Maurice Betz, the German Rilke philologist Hermann Pongs and others are valuable today for Rilke criticism. However, nothing could have been more remote from him than to see himself in historical perspective, like the aged Goethe.

There were, too, always some people who felt called upon to censure him and be hypercritical. The circle around George at that time had no friendly feelings towards Rilke, while other groups and schools took it out of him for his rejection of all ties, his proud, humble individualism. But Rilke was as 'unliterary' as anyone could be. He belonged to the company of those who do not set out to gain the world, and who by such an attitude come upon real gain. Rilke was famous. It was a fame which gave out an intense, somewhat mysterious lustre because it too had become simplified through reflecting the rays emanating from that work and that man. It was obvious that

Rainer Maria Rilke occupied a central place in contemporary European literature; he is the geometric centre, or rather, an advance guard, he stands in an intimate relationship to the streams which since 1900 have been drawing their furrows through various countries. This man who was always solitary and withdrawn from everything was among those who had a powerful effect on the mental and spiritual life of their time.[72]

If Rilke deliberately overlooked commentaries and controversies inspired by his literary work, he reacted differently (at least in letters and conversation) to the things that were said occasionally about his early life and his first youthful attempts at writing. He was really horrified when during his first Valais winter, a well-intentioned little book, privately printed, brought him a distasteful reminder of 'the young Rilke's' literary productions. 'I shall give away', he wrote to Mme Wunderly,

one *sol-i-tary* copy, this . . . yours, which you are now receiving, at least as a gesture, for Christmas. Perhaps you will be able to read in it something that is still related, still in some way valid, although (to my way of thinking) it contains only masks made up of helplessness, clumsiness, shyness, artlessness, ineptitude, a hundred uns, ins and lesses. One knew no better then. – These documents of the 'young Rilke', you know how I regard them: *inavouable*! I should like gradually to replace them . . . by the still younger Rilke, not by some of the scribble preserved from his childhood (for that too is full of helpless hypocrisy, defensively hypocritical), but by what I myself could tell of him now and later, *that* might in the end have a certain posthumous veracity.[73]

Rilke enclosed in this letter a first instalment of the childhood reminiscences he had written in the year 1914. This and other hints that his thoughts were deeply occupied with his early experiences, especially those of the Military Academy, perhaps make it reasonable to conclude that Rilke was planning to write an autobiography of his childhood. On the other hand, everything points to the fact that he still felt his childhood and Cadet School memories as a prodigious burden. It could hardly, as Kassner thinks, have been the French poetry he was writing which kept him from carrying out the project. Still under fifty, he was not yet capable of dealing with this 'material' in his art; but he had just started to get an inkling of his distance from it – and at the same time to sense the approach of a state of preparedness for starting work anew in that direction – when illness interrupted everything. During his early years in Paris Rilke used to tell his acquaintances stories which he later put into *Malte*. Presumably the stories he was so fond of telling, and told so often, during his years in Switzerland – of his Prague childhood, of the parental home, of their circle of relations, of the Military School at St Pölten – would have been foundation stones for the never-written childhood reminiscences. All these stories, despite their element of ridicule and the humourous details with which they were interlarded, revealed the sensitive child's profound, bitter suffering. Yet Rilke preserved gratefully *one* good memory of his youth: it was of the time when he was preparing for his school leaving examination (*das Abitur*). After he left the Cadet School his father sent him in the first place to the commercial college at Linz – an absurd episode on which Rilke's only comment used to be an eloquent gesture of the hand. Soon afterwards the lawyer Max von Rilke-Rüliken, the seventeen-year-old youth's well-off uncle, made it possible for him to have private coaching for this examination. Rilke passed it after an unusually short time of preparation. He told me that his favourite subject was mathematics, and that he would often discuss problems with his tutor of an evening, going far beyond the set curriculum and continuing until late into the night. Yet soon afterwards, he would add, the longing to do his own literary work prevailed, and he left the university without taking a degree. At Berlin University he had really only been interested in Simmel's lectures, but he had stopped attending these too after a while because it struck him that there were too many people in the lecture room who were there for the wrong reasons. It was obvious from Rilke's hints and from the stories he told that the decisive experience of his youth was the revolt against his home environment, the rebellious break with his social *milieu*, the violent, liberating self-'derailment' from the lines that had been laid down for him.

As Rilke himself was altogether an 'original' and had strengthened his originality by a long, self-denying process of 'individualisation', he could dispense with appearances and with every kind of façade. He acted always, and judged everything, from his own centre, never with an eye to prevailing opinions and conventions. This enabled him, as it did Proust, to live at the right 'distance from success', and to observe the literary scene only from afar; he took from art and literature what appealed to him – the rest he put to one side. For him there were no 'musts' in reading, even among the classics; the gaps in his education worried him very little, since his ideas about education and culture had nothing in common with the usual clichés. It followed that his criticisms were wonderfully fresh and unbiased. When an artist had nothing congenial to offer him Rilke noticed his work with a cool respect or not at all – even when the artist in question was Shakespeare, Velasquez or Goethe. He really asked only one thing of human beings: that they should be true to their kind and their condition. A peasant girl or a maidservant meant as much to him as a princess, a working man was as important as an artist: all were equal in his eyes, provided that each was genuinely and entirely peasant girl, maidservant, princess, worker or artist. He found it more difficult to understand the ordinary middle-class citizen than the nobleman, the artist or the beggar; for the good citizen expects the imaginative, the spontaneous and the human to be suppressed in favour of a social code. With advancing years Rilke learned to do justice to the middle classes and to value their way of life in so far as it was genuine. It was no coincidence that he learned at the same time to understand Goethe better; in his maturity he took a view of the Goethe-Bettina relationship which was the exact opposite of the view expressed in *Malte*. As all grades of society in Switzerland are stamped with the good-citizen outlook and as Rilke could not live in any environment without understanding it, he did his best to find a key to the view of life taken by this type of person. After reading a book on the history of a middle-class family in East Switzerland he wrote in a letter:

The simple and at the same time so genuine value of such family histories is very high. Switzerland, producing as she does numerous cases where material of this kind is seen in a comparatively well-preserved condition (an advantage shared with the Scandinavian states, so like her in many ways) has contributions to make to a real history of the middle classes, whose anonymous but continuous achievements have usually been overlooked in favour of more startling events, the doings of warriors and statesmen, of the loud voiced and ostentatious, out of which the mantle of history is spun. How much one learns about human beings from such a book, which in a sense could again become decisive and fruitful for the individual in his calmer existence. Here the calm of the past influences the calm of the present, and there is little doubt that the family spirit, the consciousness, as it emerges from these pages, of belonging, by inheritance not chance, to a particular group of people, has an effect on those it primarily concerns, once again calming, counselling, enriching.[74]

When he could recognise real values there, the mature Rilke did not reject these quieter aspects of human life, from which so much could be learned about humanity, nor the family spirit existing among members of a particular group. He agreed with the aged Goethe, who also developed 'his great notion of the genuine and his awe of tradition' by exercising them on objects which reveal the man of enterprise, the tradesmen, the manufacturer, in his 'dealings with the structure of the world'. Genuineness: that alone mattered to Rilke, and he acknowledged it wherever he thought that he had found it.

Rilke's completely open-minded attitude towards human beings and human affairs had its counterpart in his unbiased dealings with different languages and national cultures. A word which kept recurring very often with him, and which he used to describe a certain attitude, was 'guilelessness'. He refused to be put into any social or national strait-jacket, and he had none of the inhibitions which class-conscious or nationalistically minded people have to overcome in order to get in touch with humanity pure and simple. Plain, straightforward and unceremonious as

his nature was, he hardly took any notice of national and social
barriers. Rilke's guilelessness was that of the 'idiot' in Dostoevsky's novel of that name, a book I could never read during the
time of my personal acquaintance with Rilke without being
reminded almost forcibly, through the character of Prince
Myschkin, of Rainer Osipowitch (as Rilke liked to be called
when he was in Russia). 'It could well be said', Edmond Jaloux
remarked in a review of *Malte*, 'that the *Notebooks of Malte
Laurids Brigge* are the entries and thoughts of a Dostoevsky
character whom Dostoevsky never created'[75]: a judgment with
which Rilke gladly agreed when his friends drew his attention to
it. Of the Russians Rilke used to say that they saw Divine Providence at work behind all human destiny and suffering, even when
the suffering seemed prodigious and unendurable. Whether his
ideas about Russia were correct or simply taken over from the
former Slavophile school, he saw in this submission of the sufferer
to God the highest religious ideal. He did not think of the hero and
the saint at all in terms of the pugnacious heroism of the European warrior and religious hero. St Francis of Assisi was his
favourite Christian saint, because of his gentleness and his loving
assent to the wonders of creation and to all created things.

The service of art was undoubtedly the only law that Rilke
recognised for his own life; this it was that gave his life its hardness and its motive force, its anguish and its happiness. Being by
nature kindly and receptive (not soft), modest and open (though
neither extravagant nor eccentric), Rilke had no difficulty in
coming to terms with his environment, in forming relationships
with people and things, books and animals, landscapes and cultures, houses and works of art. Much has been said about his
shyness, his flights to different surroundings, his anxieties and his
retreats into protective solitude. No doubt the practical affairs of
life were complicated and made endlessly difficult for him by his
extreme sensitiveness or sensibility and by the fact that his
slightly built, delicate body was so easily tired. We should value
his success all the more highly, calling as it did for a sort of
heroism of endurance: tremendous exertion, self-mastery,
discipline, thoroughness in small things as well as in great. If we
are prepared to make allowance for the self-absorption of a life
completely dedicated to the art of poetry, we must also make

allowance for the social inadequacies of that life. We must not turn a blind eye: possession, daemons, played a part in this work wrested from the ore of his being. But even at the lower levels of his activity – in the side-hours and the side-achievements – Rilke left nothing to chance. The sketch showed the hand of the master. Everyday life was ennobled by art. The familiar held brightness and warmth. The sublimation of everything that happened was for Rilke a matter of course. He was transparently sincere. Hence the deep impression which his personality made on all who crossed his path, who met him, had conversations with him or were made happy by his letters. 'Happy' is not too strong a word. To be in Rilke's company, to go for a walk with him, talk to him, correspond with him, was to be happy. But everything led back to the one central thing, to poetry. (Never to the profession of literature.) One of the newer French poets, Pierre Jean Jouve, who resembled Rilke in many ways and had met him, said: 'I think the most enduring thing we have in common is our conception of poetry – understood as a priesthood and as a completely independent ritual occupation, which must unite all powers of invention, all forms of love, in one mighty effort full of humility.'[76]

It is the privilege of youth to experience everything with wide-open mind and feeling. When I first met Rilke I had scarcely read any of his work. Mutual friends had told him that I was coming to see him at Muzot. A twenty-two-year-old student arrived on the famous poet's doorstep. On that early spring day, after a winter spent in the seclusion of his château, Rilke was communicative and lively, in the mood for asking and answering questions, for walking in the open air, and for sitting up talking until late into the night. I was astonished by the youthful appearance and unselfconscious, easy manners of this lonely living poet (at a time when the pompous Stefan George was being celebrated by his followers as the ideal of the poet seer). On his slightly built, rather short body, Rilke's head appeared large, almost top-heavy, and the most striking thing about his face was the contrast between its upper and lower halves. All spirituality seemed concentrated in the magnificent vault of the clear forehead and in the wide-open mauve-blue eyes, while the nose ended in broad nostrils and the mouth was excessively large; a drooping, thin moustache made the fleshiness of the lips less noticeable; the chin was small, a continuation of the curve of the cheeks. But there is no completely satisfying portrait of Rilke, not one that he himself liked. As with all sensitive, mercurial natures, his features were extremely mobile and his expression very variable; indeed his appearance could change in the most astonishing manner. Many people observed his expression of deep sadness in unpropitious hours, when his eyelids would droop heavily over inexpressibly sorrowful eyes. Several have described the masklike, absent, extinguished look which made his face so striking when, suffering and aloof, he withdrew into himself: at such times he seemed utterly alone, quite unrelated to his environment. I have seen him like that, sunk in a chair in a big hotel lounge. It was frightening, and we know now that he was already suffering from the first ominous symptoms of his mortal illness, from general exhaustion and a tormenting sense of ill-being. But that was a year and a half after my first visit to Muzot.

Rilke always dressed carefully and avoided wearing anything at all loud. For the most part he was seen in light grey trousers, light spats and a dark blue jacket, or in a dark suit: never a coloured tie; A low, round, soft felt hat served as head-gear; always a stick with a curved handle in his right hand, sometimes a small leather case; a mixture of Austrian aristocrat and west-European intellectual; a colossal modern intelligence and manners from an earlier, more courteous age. Rilke had a second face: his hand. It was one of the most expressive that I have ever seen. It was narrow and brown and had a firm grasp: tool and physiognomy in one. With a little more strength it might have been the hand of a painter or sculptor. We know how painstakingly and perseveringly Rilke applied himself to learning from the manual or visual arts and artists (even from craftsmen: 'beside the roper in Rome and the potter in Egypt'). Every object was important and familiar to him. On the other hand he had no musical ear. When he spoke about music he expressed himself in vague, general terms. Where music was concerned he had no equivalent of the practical experience he had acquired in painters' and sculptors' studios (at first at Worpswede, but supremely later with Rodin in Paris). The music of his poems is diffuse, flowing, in contrast to the closely observed, accurate imagery. His senses of touch, smell and taste were more highly developed, or more sensitive, than his sense of hearing. In conversation Rilke's inner radiance, his confident use of metaphor, the originality, force and fluency with which he expressed himself, would hold his partner spellbound. He, who knew so well how to be silent, would talk a great deal on good days, and about a variety of things – not as other people talk, but with great directness, seeing his subject as a whole and coming at once to essentials. His keen sensuous perceptions, which he was so good at putting into words, also found expression in his talk – that talk which has, of course, begun to pale with distance and to fade from the memory of those who survive him.

Perhaps I may be allowed to witness to his ability and readiness to open his heart generously to a young man unsure of his calling and groping for his way, and to share with him his own ripeness and experience. That sympathy with an unformed, nascent mind, that interest in an unfolding destiny, that fidelity to a friendship once begun, are points which certain Rilke critics should remember, when they feel moved to underline in red his fear of human attachments and his retreat from existing relationships, in short his egotism. Kindly but never condescending, he knew how to win the confidence of a shy young man, by conversing with him quite frankly and thus challenging him to be frank also. Rilke was good at asking questions, and when someone was indebted to him he would often contrive, by requesting a favour of that person, to convey the impression that the indebtedness was all on his side.

His behaviour towards other people was regulated by a great delicacy of feeling; an exceedingly well-bred but never forbidding politeness. One example of many: piano player's neuritis had some years earlier put a stop to my piano-playing, and, in spite of being cured, I was feeling reluctant to take up the art again. Rilke did not offer advice or try to persuade me. He spoke, during those days in the Valais, about a setting of his *Cornet Christoph Rilke* which the Danish composer Paul von Klenau had written and which he, Rilke, had never heard. He was not, he said, capable of judging it (he could not read music) – could I help him? He would be glad if I would take the score with me, and write and tell him what I thought of the composition. What else could I do but take the score home, play it, and write Rilke a letter about it? Quite apart from the question of my competence to judge in this matter; could he have found a more considerate, unavoidable way of getting me to sit down at the piano again?

Often happenings which seem quite trivial can help us to know Rilke's personality better, especially as he was so punctilious in even the smallest matters (a punctiliousness which at times, of course, passed over into sheer complexity). I once witnessed at Muzot a somewhat excited to-ing and fro-ing with telegrams and telephone calls to a flag factory in Bern, carried out by Frieda at Rilke's request. (As there was no telephone in the house the housekeeper had to walk to Sierre several times.) 'Good ideas often come rather late', was how Rilke laughingly explained the commotion to me. Werner Reinhart had announced his Easter visit, and Rilke wanted to give his host a festive reception by hoisting the Swiss flag on his tower. He did not, however, possess a flag – and so the missing emblem had to be ordered in Bern at the last moment.

Soon after that holiday of mine in Sierre Rilke was expecting a visit from Kippenberg, who was a great cigar smoker (Rilke himself never smoked). I had smoked one of the last Havannas kept for Muzot guests, and Rilke asked me to procure a box of the same sort in Bern. They were, however, no longer to be had, and on receiving the news Rilke sent me the following amazing telegram – and it needs no more than this short quotation to prove his abhorrence of the so-called telegram style: 'Thanks, my dear young friend, for your good letter. With regard to the affair in question, I must in fact trouble you to do me the favour of ordering a small box of genuine Havannas, similar in value and flavour to the ones no longer available, to be sent to me by return, as the friend concerned is arriving tomorrow morning. Greetings, Rilke.'[77] In spite of the fact that he was 'expecting still more visitors', he did not omit to send me 'a word and a grateful hand-shake', and to emphasise 'the excellent contents' of my purchase, 'very much appreciated by my friend'. A triviality perhaps? But is it not well to note in the margin such trifles from a vanished world?

Many circumstances added to the relaxed state of Rilke's mind during that early spring of 1924. He was quite full of the visit that Paul Valéry had paid him at Muzot a short while previously, and I had the good fortune to hear him speak, with shining eyes and genuine delight, of his meeting with the much admired poet. When I told him that I had studied in Montpellier, Valéry's native town, and knew the French poet's brother who was a professor there, Rilke's interest in the south of France was re-awakened. The *cimetière marin*, Valéry had told him, was in Cette (or Sète), the port near Montpellier. So Rilke drew into the conversation my knowledge of that town and district in southern France (for which he longed during the last years of his life). He spoke a great deal of his Valéry translations, saying that they were more accurate than any he had done before, and remarking on the way one line had grown out of another. 'I got the same satisfaction from doing these translations as from my own work', he said in a kind of transport, as we were walking along the valley road. Many of the translations had been done while out walking, when he would scribble the ideas that came to him on any odd bit of paper found in his wallet, such as the back of an envelope. Only he could decipher these scraps and put them into the right order.

Rilke's visitors have often told of the poet reading aloud to them, upright behind his standing-desk. I look back to that homely ritual as to one of the great moments of my life, un-dimmed by the passing years. After the simple evening meal we went up to the study on the first floor and there, sitting expectantly on the sofa, I watched my host light the paraffin lamp, which he left on the table at the back of the room; two candles illumined the papers on the standing-desk. Rilke read first the French originals and then his translations of some of Valéry's poems (the *Song of the Columns*, the *Cemetery by the Sea* and others . . .). The chief impression that remains with me when I think of Rilke reading aloud, with strong emphasis and in a very clear, very musical baritone voice, is of a supreme artist. Here was not just a poet reading, here also was a man. That memory more that any other gives, for me, the lie to the over-sensitive, spoilt, effeminised Rilke presented by some memoir writers, mostly women; a Rilke whose portrait is twined about with every sort of sentimental garland. He may not have been wholly innocent with regard to these marginal aspects of his fame and legend, and no man can ever know how he behaved with women. But we must not allow the poet's posthumous likeness to get blurred at the edges; for Rilke was a strong artist, a man with a man's hardness – and this saved him, hypersensitive as he was, as well as his literary work.

The Valéry translations had an epilogue, giving rise to all sorts of complications. Rilke had copied the poems out in a magnificent book, in his very careful, very consciously formed handwriting, the titles in French, the German versions underneath. He treasured this fair copy as a valuable possession, took it with him on his travels and showed it to his intimate friends. Morisse, the owner of the Zürich bookshop, told Rilke that Valéry was very much interested in his translation of the poems from *Charmes*; Valéry could not, it was true, read German, but he would no doubt be delighted to have a copy of them. Rilke wrote to Valéry on February 7th 1924, that is, two months before the French poet's visit to Muzot on April 6th, saying that he was sending him 'his own manuscript' (*'mon propre manuscrit'*) of the translations. So Rilke, in the intensity of his happiness, gave away his own copy. He was too sensitive to ask Valéry later on to lend him the manuscript, and these circumstances gave rise to the following letter, which he wrote to me on May 9th 1924:

Dear friend,

It is certainly not so much my recollection of the quick, efficient way you made the purchase, as my wish to continue our association and my joy in doing so that prompts me to write and tell you of a plan which I have been quietly turning over in my mind since yesterday; you yourself will judge if what I am going to propose is feasible or not. If you think so, then it is another request that springs out at you from this preamble. To wit:

The other day when my publisher was here we decided to bring out as soon as possible all the Valéry translations that I have done so far. This decision means that I must produce a printable copy of my translations quickly. The thought of having to spend days on end copying things which already exist I find very burdensome (as I am still, or once again, feeling unwell, and there is no lack of other writings to be done. And so I would look to the expedient of dictation (unusual for me) as a welcome relief. Now the question is: can a person be found – a girl student used to longhand copying or typing – available to come to Sierre for a week or ten days, and work with me for a few hours daily? I would not tie this helper too much, so it might, incidentally, be a little holiday journey for her into our spring, now pushing through at last after such prolonged downpours. Do you think you could find such a person after looking round a bit? I keep speaking of 'her' because the typewriting *métier* has become a woman's profession; because my experiences of dictating so far seem to have been associated with women – and not least because the presence of an amiable girl would be the only means of relieving the dryness and obstinacy of the reproductive work (on both sides, after all). The word 'amiable' includes here, as always, some qualities of mind; for the texts are far from simple, and unless a whole lot of mistakes are going to sink from the ear into the writing hand they call for a certain practised understanding of nuances. In addition I would be very glad if the assistant in question could take not only German dictation but French too, with equal ease: for I have a few little French works also which I could put into a final state of readiness for the printer. (A Russian or Polish student, for example, might be very well fitted and suitable for such a post.) The person I am looking for exists perhaps – but how to find her? An advertisement, of which I thought this morning, would be too inexact a method; . . . perhaps, rather, a notice in the University, in a students' union or in the Lyceum Club?

It must, in any case, be someone who is able to get away (soon) for a week; for having given Paul Valéry my own clear, accurate fair copy, I have only scattered fragments of some poems, decipherable by me alone, so that I am dependent on verbal dictation and have nothing ready for a copyist.

I write of all this as of a possibility which must not be any burden or trouble to you; you are at most to make an attempt (occasionally) or ask someone for advice. Perhaps I shall yet arrange everything in a different way. . . .[78]

Rilke did, of course, arrange everything in a different way. Three weeks after I received the above letter another arrived saying that he had had a visit from Frau Rilke and her brother, to whom he had devoted himself completely until a couple of days before, so that during those weeks '. . . there would hardly have been any opportunity to dictate'. These trivialities are not recorded here for their own sakes; they are set down to illustrate the troubles and difficulties which life maliciously put in the way of this man. He met them somewhat helplessly; but the manner in which he expressed his helplessness, the carefully thought out meanderings that it left in its wake, may perhaps justify the mention of them. The reader of Rilke's works has beneath his eyes only success with no seams showing – he knows hardly anything of the small but continuous sufferings which consumed the marrow of the poet's life.

Even at the zenith of his life Rilke felt the need of a young person's company, the companionship of someone with whom he could share his memories and experiences, talk about the poets he had met, discuss religion, the Church, politics; a young person to whom he could express his ideas about the rôle of inventions and technique in the modern world. As some of those views have in the meantime been incorporated into the history of German and Western thought, I have occasionally reported Rilke's actual words in these pages. It must be said that they are obviously very consistent: remarks that he made to me correspond with sayings of his recorded in other memoirs, and especially with the views expressed in his known letters from Muzot. As I met him at the time of the Valéry translations it is not surprising that this theme was in the forefront of our conversations. But he spoke a great deal too about German poetry, language and literature. We talked often about Berlin, where I had just spent a year, and of which Rilke had many memories; but on the whole he did not like the atmosphere of that city. He sincerely pitied the fate of Gerhart Hauptmann, who was just then being made the object of endless official birthday celebrations. Rilke had known him at the beginning of his career, had witnessed his struggles and remained warmly attached to him.

He spoke a lot about Stefan George, expressing grateful appreciation of the older man whose pupil he had been for a time. The historic fact that these two important poets made spiritual contact with one another should be sufficient to put an end to the annoying habit, fashionable once among literary men, of playing George off against Rilke and *vice versa*. Rilke told me, not without a touch of humour, how once when he was a young student in Berlin he had been given a chance to attend a reading by George in the Lepsius' house. In keeping with *Jugendstil** taste, an ivy-decorated dais had been made ready for the poet in the drawing-room, and from this, at a suitable distance from his attentive audience, he read his poems. The whole process was surrounded with an aura of mystery and solemnity. Neither before nor after the reading did the master mingle with the invited guests. Frau Lepsius afterwards led a few chosen people, the young Rilke among them, into a room where they were permitted to shake hands with George, who addressed a few conventional words to each of the elect, in the manner of royalty. Later, Rilke said, he chanced to meet George in a park in Florence George recognised the younger man and started a conversation, in the course of which he reproached Rilke with having published poems too early. He was obviously a little taken aback by Rilke's ready agreement. They then proceeded to have a long, informal talk. Since then the two had not met again. But Rilke always spoke of this master of his poetic novitiate with sincere admira-tion. He saw in him one of the greatest examples of a superior, truly artistic use of the German language. Those who were young at that time, he said, felt it as a kind of deliverance when in the early 1890s, amid the general decay of taste and decline of the poetic art, Stefan George appeared and restored its dignity to German poetry. 'In my youth the *Trumpeter of Säckingen* was the Germans' poetic ideal', he continued with grim irony. Of Friedrich Gundolf's book about George, which was the circle's Bible at that time, Rilke said that the passages where Gundolf was right were admirable; there were, however, many occasions when he tried to be right without succeeding. Rilke said that he could not understand the poet's late work, *The Seventh Ring*; perhaps it had been written only for initiates, members of the circle, and could only be understood by them. The attacks made on him by the George school he ignored with a magnanimous silence. The group had derived from the master's teaching an ideal of the 'higher life' which was tinged with nationalism. They had at that time no inkling that most of them, being Jewish,

* Modern style in German art at the turn of the century. Translator.

would in less than a decade become the victims of a nationalistic
dictator, from whom George himself would take refuge abroad.
When I told Rilke that this circle (through the pen of Edith
Landmann-Kalischer) had made an exceedingly violent, malicious attack on Carl Spitteler, he replied, very much astonished:
'I should not have thought it possible that they would lay hands
on Spitteler.' He often marvelled that George let such things
happen in his name; but perhaps the master himself did not
know of them. Rilke was one of Spitteler's admirers. We were
sitting over our supper once at Muzot when, with an awe which
I had never heard in his voice before except when speaking of
Tolstoy's *War and Peace*, he remarked how extraordinary it was
that at a time when men were racking their brains over the birth
of mythologies a poet living among us should suddenly have
brought a myth into being by his own power. Rilke had most to
say about Spitteler's language, and sometimes, using the most
unlikely combination of images, he would reconstruct the
Prometheus so vividly for his marvelling guest that the latter
could almost see what was being described. With one of those
astonishing turns of phrase which gave his conversation such a
characteristic flavour, Rilke summed up: 'I believe that if man
were to give the power of speech back to nature, nature would
talk like Prometheus.' Rilke considered that the young Spitteler's
terrible experience (he was 35 when his *Prometheus and Epimetheus* appeared) of finding no echo, no recognition, after the
publication of that book, had a most unhappy effect on the poet's
life. Perhaps, he thought, the experience was to blame for the
fact that in *Olympian Spring* (which he did not care for so much)
the poetic inspiration was uncertain and intermittent. Usually he
did not pity the artist who has to wait a long time for recognition:
he even thought that in some cases it might be a good thing; 'but',
said Rilke, 'to give *Prometheus* to the world and for the world to
go on as if nothing had happened, that is terrible!' We have proof
that Rilke did not talk in this way only because he was in the
company of an acquiescent young man who shared his tastes.
At Soglio and on the Schönenberg he was never long away from
this book. He took it with him on his walks and read 'passages
of an almost Dantesque greatness' aloud to his friends. These
passages surprised him and filled him again and again 'full with

their sublime, tremendous magnificence'. 'What a poet!' he wrote in a letter. '*The Poet*, here where the great name no longer matters, one can now say Dante or Spitteler – it is the same, it is the Poet, for in the last resort there is only one – undying, manifesting himself here and there down the ages, in this or that genius from whom he exacts subjugation.'[79]

The nature of a creative artist is always revealed by what he has to say about other masters and other works. When Rilke spoke of important poets his conversation circled about the two great problems of his later years: language and myth. Talking to me at Muzot, he said that the prose of Adalbert Stifter filled him with admiration (he was rereading Stifter's works at the time); he also greatly admired Goethe's prose, which he was reading in the *Conversations of German Emigrants*. Regarding his own life, he spoke with never-failing zest about Russia, especially of Moscow and Yasna Polyana. Since Lou Andreas-Salomé published her autobiography we are so well informed about the journey that she and Rilke took together to Russia, and especially about their visit to Tolstoy, that my own recollections of Rilke's spoken account must give place to that great book by a great woman. A peculiarity of his was the way he had of talking about the characters in a novel as if they were people he had known; and as Pierre Basuchow was his favourite character in *War and Peace*, Rilke was convinced that he had met that unique imaginary person's double when he was in Moscow. It was hard to tell at the end of Rilke's story whether it was Pierre or a flesh and-blood Russian who had shown him the sights of the city on a carriage drive, taken him to the treasure room in the Kremlin, and made all kinds of extraordinary speeches. . . .

Rilke sharply rejected the aged Tolstoy's Christianity, and that of recent French poets like Claudel. He thought that of all west Europeans the Scandinavians were closest to the Russians, and that is why he loved them. In Denmark he had noticed how even the most inexplicable phenomena are allowed their freedom and that the supernatural, and therefore the poetic also, enjoys an unusual hospitality. No doubt that is why he made the hero of his novel, Malte Laurids Brigge, a Dane.

It has been observed, very rightly, that what Rilke had to say about literature and poetry was no more remarkable than the

rest of his conversation, but that he spoke always like a poet,
about everything, even the most seemingly trivial matters. His
personality and the atmosphere that surrounded him were
present in every word. It is not the subjects discussed which have
been lost from our memories of Rilke's conversations – he has
dealt with the same subjects more availably and permanently
in his letters: what have been lost are those moments belonging
entirely to the conversation, or rather to his presence, at once so
unobtrusive and so enveloping. For his reserve and his silence
were impressive also.

There was something curiously touching about the way he
came to say goodbye to me in the Sierre pension where I had
been staying for a few days. Coming back from a walk I found
Rilke in the drawing-room, where the guests were waiting for
their evening meal. He was sitting, quite inconspicuously, on a
sofa near the door, busy with some writing. 'You haven't put your
name in my visitors' book', he said, explaining his unexpected
presence. 'I have marked the day, between my last visitors.'
Then he showed me the place in the leather-bound book where
I must put my name. When this had been done, Rilke turned
over the pages on which the names and thanks of many guests
were written. Happily and proudly he showed me Paul Valéry's
signature. With a quick movement, as though he would prevent
me from thanking him, the strange man next handed me a
slender book which he had taken out of his attaché case: 'I don't
think I've given you a copy of my book. . . .' Then he rose, and
we went upstairs to my room, where he stayed for a short time,
chatting away cheerfully. He would not stay to supper; he had
some more work to do at home. From the steps outside I watched
Rilke as, with stick and attaché case, he walked briskly through
the darkening garden. The copy of the *Sonnets to Orpheus* which
he had given me was one of the first edition, published a few
months earlier, and he had written an inscription in it. I read it
from cover to cover that same night.

Illness and Death

He was a poet and hated the approximate.
RAINER MARIA RILKE
in the *Notebooks of Malte Laurids Brigge*

1

THE OTHER PARIS

RILKE'S journey to Paris at the beginning of January 1925 was an attempt to evade his illness, a mighty effort to divert his attention from it. It was the sort of revolt which an ordinarily patient, conscientious man can only make in a moment of extreme bewilderment. At that moment Rilke refused obedience to his destiny because he no longer wanted to come to terms with his creeping, hampering illness. And perhaps it was really not yet time to start the great negotiation about terms. The semi-invalid's flight from the clinic was nevertheless a most unfavourable prelude to the months which the poet was now to spend in a quiet, friendly room at the old Hôtel Foyot.

During that stay in Paris, which was to be his last, Rilke's way of life was as different as possible from the congenial routine which he had followed for long years before the war. Then he had known only a few people, lived in seclusion and worked undisturbed. He said once that he only had real social intercourse with about eight people in Paris, and we must remember that this intercourse was spread out over several years. He lived at that time, like so many unknown foreign writers and painters, in the enchanted atmosphere of the *rive gauche*, between the Observatory and the Seine quays, not far from the Boulevard Saint-Michel and the Luxembourg Gardens. He knew a few Russians, often visited Rodin at Meudon, got to know Emile Verhaeren, became friendly with André Gide. He loved the modest, rather melancholy suburban district near the Boulevard Port-Royal, visited museums, spent long afternoons in the National Library, went to the anatomy lectures in the Ecole des Beaux-Arts. One would have met him in old churches, pacing the walks of deserted cemeteries, among the crowds at the market. He would watch the animals in the Jardin des Plantes with the eyes of both a naturalist and a creative artist. He would accompany women going for walks with their children and tell them strange stories. He took loving care of a girl called Marthe, who was little more than a child. We know a great deal about this Paris – from the young Rilke's letters and from the *Notebooks of Malte Laurids Brigge*. The novel and *New Poems* were both written during those early Paris years.

Apart from the few days in the autumn of 1920, this was the first time for eleven years that Rilke had spent any length of time in Paris. His fame as a writer had hastened there before him. As early as 1911 French literary authorities had been made aware of Rilke by an article in the July number of *Nouvelle Revue française* written by Frau Mayrisch, and also by the fragment of *Malte* which Gide translated. His name became known for the first time in wider French circles in 1923, when longer fragments of his prose work, translated by Florent Fel and Maurice Betz, were published in the form of a brochure. One of the leading Paris critics, Edmond Jaloux, recognised in him a forerunner of Proust, Giraudoux and other modern French writers. And in November 1924 – a few weeks before his journey to Paris – the periodical *Commerce*, edited by Paul Valéry and Léon-Paul Fargue, published French poems by him for the first time.

Rilke would never allow himself to be fêted or excessively praised. In spite of his friends' well-meant persuasions, he refused any official meetings or receptions in his honour, such as were occasionally arranged after the war for other German writers. And yet it was inevitable that his new fame should make him very much in demand socially. It goes without saying that Rilke for his part wanted to meet certain writers who attracted him and who were known to him already from their books. Besides, Maurice Betz was working on his translation of the complete text of *Malte Laurids Brigge*, which meant long hours of work together in the Foyot room for the poet and his translator.[1]

Yet in those literary meetings and exchanges an element of the *mondaine* was present, especially during the first weeks; what with going and coming, chatting and conversing, the poet could not find a quiet hour, let alone an opportunity to write or read. 'I am meeting everyone,' he writes from Paris, 'with the exception of the only two people I should like to see every day: Valéry and Frau Pozzi.'[2] That he so seldom met Valéry during those months was a disappointment to Rilke. He excused his illustrious friend's behaviour on the grounds of all the engagements he must have

as a candidate for the French Academy. But he saw the poet
Anna de Noailles again, who remembered him, took an interest
in young Jacques Sindral (Alfred Fabre-Luce), had long conversations with Dr Mardrus, the authority on Islam, found a kindred
spirit in Jules Supervielle, visited Giraudoux in his office at the
Ministry of Foreign Affairs – and for a time frequented almost
daily the salons of the *Faubourg Saint-Germain*, which interested
him on account of Proust's *Côté de Guermantes*. With pity and
amusement he watched the miniature *Comédie humaine*
presented to his mind and eye by the social activities of Paris;
at the same time he asked himself a thousand times daily whether
he was not doing all this in order to hide from himself the memory
of his old Paris. . . .[3]

In his book on Rilke in Paris, Maurice Betz, his translator,
says:

Other witnesses confirm the annoyance that many of his acquaintances caused Rilke, and the lack of understanding that he came up
against in certain circles. Jacques Benoist-Méchin who met him for
the first time in a Paris salon says: 'From the very first moment his
expression suggested to me that he was suffering beyond measure.
Everything seemed to cause him pain: the too brilliant light from
the chandeliers, the too turbulent noise of the conversation. When I
made him break his silence it seemed to me almost as though I were
doing him some injury, being unnecessarily cruel to him. I felt that
every word I spoke made him suffer, like that plant with the marvel-
lously sensitive leaves which open or fold at every slightest variation
of light and shade.' Even in places where a less mixed company might
have made the exchange of thoughts easier for him, Rilke did not
always find the hearing he would have wished. Raymond Schwab,
who saw him at the house of a Paris writer, . . . describes as follows
the effect that Rilke's talk had on people: 'At first a circle gathered
about him in the drawing-room, but gradually the people moved
away, wearied by his loquacity. Rilke was talking as if to himself,
paying no attention to the effect of his words, and explaining how his
vision expressed itself automatically, in words quite beyond his
control, the moment he turned from prose to verse. He held that
these two creative mediums were essentially different from one
another. Never have I heard anyone lay so much stress on this

difference, never have I seen anyone drive his hearers away more rapidly and unconcernedly with a too voluminous rigmarole about highly important things. After a few minutes I was the only audience he had left, I, who must myself confess to having encountered his belief in automatism somewhat sceptically.'[4]

Rilke was never a man for salons, and conversation in a large company was not his strong point.

During the first weeks he found life in a big city difficult: 'How simple, solid and sincere dear Switzerland looks to me, compared to this everlasting sham.' The haste, the insecurity, the loveless human relationships which he found in this other Paris made him miserable: 'I'm terrified, as Malte was terrified before. . . .'[5] But in the midst of this constant change which was devouring his time he realised how little he himself had changed. His inner discords, his failing health, never ceased to prey upon him. But he concealed his suffering, bravely and shamefacedly, from everyone with whom he came in contact. Then, from March onward, he went out less often. It gave him great joy to meet again the Russians whom he had known formerly in Paris. From time to time he saw Edmond Jaloux. He met Hugo von Hofmannsthal, who was on his way to Morocco. Rilke expressed himself very indignantly about Fritz von Unruh's newly published book *Wings of Niké* (*Flügel der Nike*), which was intended to be a kind of summing up of that writer's impressions of Paris.

It is a shame that this German, received here with so much consideration and trust, should express his strange gratitude in a way that gives offence to everybody. His language, which he has built up for figures invented by himself and for allegorical magnifications, is quite unsuited to grasp even the smallest glimmer of reality: everything is exaggerated, and in what taste! Even the few personalities on whom he has deigned to bestow his pompous approval seem quite ridiculous as they issue from this pen, the pen which boasts that it can only portray heroes! For example Valéry![6]

The first anemones, which Frieda sent him from Muzot, and the news that the roses in his garden had been freed from their winter fir branches, made him long to return home soon and re-enter his 'own life'. He realised that he was 'an incorrigible *campagnard'*. And yet Rilke had only been in Paris for two months; he was to remain at the Hôtel Foyot for another half year. True, he was often 'on the point of going home': the tower, his garden, the books, the study – all these were drawing him away. Again and again he urged the Swiss friend who kept a motherly eye on him and his affairs to see that Muzot was kept in a state of readiness and to prevent the housekeeper, who was growing impatient, from leaving. But then, once again, he would feel that Paris had something in store for him. In the continuous plenitude of his sociable, conversation dominated life, he was aware of a strange lack. He longed to discover, behind all the changes, his former Paris and his old life. Then, in the spring, a letter from Emile Verhaeren's widow broke the spell. She invited Rilke to visit her at Saint-Cloud. The circle was complete at last. The poet side-tracked by success found his continuity again. He could stay on. And in the Luxembourg Gardens and the Champs Elysées the awakening glory of blossom seemed like a response to his mood.

Two things, however, Rilke could not alter: the permanent change resulting from the new claims upon him, which he thought of as an atonement for the excessive freedom he had enjoyed during his recent years of solitary work; and that innermost, secret distress which clung to him so closely and from which there was no escape. His one consolation: 'that our dear Muzot exists, and that I shall soon be there, to set in order the spoil of my innumerable memories, or, who knows, to drown them in a productive oblivion. What should I do without Muzot?'[7] But in the meantime he continued to comfort himself with the society of agreeable and important people, who received him amicably and confirmed his great admiration for contemporary French literature. 'Many questions and references' says Maurice Betz,

showed how much it attracted him and how familiar he was with it. Not only had he loved Proust from the very first moment, but he read the works of many young post-war writers. He sensed in these books an urgent endeavour, a growing power, which seemed to him to justify the highest expectations. Even the youngest of these writers, deeply disturbed by the war and presenting their first experiences with vehement bitterness, made a strong appeal to him. He had none of that exaggerated self-importance which one so often finds in outstanding writers, who end up, old and famous, by having no knowledge of anything but themselves. Although, of course, his reading was regulated by his preferences and by his passing moods – so that books often had to wait months for the propitious hour – he read all sorts of books with enjoyment. During his stay in Paris he read haphazardly, as the mood took him, Giraudoux, Colette, Saltykow-Schtschedrin, Ramuz, Aragon, Emanuel Bove, Supervielle, Alain Fournier. Far removed as Colette was from him, he nevertheless appreciated her sensuous fire, her natural freshness, and the originality of her images. Giraudoux he regarded as one of our best writers. He found fault with him, however, for misjudging his own best qualities and squandering his powers on diversions which were altogether too cheap.[8]

When he learned that Ramuz was in Paris he went twice to call on him but did not find him at home. Then, as Ramuz failed to respond in any way to his calls, he gave up trying to make his acquaintance. Rilke admired Ramuz's works; he spoke to me once of 'our two great Swiss writers', meaning Ramuz and Spitteler.

Never at any time during his later years had the poet written so few letters and made so few notes as during those eight Paris months. He regretted it, but there were too many other claims on his time. The life he was leading was in every respect a complete breakaway from his former habits, and one may suppose that he had to satisfy a tremendous craving for distraction, the result of his long years of solitude. Perhaps Rilke would have suffered less from this kind of urge to sociability and change if it had not over-taxed his strength; as it was he never ceased to be conscious of his *malheur tout intérieur*, immovably established at the centre of his vitality. Even in the few confidential letters he wrote he did not want to talk about himself – '*pour ne pas trop tristement me répéter*'.[9] He was still undecided whether to return to Muzot by the most direct route or to travel through southern France in order to have a look at Valéry's native district – Montpellier, Cette. He had put off seeing Marthe again until the end of his time in Paris; she meant for him the tenderest spot among his early Paris memories, as well as his intimate bond with the great city. Rilke left the city as he had arrived there: suddenly, astonishing his Paris friends, to whom he had not said goodbye. Gide, who had started to take an interest in political and social problems, had left for Africa, where he wanted to study conditions in the French colonies: his departure, combined with Valéry's lack of time and slightly — as Betz says — too formal politeness, may have made Rilke aware of the distance which everyday life had opened up between himself and these two active men whom he knew so intimately as creators of works of art. On September 5th Rilke is once again dating a letter from Sierre. The mail which had arrived meantime lay in mountainous heaps on his table at Muzot.

In Bern one autumn evening of that year 1925, I returned home to find Rainer Maria Rilke's visiting card. On the back of it he had written in pencil: 'Dear friend, I have a bad conscience; let me make amends, as many of them as your forbearance will permit. You will find me at the Bellevue this evening after dinner, about 8 o'clock.' It was to be my last meeting with the poet. When I came into the hotel lounge a strange sight met me. A curious absence of expression had removed all of Rilke except the impenetrable outer shell of his striking, almost ugly face. One realised with a heavy heart that this man was no longer young, yet could not look old. Small and shrunken looking, wearing a dark suit, Rilke was sitting plunged in the cushions of a vast armchair; his closed, masklike face had a suffering, remote look. He obviously found it difficult to smile; he seemed very tired. Only after his death did I learn, from letters to intimate friends, that he was already at that time living 'immured with his fate'. Nevertheless I remember clearly and with pleasure Rilke's accounts of his Paris experiences. Specially vivid is my recollection of his visit to André Gide in a clinic where the latter was recovering from an operation. The broad forehead, the godlike head, looming up from the pillows, made a deep impression on Rilke. When the nurse brought the hungry convalescent his meal on a tray it looked 'comme une offrande'. (We spoke German, but Rilke sprinkled his talk with French expressions.) He had been deeply moved, almost alarmed, by his old friend's sudden departure for the Congo on July 14th. About the city of Paris, its light, its life, its magic, Rilke spoke with the verve we are accustomed to find in his letters whenever he discusses that subject. He questioned me about German books published during the course of the previous months, which he had not seen owing to his absence. So I was able to tell him about Thomas Mann's *Magic Mountain*, which was the literary event of the year and dealt with problems which were highly topical in that post-war period; Rilke had told me earlier on, at Muzot, of the importance that *Buddenbrooks* had for him in his youth. One thing at any rate these two German writers have in common: they are the best known outside Germany of all their generation of German men of letters; but perhaps they had hardly any personal link other than their common year of birth: they were both fifty at the time.

I took leave early that evening of my great, admired friend; and as I myself went to Paris a few weeks' later, a thing he had encouraged me to do, I never saw him again.

2

DESPAIR

In September Rilke went to Ragaz to recuperate, via Sierre – where he stayed in the hotel, to see that all was well with Muzot – and Bern where, in spite of his tiredness and low spirits, he gave wonderful accounts of Paris, the people he had met there and the new French books. But instead of finding the hoped-for relief, he developed a painful affliction during his time of treatment. Swellings appeared inside his mouth, in the mucous membranes and on the palate, making speech very difficult, so that he could no longer read aloud, as he had been in the way of doing. The 'phobia', as Rilke called this inhibition about speaking, which lasted longer than the mouth trouble itself, tormented him for months and gave rise to a neurotic dislike of meeting people. It was a peculiar feature of his sensibility, and a result of the way he looked at illness, that he attached a feeling of shame to physical suffering, experiencing it as an humiliation – worse than any that could have been inflicted on him from outside.

Very few people knew anything of Rilke's illness at that time, and the little he told his friends, although it hinted at an oppressive grief, was worded with such restraint and dignity that one never ceases to be moved by the strength of this man engaged in his hopeless struggle. And yet he must have been indescribably tortured by horrors and anxieties during that endless descent into the hell of illness. Monique Saint-Hélier in her *Souvenir de Rilke* gives us in a few vivid words a picture of the afflicted poet at that time:

He knew a lot about life, a lot about fear, but anxiety was his familiar acquaintance, his painful, restless world, and nothing concerning it escaped him. But his self-control was so great that he succeeded in observing the anxiety with that clear look of his – such a look as, had he been a doctor, he would have turned upon someone else's illness; he made no movement, was dreadfully present, and yet at the same time gave his full attention to that world of which we know so little; only at such moments his hands were like the hands of a corpse.[10]

That his sufferings were not the result of imagination, of auto-suggestion, is clearly demonstrated by the fact that a year later, when his leukaemia had become acute, the patient's most striking symptom was again the swellings in the mucous membranes of mouth and nose – albeit in a much more virulent form. At Ragaz his mouth condition was already very painful and it worried him a great deal as he was afraid it might be cancer. At the beginning of October he went, in a very distressed state of mind, to Meilen, where he stayed for a week in the Wunderly's house; from there he travelled to Zürich to consult two doctors, who tried to convince him that his fears of cancer were groundless.

It is now known that Rilke was suffering from leukaemia, a rare disease of the blood characterised by an increase in the white and a decrease in the red blood corpuscles. Acute leukaemia is a trouble which medical science has no real means of combating. This knowledge is anticipated here in parenthesis, to help the reader to a better understanding of Rilke's illness, which in that autumn of 1925 was still mysterious and inexplicable.

After his Meilen and Zürich visits Rilke returned to Muzot on October 14th. A year had passed since that heraldic device of the house, the poplar, had been felled by resounding axe strokes and had fallen 'on to the level', bringing the landscape down with it. A new trouble awaited the poet in the disenchanted tower: his housekeeper, Frieda, broke the news that she would have to leave him. 'Frieda's departure was strange this time,' Rilke reported; 'she really was, as she called herself once in the early days, "a little pixie", and it was extraordinary how she looked to me at last in the mirrors by which I am surrounded.'[11] There were no mirrors in Muzot. Asked to explain, Rilke replied: 'When I spoke of mirrors I did not mean, alas, those mirrors I once thought to acquire but. . . . But why keep depicting and describing what is simply there and has to be endured.'[12]

A few days after his return to Muzot Rilke made his will. He sent it in a large, sealed envelope, together with some other important packets, to Mme Nanny Wunderly-Volkart. In an explanatory letter which accompanied it he asked his friend to open the big envelope later on if necessary; it contained, he wrote, '*quelques indications pour le cas qu'une grave maladie, me priverait de la possibilité de prendre certaines dispositions. De savoir ce papier, Chère, entre vos mains, fidèles entre toutes, est une de ces rares consolations que je peux m'offrir en ces jours infiniment douloureux et difficiles. . . .*' The will itself is written in German. It is in the possession of the executrix he appointed.

The complete text runs as follows:

On the envelope: 'A few personal requests in the event of a more or less incapacitating illness.

(Muzot, October 1925)'

On a big sheet, written on both sides:

'If I should have a serious illness affecting my mind, I request, indeed implore, my friends to keep away any priestly assistance which may seek to intrude itself upon me. Bad enough that in my physical emergency I had to admit the mediator and negotiator in the form of the doctor; any spiritual middle-man would be offensive and nauseating to my soul as it moves towards the open.

2. If I happen to die at Muzot or anywhere in Switzerland I do not wish to be buried either in Sierre or in Miège. (The latter should perhaps be avoided in view of the unknown old woman's mysterious tale, so as not to start poor Isabelle de Chevron off on her restless night wanderings again.)

3. I should prefer to be laid to rest in the high-up churchyard of the old Church of Raron. Its enclosure was one of the first places from which I experienced the wind and light of this landscape, together with all the promises it helped me to fulfil later on, with and in Muzot.

4. I detest the geometrical art of modern stonemasons. It might perhaps be possible to buy an old stone (something of the Empire period, like the one on my cousin's grave in Vienna). When the earlier inscription has been erased, this should have on it:
the coat of arms
(: in the form used by my great-grandfather, reproduced on the silver seal brought back recently from Paris),
the name

and, some way below, the lines of verse:

Rose, oh pure contradiction, delight
in being no one's sleep under so many lids.

5. I do not regard *any* of the articles of furniture and other objects in Muzot as my personal possessions; apart from any family portraits which may be there: which should go to my daughter, Frau Ruth Sieber, Vorwerk Alt-Jocketa bei Jocketa (in Saxony). Everything else, in so far as it does not belong to the house, shall be disposed of by Frau Nanny Wunderly-Volkart of the Unteren Mühle, Meilen, in consultation with her cousin, Herr Werner Reinhart, Rychenberg-Winterthur: my generous friend and the owner of Muzot.

6. As it has been my habit now and then, for a certain number of years, to divert part of the productivity of my nature into letter writing, there is nothing to hinder the publication of any of my letters which may be in the hands of the addressees (if the Insel-Verlag should suggest it).

7. I do not think that there are any really good likenesses of me except those which remain in the thoughts and feelings of particular friends.

Rainer Maria Rilke.

Château de Muzot,
evening of October 27th 1925.'

Rilke had written out his last will with a clear mind, in legal form and in the required words, and had set his house in order. And yet he had not mentioned what was to be done with his poetic estate, with his own manuscripts and books and the letters he had kept from correspondents of both sexes.

His will written, Rilke began to think again about having some medical care. It should be stated here that the 'incapacity' of will power or mental faculties which he so obviously thought of as a possibility, did not in fact ever take place, even temporarily, during his last illness. He preferred to endure the most agonising pain rather than let his doctor give him narcotic drugs. During the whole time of his suffering Rilke was uninterruptedly able to give orders and ask for what he wanted, and he followed the course of his illness until the end with a perfectly lucid mind.

In November he received some boxes from Paris containing his papers of pre-war days. 'Many strange things are coming to light,' he wrote of this trivial occurrence, 'many which lay open my memory before me.' It is 'sad, often alarming', but 'strangely, even more "me": a dead me, but, even so, more "me" than the self I would find in the letters and papers of my last Paris visit, had I kept them'. For, Rilke confesses, during that short time spent in Paris, 'I was already he whom I have more and more been becoming, a person unknown to me, so unknown that I have to rely for months on end on someone *outside myself*, who ought, that other, to have been "me", and also within an obscure me somehow more deeply authentic than the former self whom I had no difficulty in recognising.'

From now on everything in Rilke's life leads to the ever-present affliction, within which he finds it hard to be alone, although at the same time he is unable to think of anyone whose company he could endure.

I am like an empty space, I am not, I have never been, identical with my suffering, which I can only up to a point regard as legitimate. As my mouth condition makes talking an effort (the disorder and the particular phobia always go together) I cannot even read aloud, a practice which more than anything else used always to help me towards myself.

Yet Rilke tidies his papers, reads books, and is full of praise for *Grande Peur dans la Montagne*, the new book by the 'great Ramuz'.[13]

Weeks passed in Muzot, where Rilke felt himself to be immured along with his fate. But his anxiety kept mounting, mounting. At the end of November he at last made up his mind to go to Valmont again, only to learn that Dr T. Haemmerli – his doctor there – had just gone away.

On December 4th Rainer Maria Rilke completed his fiftieth year. He had begged his Meilen friend beforehand to keep away from him everything concerned with that date. For now at last – what a struggle it must have cost him! – he admitted that he was really feeling ill. He no longer looked to his own nature for consolation; he was having great difficulty in keeping his balance. He refused to receive any visitors on his birthday because he was afraid that he might not be able to hide his despair any longer.

And yet: there are unmistakeable signs to show that this man preserved his self-control, that he struggled against his affliction with all his might, and that all this effort was in vain.

On December 4th, of course, piles of letters and telegrams arrived at Muzot. Thanks had to be sent in every direction: '*Quelle corvée, quelle inutilité!*' he exclaimed. 'A warm sun is shining on quantities of snow, and I have to sit in my room rustling paper. Of course, looked at in the right way, it shows love, but where is the love that does not give some trouble?'[14] To crown everything, the presence of his housekeeper was an added source of distress to Rilke. On no account had she to learn anything about his ill health – the thought that she might start to nurse him he found horrible. She was a good soul, but not as tactful as Frieda, whom he called *irremplaçable*.

To commemorate his fiftieth birthday Rilke made a pious foundation. He gave 1000 francs from his own pocket (a mad expense, he called it) for the restoration of St Anne's Chapel, opposite Muzot. His financial circumstances were such that he had afterwards to ask his publisher in Leipzig to refund him the amount; but he counted on having, from 1926 onwards, a regular income from a Czech legacy, and also on his latest publications bringing in something from the Insel-Verlag (which would then pay for Valmont). The poet had been grieved for a long time at having to watch the nearby chapel falling so rapidly into decay; and lest the winter (which was specially hard that year) should make the damage worse, he quickly ordered the necessary repairs to be done. The little sanctuary belonged to one of the local families, the Winkelrieds, and Rilke was cheered by the thought that Mass could be said in the chapel the following spring, to the great joy of good old Frau Winkelried and the people of Veyras, Miège and Venthône.[15]

Shortly before Christmas, Rilke at last went into the Valmont clinic, where he was to undergo treatment for five months. His doctor, who had returned and could look after him again, had long conversations with him, listening attentively to all the patient's theories and accounts of his symptoms; and the patient on his side, turning his powers of observation away from his own condition, watched Dr Haemmerli making characteristically sympathetic attempts to understand the ins and outs of his constitution and sensibility. For this gravely ill man was so free spiritually that he found a certain stimulus again in these dialogues with his doctor, and in the careful examinations which the latter carried out.

From the point of view of literary criticism also Rilke's attitude to his own illness is illuminating; for critics have often found fault with his work for betraying an unhealthy personality attracted by the morbid. Jaloux held that this view was quite erroneous, and wrote, apropos of the *Notebooks of Laurids Malte Brigge*, that writers were often accused of morbidity because they wrote about death and illness. 'Many people', says Jaloux,

confuse the subject and the way it is treated. There is nothing brighter, stronger, more fitting, i.e. healthier, than the way in which Rilke describes certain states of anxiety or certain nervous disturbances. His greatness lies in taking the measure of the soul at those moments when it leaves its accustomed tracks and moves towards the unknown. . . .[16]

These remarks are undoubtedly correct in so far as they refer to the poet's lucidity of mind and powers of truthful observation; but of course he could only describe such psychical disturbances as he himself had lived through, which in fact amounted to describing his own pathological tendency. What this critic had once said of Rilke's prose work applied now to the very different, harrowing circumstance of the poet's own illness. Perhaps the sick man suffered less from the subjectively painful, objectively present symptoms of his malady than from an all too clear awareness that his nature had been violently turned aside from its accustomed path and that he could no longer follow it into the unknown. But this was precisely what the doctor would help him to do. According to Rilke, the doctor's vocation was to give enlightening advice and to be a mediator between the patient's true self and the 'nature' which was slipping away from him.

The first examination carried out at Valmont showed a serious condition. On the very first day Rilke wrote an account of it:

The swellings in my mouth, which are so troublesome and painful, are more widespread than I thought, though as he (Dr Haemmerli) assures me again, they give no occasion for the phobia which I attach to them. . . . These nuisances upset and inconvenience me more than anything else now, and it is a pity that nothing can be done, or so it seems, to mitigate the discomforts they cause me.[17]

The doctor was kind and attentive, he said, but could give him no explanation. On December 29th Rilke speaks in a letter of the rather monotonous life to which he is condemned; for in spite of the innumerable books with which he has surrounded himself, he feels cut off, as it were, from real life. However: '*il y avait quelques instants supportables de temps en temps*'.

The patient was somewhat alarmed by his rapid gain in weight. When he arrived he weighed about eight stone, while sixteen days later he had put on five lbs. Rilke was afraid of becoming '*un personage lourd*'. At the end of January he speaks of the great discrepancy between the doctor's view that some objective improvement could be discerned, and his own feelings, unable to detect the slightest change for the better in any one of his several ailments. – An attack of laryngitis had given the patient another bad setback. – By the middle of February he is saying that there is never a day when he feels the least bit 'me' and on good terms with himself: 'I am worried, the state of my mouth still makes me apprehensive, and as reading and working are for me identical with the use of that very commonplace apparatus, I feel constantly hindered from living my normal life. . . .'[18] Dr Haemmerli was of the opinion that there was no need for the patient's established symptoms to incommodate him to this extent; on which view Rilke made the fine comment: '. . . *personne ne peut changer le degré de sensibilité d'autrui, ni arrêter les combinaisons d'esprit et d'humeur que cette sensibilité entraine.*'[19]

At Easter (the beginning of April) Rilke was looking to a visit from Mme Wunderly for advice and help. 'For really', he wrote to her,

I am at my wits' end. Even when the good Dr Haemmerli sits there enumerating his reasons for taking heart (I am quite prepared to believe that they are honest and objective), even while he's speaking, I'm not aware of the slightest improvement at any of the trouble centres of my damaged being: mouth, stomach and all the rest . . . still cause me as much distress as ever, and terror is lurking just round the corner. Rather (from my point of view) everything seems to have grown worse (after more that three months!) since I came here, and

I feel that my whole condition unfits me for living in freedom . . .;
so far *behind* the still quite nice sum of neutral nature available to me
last year, which enabled me to manage Paris almost without any
bother. This mouth misfortune, which began in Ragaz, has made me
nervous.[20]

All the same, the invalid longed to escape from the atmosphere
of the clinic and venture on a few free steps. As his doctor had
to go away he would take advantage of the occasion and move into
a nearby hotel. In fact, the objective improvement which had
been observed for some time now gradually began to extend to his
own feelings. A despatch of April 26th, in which he says that he
has 'flown out', sounds freer and more cheerful in tone. He has
travelled down to Lausanne and been to an exhibition of pictures
by the painter Auberjonois; of these he says: '(*ils*) *compteront
dans l'histoire picturale de cette époque embrouillée*'.[21] On the
same occasion a meeting with Edmond Jaloux was a great joy
to him; friendship with this writer was one of his consolations
during his years of suffering.

In fact, Rilke's condition had improved so much by the spring
that the doctor advised him to have a complete change and to
accept an invitation from the Princess Taxis which would have
enabled him to go to Rome. On the other hand Rilke wanted to
visit Vienna in the summer, to see to business connected with the
Czech legacy. But his mouth trouble, now better, had left him
with feelings of apprehension which restrained him from ventur-
ing on such a long journey. He felt that his 'secret illness' was still
within him, giving him again and again a sense of ill-being and
robbing him of the '*élans*' which he longed to find again for his
own and his friends' sakes. '*Quel mystérieux malheur où je me
traîne*', he was writing in May from Valmont, '*tournant en rond
dans un cercle mortel.*'[22]

The best hours were again those spent in the Jaloux's house in
Lausanne, where he met at table a famous Swedish neurologist.
'Was this only Lausanne?' Rilke exclaimed afterwards. 'It was
almost Paris!'[23] On June 1st we at last find him back at Muzot,
in better spirits, even happy because of the return of the creative
mood. He was to spend several weeks living alternately in his
tower and at the hotel in Sierre.

3

PHYSICAL AND METAPHYSICAL

WHEN, two years previously, at the beginning of 1924, Rainer Maria Rilke had looked back to his first illness and speculated on the possible causes of these sudden 'fluctuations and insecurities', he had written the following significant words to an intimate friend: 'But above them both, however they may be, stands authoritatively *what I never forget*, the single miracle of life and death!' – It is, then, remarkable that the more illness devastated his being, the more silent did he become on the subject of those last questions now pressing so inescapably upon him. A sentence like the one just quoted could hardly have come from his pen when the cruel fangs of his illness had him in their grip. This attitude he maintained right to the end. He seldom uttered the word 'death': even when writing his will he made detours round about it, using other expressions. When his talks with the doctor approached the inevitable question, he would change the subject. Almost until the last he spoke of the future to those around him in a way that implied his hope of recovery. No word of farewell ever passed his lips.

The man who from his youth had appeared before the world as the poet of suffering and death avoided as far as possible making any mention of the great enigmas when they laid hold upon his own life. We can never know what conversations he had with himself, unhinted at to others. We should beware – beware with the same humility in face of the unutterable which he observed throughout his long illness – of speaking about 'his own' death in images and words taken from his poetry. Perhaps the death he fell victim to in the end was not the death of which Malte wrote. We do not know. Our memory is haunted by that prayer from the *Book of Hours*: 'O Lord, give each one his own death. . . .' The idea of each man carrying his own particular death around with him throughout his life was one that Rilke never disavowed. But it is strange that in his later years and most mature work he never used the famous old image that he coined to depict death in *Malte* and the *Book of Hours*. Death as 'fruit', which man always carries inside him, covered only by the husk and leaf of life: *that* death he never, as far as we know, mentioned again. Nor should Malte's somewhat literary effusion about the 'well finished' death be brought too close to the elemental happening which tore Rilke like a tornado in his last illness. It was no literary illness, no literary death, which overpowered him, and he suffered both illness and death with a manful courage.

Like death, but even more so, the name of God was for him 'something indescribably evadeable'. In this respect, too, the poet of the *Book of Hours* had changed (at any rate as regards his use of words). God is only mentioned once in the Elegies. The statement so much favoured by Rilke critics – that the angels of the Elegies are a 'pseudonym for God' is not quite correct, for these angels are related to man rather than to God, an allegory of the perfection unattainable by human kind. Two acts of Rilke's are all we have to indicate his attitude to religion during his illness – acts which, incidentally, speak more clearly than words, and between which there is an apparent contradiction: his will, in which he implores his friends to keep away all priestly assistance from his death-bed, and the restoration of St Anne's Chapel at Muzot. It is well known that Rilke emphatically rejected belief in Christ as mediator and in the dogmas of the Christian churches. He felt that dogmas and rituals were obstacles on the road to God. Practically the only occasions on which he overcame his antipathy to Church and dogma were when he encountered a simple, ancient popular belief. At Muzot he told me that he had seen religious actions in Spain and North Africa which he could understand and in which he could take part. He mentioned especially the procession through the underground passages of the monastery at Kiev, where the faithful, with lighted candles in their hands, moved past the undecayed bodies of saintly monks; and certain mosques had made the same moving impression on him. He thought that he had found a similar relationship to the popular beliefs of the Valais. This fundamentally very devout, religious man took pleasure in the thought of the pleasure he had given to the valley people by restoring the altar in St Anne's Chapel. For such was his direct belief and his own special brand of piety that he was ready to share in any religious experience which was free from denominational conceptions confining, so it seemed to him, the presence of God. The simplicity of their religious beliefs, the self-evident unity of life and religion in the Catholic Valais, were among the things which had made Rilke feel at home on this alien soil. For that reason he wanted to entrust his body to the earth there, at the foot of a Valais church, and his friends were allowed to arrange a funeral in accordance with the religious customs of the country.

The Protestant form of Christianity was more alien to Rilke than the Catholic, to which he belonged by birth and tradition. In Flaach parsonage, which he sometimes visited during his time at Berg, he became aware of the distance separating him from the local Protestantism with its puritanical flavour. There was hanging in the house an old picture of a gentleman with a bunch of flowers: 'the glorious bunch of flowers before the man in the brown coat', Rilke said, 'was described on the little label as a "symbol of transitoriness", without any right understanding *que cette gerbe magnifique et joyeux voulait dire en même temps: comme ce qui passe est beau pourtant!*'[24] He explained to the local clergyman, with whom he was still keeping up a correspondence at Muzot, why it was that he had to reject Christianity, especially in its Protestant form. Looked at from a higher viewpoint, the Christian conception

still certainly appears as one of the most marvellous attempts to keep open the way to God. That it is the most *successful* attempt we and our contemporaries are quite unable to prove, since it is constantly failing before our eyes to provide the pure counterbalance to the inordinate weight of suffering. All those religions in which the mediator seems to be quite unimportant or to have almost ceased his activities, are nearer to *me* personally. . . . There are such wonderful ways of grasping God, and if I watch humanity I think that it is only a question of keeping ready for it the countless possible ways of catching hold of him or of being surprised by him.[25]

Hearing Bach's St Matthew Passion in the cathedral at Basle confirmed the poet again in this belief: 'The difficulty I more and more find in unreservedly sharing the Christian experience inhibited for me that abandonment to the subject itself which must have made listening to the whole an event.'[26]

Always it is the figure of the suffering Christ which seems to him to contract the mystery of God as well as of man; for if the Passion does indeed bring deliverance to men, then God 'who always has new ways of rescuing', is tied to this one path of salvation, according to Christian ideas. As Rilke saw it, the power of God, which overflows every measure, cannot tolerate being compressed into the channels of ecclesiastical and theological conceptions, nor being attached to the figure of a unique redeemer, who blocks the entrance to all other roads. But to return to the Matthew Passion:

And this very, elemental superabundance of God is so closely related to the nature of music that I wanted to reproach the immensely great and yet so programmatically restricted Protestant soul from which this music sprang, even though one has continually to admit that it is so pure and honest in its *métier* that it could reach to the mightiesι, transcending all systems.[27]

It was not Rilke's way to fit his experiences and insights into a philosophical system and then to deduce theories from them. He had read no philosophy. Conceptual thinking was alien to him, and he was without any scientific education. He needed complete freedom for the full flow of his powers. He sought out and uttered wonderful things like an astrologer in the night, but his ability to order and explain them intellectually lagged far behind his powers of intuition. Neither bound nor binding, Rilke belonged to no philosophical school, no literary group, no political party and – strictly speaking – no religious denomination. No ideology can lay claim to him. He was too transparently sincere to put up with any of the compromises, half measures and conventions called for in adapting oneself to programmes and orthodoxies. His humility did not extend to obeying the laws of earthly authorities, among which he counted the churches. 'He was a poet and hated the approximate', wrote Malte Laurids Brigge, speaking of the poet Félix Arvers.

In his *Young Workman's Letter* Rilke developed his arguments against the traditional dogmas of the Christian churches, unsystematically, interweaving the intellectual element and the world of the modern factory worker's personal experience in a wonderfully skilful way, but without any attempt at reasoned argument. The way in which, unencumbered by philosophical, theological or sociological reading, he puts his finger on a sore spot, that is to say the historical limitation of the Christian faith, shows, incidentally, how surely this genius moved in his own time, from which he seemed so detached. No sociologist could have had a surer feeling for the contrast between the Valais peasant's simple, traditional faith and the scepticism of the factory worker in a modern city than this 'naïve' poet; and he knows well how to imply it without mentioning it directly: 'I feel bound to say,' writes his workman,

who – I can't express it otherwise – *who* then is this Christ, who interferes with everything? – Who knew nothing about us, nothing of our work, nothing of our sorrow, nothing of our joy, as we do, endure and feel them today – and who still, so it seems, keeps on asking to be the *first* in our lives? Or has that only been put into his mouth? What does he want of us? He wants to help us, they say. Yes, but in his dealings with us he seems strangely at a loss. His conditions were so completely different. Or don't the circumstances really matter; if he came to me here in my room or there in the factory, would everything suddenly become different, good? Would my heart beat more strongly in me, and, in a manner of speaking, move up a stage higher, always moving in his direction? My feelings tell me he *cannot* come. That it would not make sense. Our world has not only changed outwardly – it has no entrance for him. He would not shine through a ready-made coat, it isn't true, he would not shine through. It isn't by chance that he went about in a garment without a seam, and I believe that the kernel of light in him, that which made him shine so powerfully by day and by night, has been extinguished for a long time now and distributed in other ways. But it seems to me that the least we could ask of him, if he was so great, was that he should vanish somehow without residue, yes, quite without any remains – traceless.

The worker's letter, to which we must always turn if we want to find out Rilke's attitude towards religion, is a rich paraphrase of this theme.

The intelligent, somewhat fanatical workman speaks here of his own religious experience, of his own conception of Christianity

of beautiful churches which he has visited with his young friend
Marthe. Marthe's idea of freedom had been boundless, and so she
had been afraid of God as of the *patron* in the factory, until she
discovered 'that God leaves one alone in the churches, that he
asks nothing', and that *everything* is there in the old churches
and in their stained-glass windows, 'the bad and wicked even, and
the frightful, the crippled, the suffering and the ugly – and
injustice, and one might say that it is loved somehow for God's
sake'. In these churches, between the angels and the devils, who
did not exist, man, who did exist, seemed in a sense more real
to him . . . .

In this prose work, meant to be a letter to Verhaeren, the name
Marthe – that of the little Parisian working girl with whom he
visited churches in his youth – is a hint that Rilke identifies
himself with the letter writer. That he should make his workman
say that angels and devils do not exist, while man does, is very
revealing.

Man, as he is and lives and works, should above all be 'available
for God' and must not be pushed away from him all the time.
To God, says the workman in his simplicity, one can bring everything, one can bring the machine with its first fruit, 'just as
it was easy once for shepherds to bring to the gods of their lives,
a lamb or the fruit of the field or the most beautiful grape'. But
that one cannot do to Christ: 'he does not retain'. – Very strange
are the words in which Rilke formulates here his lifelong protest
against Christianity: 'I don't want to be made bad for Christ's
sake, I want to be good for God. I don't want to be addressed as
a sinner from the start, perhaps I'm not one. I have such pure
mornings! I could speak to God, I don't need anyone to help
me to write letters to him.' – And the last word from this
workman, whose letter is addressed to a poet: 'My friend once
said: Give us teachers who praise this world for us. You *are*
such a one.'

If there was one thing we needed at the moment of setting out
to accompany Rainer Maria Rilke on the last stretch of his earthly
way, it was this: to hear from him once more how he explained
and justified the great venture of his life as a poet. In his worker's
letter to Verhaeren, that inspirer of his own literary beginnings,
Rilke turns a bright light on to much that seemed strange or

even inexplicable in his life and poetry. The life and earth affirming spirituality peculiar to Rilke finds expression in this piece of prose.

Existence, this world, the business of learning from life, man and his gifts, the ego – which, as it were, increased in size as life was rightly used – these things had outstanding importance for Rilke, and we must recognise that they were his chief concern. He refused to relate the soul's experiences to a 'beyond'. But as, fundamentally, he was a religious man and a believer in God, there is a contradiction in his view of the world which nothing can bridge – nothing save wonderful poetic images, magical incantations, and the word clothed visions of a poet of genuine imaginative power. For what is external to man and the things of earth has no part in Rilke's conception of God. He always spoke disparagingly of all 'oppositeness' and had no use for actual instances of it: the division into heaven and earth was displeasing to him even in a landscape; he preferred the buoyant light which includes both in its vibrations, bringing them into relationship with one another. His denial of a 'beyond' in the transcendental sense arose from this way of feeling about things, so characteristic of him and evidently with him from the beginning. However, he did not carry it to its logical conclusion – whether that of philosophical materialism, which erases metaphysics from its cosmogony (for Rilke was a metaphysician by instinct), or that of Nietzsche, who affirmed that God was dead (which accounts for the fact that Rilke silently but decidedly repudiated Nietzsche, whose theories he must have known, but whose name he did not mention and whose works he would not read).

With his profound belief in the existence of God Rilke combined rejection of the Christian faith, because it seemed to him that Christianity had declared eternal warfare against the world and its creatures; it had made the world evil and the enjoyment of love suspect. The God who was always revealing himself in his creatures, in their suffering and in their joy, that God he sought and loved. Rilke's search for God started from creatures, and this led him to the belief, expressed more than once, that if mankind's religious feeling should ever again become powerful enough to crystallise itself into images and myths, the first deity to come into being in this way would be a phallic one; for in sexual love he thought that he had discovered a human capacity for the supreme delight, and he passionately denied that it was sinful or shameful. If Rilke was spiritually at home with the saint and the poet, he was for all that no mystic aiming at union with a transcendent God but a worshipper and singer of the earthly and the creaturely. God, he believed, was somehow contained in creation and in created beings. Rilke himself was a genius full of all kinds of insights, the creator of work which is full of signposts, a genius who showed the way, and opened up paths into, the depths of the soul. He was full of intuitions about man's place in the cosmos; but, as he said of Christ, he had no room within him, 'like everyone who points the way, who is a gesture and not a stopping place'. He too received nothing into himself – he did 'not retain'. It is just this, however, which makes people distrustful of his ideas – those ideas from which he removed every fixed landmark by which men can steer and hold, every fixed centre which can help them to the endurance of life. His element was movement, pure relation, and in it he attained to an ease and an ingenuity unequalled by any poet before him. But the question remains: what is to be life's motive power and to what shall it be related?

4

RESPITE

AFTER leaving Valmont, Rilke lived alternately at Muzot and at the Hotel Bellevue in Sierre. His poor health made living in the inconvenient little castle more difficult than in former days. It seems, too, that Muzot had begun to play a new and rather different rôle in Rilke's imagination. The old walls still meant home to him, a refuge, the shelter of a roof and the comfort of a garden; we know how, during the long months in Paris, he was seized with homesickness for them again and again. But while in earlier years he had made the old tower the centre of his existence, finding in its enclosure security for his life and shelter for his work, he later looked upon it more and more as a place of transit. He would now mention to his visitors something which had not struck him before: Muzot lay on the route to Italy, on the way to the south for which he longed. The thought comforted him, and he said that he would take advantage of this circumstance, and go and stay in Milan, no distance away, now and then in the winter. Earlier on he had delighted in the 'great valley' and enjoyed the remoteness of his mountain château. Now he observed with satisfaction that the Orient Express passed through Sierre station and that his house was near the Paris-Constantinople line. The vertical of the vanished poplar was gradually replaced in his imagination by the horizontal of journeys through the world. At other times he would talk of going to stay in the South of France or the Mediterranean. He knew Provence well; its famous cities appear in his work: Les Beaux in *Malte*, Arles (where he had seen the 'antique sarcophagi') in the *Sonnets to Orpheus*, Avignon in the *Young Workman's Letter*. But he did not know the Languedoc yet, and that plain, that sea-shore, had acquired a new significance for him as Paul Valéry's native district. He wanted to see the *cimetière marin* with his own eyes, to visit Cette and Montpellier. . . .

The weeks of June and July 1926, which Rilke again spent in the old familiar Valais surroundings, can be said to have been tolerable, almost, indeed, good. The first copies of his French poems *Vergers* arrived, making him very happy. While he was staying at the hotel his study up at the château was redecorated on his instructions: *'mon cabinet de travail est une merveille à présent'*.[28] What gave him most pleasure, however, after his return from Valmont was translating Valéry's *Fragments du Narcisse*, which had appeared shortly before in the new edition of *Charmes* (1926). How happy this work made him – giving him the same satisfaction as his own creative writing – is shown by the following passage from a letter: – *'Ma traduction est terminée: c'était, – vous l'avez deviné – de Valéry encore: les trois fragments de "Narcisse" qui se trouvent dans la nouvelle édition de "Charmes". C'est beau, c'est magnifique, et ma traduction me contente à souhait. De la faire était une félicité entre toutes les félicités.'*[29] – At the same time his mouth trouble and the 'phobia' connected with it had improved to such an extent that, at Ragaz in July, the poet was able to read his new work aloud, just as he had been in the way of doing: always the French text first, then his German version. These translations are at the same time elegant and strong, and again there is something of his own in them, something of the unique tone of his German lyric poetry. There is nothing here to indicate that his craftsman's powers were failing.

On July 19th Rilke had gone to Zürich, and on the following day, accompanied by Mme Wunderly, he went to Ragaz, where the Princess Thurn und Taxis was expecting him. He had so far overcome the nervousness due to his mouth trouble, and his consequent dislike of meeting people, that he was able once more to take up the intimate social life of the Ragaz cure and of the nearby Grison châteaux. The district and *'cette vie au ralenti'* charmed him as much as ever; after staying for some weeks in this spa he found it strangely difficult to tear himself away. Although he thought of himself as *'abîmé dans mon secret et ridicule malheur'*, his friends at Salenegg Castle in Maienfeld had no idea how ill the poet already was when, on August 6th, he wrote a poem called *The Willow of Salenegg* in their visitors' book. It was the last of Rilke's poems to appear in a Swiss periodical during his lifetime and with his consent.[30] Its twelve stanzas, faintly reminiscent of 'Count C. W.', are reproduced here not because the poem was one of his last, nor because he said to his hosts with a humourous smile: 'I have written a real poem for you, not just improvised one.' They are given because this vivid, objective poem, which seems to be bathed in clear autumn sunlight, expresses an image and a thought which were close to Rainer Maria Rilke's heart.

A tree – a willow – which had been planted almost three hundred years before by the then owner of Salenegg, one of the Salis family – whose crest it represented – had withered in the course of time; a wide cleft had opened in its trunk. The tree was to all appearances dead; but then

astonishingly enough, new life began to stir; some quite young growth and fresh foliage appeared in the crown, which no one could account for. When the mystery was investigated, it was discovered that the crown of the tree had thrust a young root down through the rotten interior of its own trunk . . . the decayed wood inside the trunk gave way here and there, the root emerged into the air, it formed a bark and became itself a new trunk, nourished by the old crown. Of the old trunk only the quite lifeless bark is there now, held together by the ivy twined about it. . . . The new trunk is growing quickly in the shelter of the old bark and could within forseeable time entirely replace the old trunk.[31]

The symbolism of the tree trunk (he had already used this motive in his tree trunk poem in the *Sonnets to Orpheus*: 'Undermost he, the earthbound . . .') had for long fascinated Rilke. The natural phenomenon at Salenegg must have impressed him deeply just then. He thought of himself as the last scion of an ancient line, at whose death the family tree itself would come to an end. The poet was the last male descendant of his great-grandfather, and the name Rilke would die with him. Rilke was distressed by his impaired health, yet still full of the will to live; he believed in nature, that it would never really let him down, and in the 'sovereignty of the miracle': so it was not surprising that the fate of the willow, the armorial tree drawing new life from its own decay, should provide him with a welcome pretext for writing a poem wholly attuned to hope and confidence. Here it is:

RESPITE

THE WILLOW OF SALENEGG

Long since the armorial willow started
as a question to futurity.
Both, it seemed, the live and the departed,
shared the hope of its increscency.

Throve. The rich soil gave its confirmation
to the race united with the tree.
Heaven each spring-time without hesitation
justified its spontaneity.

How but anchor to the tree's endurance,
to the trunk's sheer power to resist,
some signification, some assurance?
When we see familiar things persist,

we persist with them. It grew apace,
from an ever-stronger trunk-foundation
flinging yearly its green jubilation
into joyfully assenting space.

Growing, though, means growing old. The failing,
grizzled form had spent its last resource,
and one had to gaze in unavailing
sorrow at its self-consuming course.

Now the bark of that dried trunk was gaping:
through the arid crack one came to see
more and more the wholly life-escaping,
sap-forsaken void obscurity.

Under storms' and winters' desolation
ever wider open gaped the rent;
finally to that dark habitation
crept a strange and shelterless descent.

Only through a single root's transmission,
hanging in the cleft as though abjured,
did the cheerful foliage's emission
seem for yet a little while assured.

No one paid the withered shreds attention,
even the careful gardener failed to see;
for we're more alert to detrimention
than to growing marvel's melody.

None the less, it happened. Marvel here
breathed in ruin's poverty its note;
secretly its voice rose every year
from within and fortified that throat,

till it swelled into a trunk; the old one's
ruinous encirclement became
its protection, just as one will hold one's
hollowed hands around a fighting flame.

Envoy: May the mighty willow's sloughing through all
time hold good for the ancestral tree,
with the tree the meaning find renewal
and the undiscerned confederacy.

This poem which, like the verses written at Berg by the Irschel in the winter of 1920-29, is technically inferior to Rilke's most inspired works, stands near the end of his earthly road as a great, joyful affirmation of life.[32] He had not ceased to hope for a harmonious, artistically fruitful old age. The memory of the aged Rodin still gave him assurance 'that one will have time and that, hard and patient, one will keep moving towards perfection, if life is not interrupted too soon. But oh', he adds reflectively, 'one must not wish to last too long, neither the individual nor the family: . . . Nature is gentler with things that outlast. Muzot's *dementia senilis* – if people dont clumsily prevent or divert it – can be a benign, untroubled state that will not scare the birds or the roses.'[33]

Early in September Rilke again went to stay with his Vienna friends the Weiningers at Ouchy on Lake Geneva. From there he visited Valéry who was staying on the Savoy side of the lake, and with whom he discussed the Narcissus fragment and certain difficulties that he had encountered in making his translation. It was the last meeting between the two poets, and Valéry found Rilke in an expansive, talkative mood. Of course this visit was also a chance to meet Edmond Jaloux again in Lausanne. – At the beginning of October friends who went to see Rilke at the Bellevue in Sierre found him no better, but no worse either, than he had often been in earlier years when he was out of sorts. He told them that he was quite absorbed again in his early memories and impressions of Russia, and was getting his new secretary, a Russian woman, to read aloud to him, in Russian, the memoirs of the late manager of the Imperial Theatres, Prince Wolkonsky. Incidentally, this gives us some idea of how familiar Rilke was with the Russian language. His visitors noticed that he did not accompany them to the station as on previous occasions, but waved goodbye instead from the hotel window. However, they did not leave with the impression that there was anything to worry about.

Rilke became ill after pricking two fingers while cutting roses in his garden at Muzot. The pricks turned septic, began to suppurate, and became intensely painful. It was soon apparent that these were the first symptoms of an acute leukaemia. Rilke wrote on October 30th that he wanted to spend the winter 'in the world' and avoid a repetition of the endless months in Valmont. But the whole letter sounds very unhappy. Rilke says that he is making a great effort to recover from his indisposition. The dreadful noise made by the workmen in the hotel is upsetting him. Yet he is afraid to return to Muzot, even though he longs more than anything to shut himself up at home. But could he, in his nervous state, endure *'l'endroit rude et solitaire. . . . Et puis, et puis . . . je filerai vers la mer, vers le midi de la France . . . Peut-être qu'un grand changement me sauve de tous les démons dont je suis le jeu par trop facile.'*[34]

On November 7th Rilke's last publication appeared. It was the translation of Paul Valéry's prose piece *Tante Berthe*, which was published in the columns of the *Neue Zürcher Zeitung*.

The illness spread rapidly. The swellings which had re-appeared in the mucous membranes of his mouth and nose were now giving him a sore throat and a fearful cough. His digestive organs were giving trouble also. The poet had the impression that he was suffering from a severe attack of poisoning or influenza; he felt that his constitution *'se débarasse de quelque choses'*. But he would not see a doctor or take any medicine. He could not bear the idea of having to call upon his secretary to nurse him. In the same letter this everlastingly busy man tells his correspondent that he is reading with great interest the novel *Le démon impur*, by his French translator, Maurice Betz.[35]

Another letter in the poet's hand to Mme Wunderly – and then, on December 1st, his secretary Mlle Genia Tschernoswitow is writing to tell her that he is much worse:

I am writing to you in the deepest distress. Herr Rilke is in Valmont again, since yesterday afternoon. I went there with him. . . . That waiting for an improvement which never came, the pains which grew worse from day to day – what a nightmare! I shall never be able to give you an idea approaching the reality of what he has suffered during the last fortnight. Since last Saturday, when he saw Dr T., Herr Rilke suffered appallingly; he did not have a moment's respite until towards the end of the afternoon – but the evening, but the night, but the morning, especially the morning! As he had a terrible aversion to sending for a new doctor – whoever he might be – when he was in such a state of pain and apprehension, he saw that he had no choice but to go to Valmont.

. . . When I left him yesterday evening he was ashy grey and could not rest in any position. . . .

During the whole time in Sierre he showed extraordinary courage, and in spite of his weakness in face of physical pain – which he frankly admitted – he fought like a strong man.

PS. He was in such severe pain that he could not be examined this morning. It is unutterably terrible to leave him in such a state.[36]

5

DEATH AND BURIAL

DURING the first days in Valmont Rilke was not treated by his usual doctor, who returned from abroad, where he had been attending a medical congress, on December 9th. Rilke wanted to hide his illness from everyone. The only indication the public had that anything was wrong, before it heard the news of his death, was a short notice in the papers to the effect that Rainer Maria Rilke would not be standing for the German Academy of Poetry. Until the end he remained faithful to his freedom. On December 8th he wrote a letter in pencil to Mme Wunderly, in which the writing is laborious and completely irregular, almost unrecognisable. The recipient left for Valmont at once. Rilke had written (in the morning):

Très Chère,
  jour et nuit, jour et nuit: . . . l'Enfer! on l'aura connu! Merci que de tout votre être (je le sens) vous m'accompagnez dans ces regions anonymes.
  Le plus grave, le plus long: c'est d'abdiquer: devenir 'le malade'. Le chien malade est encore chien, toujours. Nous à partir d'un certain degré de souffrances insensées, sommes nous encore nous? Il faut devenir le malade, apprendre ce métier absurde sous l'oeil des médecins. C'est long! Et je ne serai jamais assez rusé pour en tiere profit! Dans cette affaire je perds.[37]

The rest of the letter is in German. It contains various requests and commissions. Rilke writes that for the time being he will have to call upon Werner Reinhart to help with the Valmont expenses; and that, with regard to the investment of his small legacy, he agrees to a proposal made by his Vienna friend Weininger and wishes to sign a declaration to that effect which Weininger has drawn up. Only he can 'do nothing now, not even sign properly. To think of business affairs impossible.' He had been asked a short while before to help with the founding of an international prize for literature, but he writes that he is too ill to promise anything at present, although he is ready to help Valéry with the judging – if that can be arranged.

On the same day (several hours later) he finished the letter. There are some more requests and then the words in brackets: '*encore un autre chapitre d'Enfer depuis ma lettre de ce matin!*' The last words:

Le Dr Théodore Haemmerli doit rentrer demain. Quelle surprise que je lui ménage là

> Le pauvre,
> > Adieu, Chère,
> > > Merci Merci
> > > > R.

In Valmont only the doctors, the nurse and Mme Wunderly were witnesses of the long, difficult death. Repeatedly, almost imploringly, the sick man asked that all visitors should be kept away from him, no matter who they might be, even those who had been closest to him. The thought that anyone might come to see him in that state, and commiserate with him, he found unendurable. Once again he expressed the wish not to see a priest. In the midst of the fearful agonies he was suffering he kept making plans for his journey to the South of France, to the Mediterranean. He himself dictated all the orders to his housekeeper at Muzot, with his usual exactness: above all he wanted clean linen and a quantity of books for the journey, which he intended to make as soon as possible.

The way he spoke to the intimate friends who were with him in those last days varied with the situation and with the phases of his illness. He welcomed his motherly friend on her arrival at Valmont with the joyful cry 'You are bringing me life!' But on another occasion: 'Help me to my own death, I don't want the doctor's death – I want my freedom ' And in the inferno of his illness he found strength to say, 'Don't ever forget, dear, life is a glory!' – As Christmas drew near he asked for a writing block and pencil, so that he could send news to some of his friends. None of these fairly numerous notes, written in a high fever and with a painful, bandaged arm, is in the literal sense a farewell letter; and yet these last lines, these faithful, unutterably sad tokens of remembrance, could hardly have been mistaken by the recipients for anything else. Accounts of his illness were only allowed to be sent to Lou Andreas-Salomé, whom Rilke trusted to have an almost supernatural understanding of what was going on inside his body and of the nature of his illness. Three letters came from her, but none contained a solution of the mystery that engrossed him – and his only comment on his old friend's letter as he held it in his hand was a rueful shake of the head. No, human beings could not help him any longer.

While there had been no definite symptoms of a blood disorder during his earlier attacks, after his arrival at Valmont an acute leukaemia was diagnosed – an incurable disease which in his case took a specially virulent form, unfamiliar to medical science. The illness began as an acute leukaemia often does: with a slight external injury leading to a septic skin infection. For Rilke it was a sad thought that his illness was caused by the prick of a rose thorn. As the illness took its course small black blisters, which burst open and bled, formed on different parts of his body. The mucous membranes of the nose and of the mouth right down into the oesophagus were full of these tiny blisters, so that it was a difficult matter to quench the invalid's thirst. (An attempt was made to feed liquids to him through fine glass tubes.) According to the doctor who attended him the pain he suffered was frightful. The black pustules were swabbed daily and the pustule-bearing areas treated lightly with cocaine. He twice asked to be shaved, and this was done for him with great difficulty. The nurse and Mme Wunderly had to take it in turns to read aloud to him. Sometimes when Mme Wunderly was reading to him in the afternoons from a volume of the *Cahiers verts*, which she often did for hours at a time, he would seem to fall asleep and she would stop; but then, in a tone almost of command, he would call out '*Continuez!*'

He had greeted Dr Haemmerli on his return with the words: 'Dear friend, how good that you are there, that you know what it is and that I can rely on you not to tell me.' And again: 'It is a comfort to me that you know what unheard-of tortures I am going through.' Although he refused to listen to words of comfort he wanted people to know what he was suffering. Rilke did not judge his illness by medical or physiological standards. He believed that tremendous happenings had occurred within him, which were now using this physical attack as a disguise in which to manifest themselves: 'We used to be such good friends, my body and I; I don't know how it is that we have drawn apart and become strangers to one another. For the past two years I have had the feeling and the absolute conviction that something immeasurable has been gathering force, which is now erupting.' The appearance of the pustules had frightened him, but it had also confirmed his belief that every man has his particular, unique illness. At the same time he did not on any account want to know what disease he was suffering from. He did not believe in bacteriological causes; he sublimated even this dreadful thing as he had sublimated everything else in his life, seeing it as part of a metaphysical occurrence. He did not want to be told of any deterioration in his condition or to be given any medicines or narcotics. For this reason when narcotics were used, as they had to be to deaden the pain of his treatment, great care had to be taken that he should not be allowed to cross over the borderline of consciousness.

It took a great deal of persuasion to get him to agree to a visit from a consultant. Dr Haemmerli had to promise that it would not be a doctor so conceited as to classify his illness like a schoolmaster: 'he can examine my blood if you like, but for God's sake do not let him give a professional explanation. Just think how terrible it would be if some pedant were to come and ruin all this with the banal comfort of a doctor's visit.' Two professors came to the poet's sickbed for a consultation, one from Zürich and the other from Leipzig, the latter at the request of the Insel-Verlag. Medical examinations caused him the greatest agony. It was literally a case of being flayed alive.

In his conversations with his doctor Rilke continually expressed anxiety lest this should be a no man's illness. That sickness and death are mysterious, tremendous happenings which have a reason and a meaning at some profound level and are not, therefore, likely to be identical in different men: this old idea of Rilke's seems to have occupied his thoughts continuously until the very end. It was remarkable, Dr Haemmerli says, how the sick man would always warily break off these conversations, all of a sudden, just as they reached the danger line beyond which death would have had to be mentioned. He was afraid, maybe, that the inconceivable was going to be pinned down by a medical term or even interrupted by a word of sympathy. The doctor was always pleased and moved to hear Rilke say, when he entered the room: 'There you are, my dear friend. You keep everything away, don't you?' Several times during the last few days he said to his doctor: 'Perhaps even yet Lou Salomé will understand what has happened.' Only by her, he thought, could the causes of his malady be understood.

For the above description I am indebted to Dr Haemmerli, who dictated it to me. As he wrote a full account of Rilke's last illness for the Princess Marie Taxis on February 25th 1927, a few weeks after the poet's death, I shall now give part of that statement (translated from the French) by the doctor who attended him:

. . . The disease was a very rare one, which in Rilke's case took a particularly painful form localised in the intestines, and presently causing black pustules to break out on the skin as in cases of general septicaemia. Later the mucous membranes of the mouth and nose were attacked by the same eruption; in short, our poor friend suffered for three weeks from the most painful symptoms. A simple nurse from Lausanne, whom he liked very much, looked after him, and Mme Wunderly, who stayed in Valmont, saw him for a few hours every day. In spite of his sufferings, he never thought until the last three days of his illness that he could not be saved. He was even planning to spend the winter by the sea. The thought of having to die was so terrible to him that he put it away, never once asking what disease he was suffering from and never once mentioning the possibility of dying – although at his request I would spend some time alone with him every day, when we spoke very intimately about his condition and his friends. In the course of these conversations I begged him to allow me to send you word of his illness, and Mme Wunderly did the same, but the idea horrified him. His only wish was not to see anyone who might make him realise the gravity of his condition, which he deliberately concealed from himself. In fact, I had the impression that he was longing every morning for me to assure him that he could be saved. He was so extraordinarily sensitive that the slightest doubt, which would sometimes strike him if I hesitated, caused him more suffering than his frightful malady itself; and the only way one could help him in his terrible situation was by leaving him until the last his serene plans for a convalescence. One managed, in accordance with his wish, to relieve his pain by the use of sedatives (*calmants*) without making him lose consciousness. For the last week he lay quietly with half-closed eyes, his mind lucid in spite of an almost unvarying temperature of 105 degrees. Until the fifth day before he died he would ask the nurse to read to him a little in the afternoon, nothing deep but things such as items of news from literary magazines, the *Revue des deux Mondes*, etc. He liked to spend the greater part of the day thinking, lying quietly with his eyes shut.

He resigned himself to his illness, more or less, as to an inevitable mystery which should not be analysed too deeply. In the morning, after I had dressed his wounds and examined him he liked me to stay with him, sometimes just to hold his hands and to give him my views on his constitution, his illness, and, above all, the possibility of a cure; while at other times he would tell me what he thought about medicine and doctors and, above all, about what was taking place within him. Having attended him very often and over a long period I knew how thoroughly he disapproved of the medical profession; our poor friend liked being able to express himself freely about this, as he knew that it would never give me offence nor impair my doctor's imagination in its attempt to save him.

As you perhaps know – and he knew it too – he was quite illogical in this respect. He liked you to know his opinions and at the same time to continue your efforts to cure him, on the condition that you did not let him feel that what you were doing was contrary to his ideas. . . . When we had come to an agreement he always took hold of my hands and said in an encouraging tone: 'Yes, my dear friend, now we will do everything in that way.'

On the last two days he was extremely weak. On December 28th from about 3 p.m. onward he began to doze, and he asked us to leave him in that state as long as possible, without letting him lose consciousness altogether. We had arranged that he should press my hands instead of answering me, as answering made him breathless. This dyspnoea was easily relieved by inhalations of oxygen. He dozed like that until coming on to midnight, when he lost consciousness; for three and a half hours he lay there unconscious with his eyes closed, breathing quietly but more and more feebly. At 3.30 a.m. he raised his head a little, his eyes wide open, and fell back dead into my arms. Mme Wunderly and the nurse were in the room.[38]

It is permissible to ask whether there are not certain contradictions in the accounts of Rilke's last illness. Dr Haemmerli was convinced that his patient had no thoughts of death until three days before he died, or that he found the thought of an early death terrible and waited longingly for an encouraging report from his doctor. There is also evidence that he made plans even from his sickbed to travel south and spend the rest of the winter in the mild climate of the Mediterranean. Furthermore, in the short greetings written laboriously in pencil to his closest friends before Christmas there was not a word of farewell nor a hint as to the gravity of his illness. All the same, when I received one of those friendly cards in Paris, in the second half of December, I had the feeling that Rilke was mortally ill; one could not explain his sad words in any other way. He had, too, spoken of death to Mme Wunderly-Volkart: 'Help me to my own death – I don't want the doctor's death – I want my freedom.' The truth of this report by his most intimate friend cannot be doubted. But why should he not have fostered and cherished the hope that the doctor could save him? He expected the doctor to help him, and he himself wanted to be helpful to the doctor. Rilke had reached the age when a healthy man is at his best: on December 4th he had completed his 51st year. Extraordinarily sensitive though he was, there was nothing of the hypochondriac about him. We know that he would have liked to go on living; when he had been feeling very bad in the autumn he had called, as it were, on the aged Rodin to witness posthumously to the fact that an artist's old age can still be productive. Rilke was, however, also aware that he had experienced all the heights and depths of life and that life, perhaps, had nothing more to offer. But right to the end he was convinced that life is a glorious thing. Far from yearning to leave it, he struggled against that cruel fate, but gradually he was made to feel that life was leaving him: Dr Haemmerli himself wrote to the Princess Taxis (and said to me also) that three days before his death the sick man had realised in his inmost heart that he was going to die. Rilke's strange ideas about sickness and his aversion to the medical conception of it made him anxious that the doctor should not tell him what illness he was suffering from; those labels with the foreign names which the profession attached to the different illnesses were profoundly repugnant to him.

According to a statement by Dr Haemmerli, which I took down at his dictation, Rilke asked him on one of the last days of his life:

You won't tell me how I am, will you? If I'm asleep when you come into the room, don't speak to me. But press my hand to let me know that you are there, and I will press your hand in return – like this – then you will know that I'm awake. If I don't press your hand, promise that you will sit me up and do something to make me regain consciousness.

Early in the morning of December 29th 1926, a Wednesday, Rainer Maria Rilke died. When one of those present opened the window, a cold wind blew in from Lake Geneva and the winter night outside.

On all who saw it the poet's dead body made a deep impression: the thin, almost brown face on which the blisters had left black specks, the wonderful forehead, still seeming in its nobility to be giving expression to the departed spirit, the almost black, few days' beard on the chin and the heavy eyelids closed over the great mystery – a hieratic head, which might have been that of a high-born Persian or Indian, a sage who had come from far to live a short life and who now, his martyrdom endured, was unbelievably lying lifeless on his deathbed. . . . A small, silver Russian cross, which he always had with him when he was alive, adorned the dead man's breast. Sprays from a laurel tree, then flowering in the midst of the Valmont snow, framed his face.

On a raw winter's night the coffin was carried from the clinic and lifted onto a sledge. The three people who, selflessly and faithfully, had stayed with him and tended him until his last breath, accompanied the body to a chapel where it lay in state. The old year had departed and the new begun before the poet's mortal remains left this spot, and were taken to their final resting-place in an automobile.

In accordance with the wish expressed in Rilke's will, his Zürich friends had reserved a grave for him 'for all time' at the foot of Raron Church. Although he had entrusted them with arranging for a grave and with the disposal of all his belongings left at Muzot, he had said nothing definite about the sort of funeral he wanted. That it would be Roman Catholic, however,

followed from the position of the grave against the wall of the
little old Church of Raron and from the fact that Catholicism
was the poet's own inherited religion. This church high up on
the mountain with its humble churchyard from which, with
whole-hearted response, he had once admired the broad valley
and the silver Rhone, had seemed to him the resting-place to
which he could entrust his tired body as to its native soil.

On Sunday, January 2nd 1927, those friends of the poet who
had not shrunk from the journey and who had to represent a
mourning world gathered in the little Valaisan mountain village.
Rainer Maria Rilke was laid in the ground without pomp,
without any official honours, as befitted one who all his life had
been free from worldly vanity.

The Valais is full of ringing bells, really full of chimes and melody.
It is almost frightening to look up at the towers, where men who
know nothing of giddiness are standing on the bells and swinging out
over the tower walls. Four men carry the coffin up the steep, icy
footpath to the little Church of Raron, while in front of them walks
the local magistrate with the wooden cross. The beautiful old customs
have to be observed. Not a soul in Raron knows the poet, yet how much
reverence surrounds the dead man.[39]

The coffin stood in the church during the quiet Mass. Organ
notes and Alma Moody's masterly violin playing made the
building resound with the music of Johann Sebastian Bach. It
had taken the sturdy gravediggers all their time to break through
the frozen soil. According to peasant custom children formed a
circle round the open grave.

Mercilessly, the clods of stony earth rumbled and thudded on the
lowered coffin. But those who were harrowed by these ruthless
moments may have been consoled to see the children holding up the
heavy wreaths, in hands blue with cold, throughout the stranger's
interment: with touching endurance holding them so high that they
did not touch the ground till we laid them on the grave, not to over-
burden it but to green it over.

In response to a request from the Swiss Writers' Association
and the Swiss Schiller Fund, Eduard Korrodi spoke some words
of praise, mourning and farewell[40]:

'. . . We stand here now, a few of us, at the grave of the poet beloved by countless numbers. In the courtesy of his heart he would not have wished to trouble his far-distant friends, who were yet so close to him, by calling them to his grave, because it was he himself who had put the distance between them, that distance which was never 'difficult' for him. Each of us therefore stands proxy for many distressed spirits, scattered over many lands, drawn into fellowship by the question: where shall he who never had a home find lodging 'for all time'? If I venture to utter a deeply felt word here in anyone's name, on whose behalf should I utter it if not of those countless anonymous people who entrust their grief and love to a voice, be it never so inadequate, longing to call after the dead man into the open ground that 'love which is stronger than the world' clings indestructibly to him, to him who in his generosity never failed to befriend and help people; and they, now that he is no more, have to comfort themselves with the fugue of his work, which outsounds and outlasts him.

With a word the speaker turned to 'those whose beloved dead the stranger now joins in the fellowship of the ground'. He laid to the heart of the Valais this nobleman, this poet 'before whom every praising voice falls silent', who had praised their country-side in his *Quatrains valaisans* and wished to rest in its rural peace from his great, quiet life. To Rainer Maria Rilke, who had sung of the Valais in a French poem, the speaker wished to bid farewell in the German language, faithfully preserved as the native speech of Raron. He ended his valedictory words with the lines from the First Elegy:

> They've finally no more need of us, the early-departed,
> one's gently weaned from terrestrial things as one mildly
> outgrows the breasts of a mother. But we, that have need of
> such mighty secrets, we, for whom sorrow's so often
> source of blessedest progress, could we exist without them?

René Morax spoke on behalf of friends from the French part of the country when he said at the edge of the open grave:

> '*Adieu, grand poète!*'

The harsh winter soil of a simple churchyard closed over this universally loved human being. His solitude had been restored to the poet, the deepest yet, never more to be broken. A grave

'for all time' had been reserved by his friends for this man who
in life had never laid claim to a permanent home.

The commotion and grief caused everywhere by Rilke's
passing exceeded anything that could have been expected. It is
impossible to conceive the extent of the echo which answered that
death knell from a remote little mountain church. There are only
a few instances in the history of poetry of a poet being so unani-
mously venerated, having written or verbal homage paid to him
by someone somewhere in almost every country in Europe. In
Austria and Czechoslovakia, in Germany and Switzerland, in
France, Italy and the Scandinavian countries, in Poland, even
in England which Rilke never saw, voices were uplifted in
mourning and homage. Many newspapers and periodicals had
pages or special numbers devoted to Rilke. All contained obitu-
aries. Commemorative gatherings were held in numerous cities.
In Vienna, in the Josephstadt Theatre, a memorial scene by
Alexander Lernet-Holenia was performed on January 23rd 1927.
In Paris, Edmond Jaloux spoke to his readers again about this
poet, telling them once more 'how great a phenomenon his
presence was; he seemed to be here in the world in which we live
as a continual miracle . . .'. In a commemorative speech in
Zürich Robert Faesi made some subtle and truthful observations
which, prior to any research, give the poet's image its final
stamp:

We must not deceive ourselves: this life was passion; quietly but
emphatically he gave his assent to a hard existence. Anyone born
under such a constellation is doomed to suffer. The extent of his
suffering he concealed in a way that was inexpressibly noble, proudly
modest, humbly chaste. Where his poetry is elegiac, is lamentation, it
laments not for himself but for the world.

'I was rather exhausted, one might almost say knocked up . . .',
'I am finding it rather difficult just now . . .'. In the notebooks of the
martyr-like Brigge these confessions of suffering, muted by weakness,
correspond almost literally with the discreetly veiled phrases in
which Thomas Mann's 'Royal Highness' hints at the exhaustion
which he finds it such an effort to bear. And the way in which the
greatest German novelist of our time wants us to see his hero is the

way in which we must see Rilke, that is, as an eminent example not of robust greatness but of what may be called highness: 'elect, melancholy isolated forms of life whom one is asked to approach with the most delicate sympathy': as a hero of weakness, of endurance.

In the same way that he interiorized everything, Rilke interiorized the conception of bearing. When he brings the calm, controlled dignity of the aristocratic cultures to life again in his poetic portraits of cornets, generals and doges, in his evocation of Biblical kings and western grandees, it is his own dignity that he is portraying. Simpler, quieter, without the least trace of pomposity, never for a moment exaggerated as it was never for a moment abandoned, that dignity of his was yet unmistakable.

It was an attitude which clothed the downward trajectory of his fate, even his long dying, with knightly steadfastness. At no time did he seek to break away from the fearful clutches and purgatorial fire of 'this world'!

Without the slightest resentment against life, even with a painful tender love for it, he remained faithful to the world. Truly that is a decision of the utmost importance, and if we consider how sensitive to pain he was and how full of ardent desires it becomes doubly meritorious. To him the world was his task, the task which had been set him. His ethos: not to resist, more: to be willing, ready, open. It was the passive heroism of the destiny lover, the feminine surrender.[41]

The most striking thing about Rilke's obituary notices, the speeches and expressions of sorrow following his death, from wheresoever or whomsoever they came, was their astonishing uniformity. The most dissimilar people said similar if not identical things about this unique soul, this poet who gave so much delight. They spoke of his wonderfully balanced humanity, the expanse and gentleness of his spirit and his incredibly subtle art. All testify that he taught his contemporaries to see things, to recognise relationships, to love what is fine, to be aware of depths, and to discover the hidden ways of the human soul, and that he did this with a gentle but sure conviction. The dead man remained among the living as a signpost, as one who sees and knows, but at the same time as an inimitable example of noble nature and bearing; and it will be as unnecessary as it is impossible to imitate him if only we move in the direction in which he pointed, developing those quieter, deeper regions of the human psyche which were his marvellous realm.

We must never forget those words spoken by the dying, patiently suffering man on his bed of anguish: 'Life is a glory!'

AUTHOR'S NOTES

SPELLING AND PUNCTUATION

When quoting from original MSS. or photostats of these we have in every case faithfully reproduced Rilke's spelling and punctuation. Ernst Zinn did the same when editing Rilke's *Briefwechsel mit der Fürstin Marie von Thurn und Taxis*, so that our quotations from that edition may be taken as philologically accurate. When quoting from published sources, in particular the Insel-Verlag letters, we have had to keep the publishers' emendations, as the originals were not available to us.

ABBREVIATIONS

A.W. = Rainer Maria Rilke's *Ausgewählte Werke*, edited by Ernst Zinn, 2 volumes, Insel-Verlag 1948.

G.Br. = Rainer Maria Rilke's *Gesammelte Briefe* in six volumes, Insel-Verlag, Leipzig (chiefly vols. IV, V and VI, published in 1936, 1937 and 1938).

Briefwechsel Thurn und Taxis = *Rainer Maria Rilke und Marie von Thurn und Taxis, Briefwechsel*, 2 volumes, edited by Ernst Zinn, Niehans- & Rokitansky-Verlag and Insel-Verlag, 1951.

Bassermann = Dieter Bassermann, *Der Späte Rilke*, 2nd ed., Verlag Dr Hans von Chamier, Essen and Freiburg i. Br., 1948.

RAINER MARIA RILKE IN SWITZERLAND

1. R. M. Rilke, *Briefe*, Insel-Verlag, 1950, Vol. II, 14
2. To Dr Wilhelm Mühlon, Soglio, August 19th (unpub.)
3. *Briefe an eine Reisegefährtin, Eine Begegnung mit R. M. Rilke*, ed. Ulrich Keyn, Alfred Ibach-Verlag, Vienna 1947
4. *Briefwechsel Thurn und Taxis*, pp. 430-431
5. Ibid., 521-522
6. Ibid., 557
7. Ibid., 541
8. Quoted by Bassermann, 172
9. Ibid., 51, and G.Br., II, 336
10. *Bassermann*, 70
11. *Briefwechsel Thurn und Taxis*, 345
12. R. M. Rilke, *Briefe*, Insel-Verlag, 1950, Vol. II, 201

13. Ibid., 61

13a. On the years 1914-16, i.e. on Rilke's life in Munich, in Vienna and Rodaun and his relations with the Hofmannsthals, cf. Lou Albert-Lasard *Wege mit Rilke*, S. Fischer-Verlag, Frankfurt a.M., 1952.

14. Cf. the special Rilke number of the Paris periodical *Les Lettres*, anno IV, Nos. 14, 15, 16, Paris 1952.

15. *Briefwechsel Thurn und Taxis*, 543

16. *Bassermann*, 61

17. R. M. Rilke, *Briefe*, Vol. II, 109

18. Ibid., 110

19. Ibid., 111

20. To Dr K., Munich, November 1918 (unpub.)

21. R. M. Rilke, *Briefe*, Vol. II, 113

22. Ibid.

23. *Briefwechsel Thurn und Taxis*, 570

24. Lou Andreas-Salomé, *Rainer Maria Rilke*, Insel-Verlag of Leipzig 1928, 87

25. G.Br., VI (*Briefe an seinen Verleger*), 303

26. Quoted by Bassermann, 142

27. G.Br., IV, 251-252

28. Ibid., 269

29. Ibid., 264

30. *Briefe an eine Reisegefährtin* 22-23. Dated: Zürich, Eden au Lac, June 13th 1909

31. G.Br., IV, 259

32. G.Br., VI, 292

33. *Briefe an eine Reisegefährtin*, 39-40

34. G.Br., IV, 271-272

35. *Briefe an eine Reisegefährtin*, 66-74. The reference is to Alexander Sacharow, a dancer who was very successful at the time, and whom Rilke had known since his Munich days. – Ferruccio Busoni has dedicated an essay on the aesthetics of music to Rilke.

36. See 2

37. Inga Junghanns, *Persönliche Errinerungen an R. M. Rilke*, 'Orplid', Rilke special number, anno III, 1927

38. G.Br., VI, 304

39. *Der Kleine Bund*, Bern, January 9th 1927 (not included in the G.Br.)

40. See 2

41. G.Br., VI, 248

42. G.Br., IV, 253

43. G.Br. 259

44. See 2. At Soglio Rilke made the acquaintance of Frau G. Nölke, who, with her children, was staying in the same house as the poet; he kept in touch with her afterwards and they exchanged letters. His letters to her are among the best, clearest and most revealing of all those belonging to his years in Switzerland. They will be published shortly by the Insel-Verlag under the title: *R. M. Rilke, Briefe an Frau G. Nölke, Ein Beitrag zur Biographie von Rilkes Schweizer Jahren,* * edited by Paul Obermüller. I am grateful to the publishers for their co-operation in allowing me to see copies of these letters before publication and to make use of them in this new edition of my book. I cannot, of course, refer to page numbers in the published book, and so am confining myself to giving only the dates of my quotations. I express my thanks to Herr Paul Obermüller for this outstanding piece of helpfulness, and for his generous co-operation.

45. *Erinnerung*, in A.W., II, 271

46. Ibid.

47. *Ur-geräusch*, in A.W., II, 248

48. *Bassermann*, 204

49. To Frau Nanny Wunderly-Volkart, Locarno, undated (February 1920) (unpub.)

50. See 39

51. G.Br., IV, 273-276

52. G.Br., IV, 275. Marthe Hennebert later married the painter Lurçat

53. *Briefe an eine Reisegefährtin*, 103, from Zürich, November 4th 1919

54. MS. in the Rilke Archive, quoted by Bassermann, 375-376 (italics Rilke's)

55. *Briefe an eine Reisegefährtin*, 101

56. G.Br., VI, 298

57. To Mme Nanny Wunderly-Volkart, Bern, November 1919 (unpub.)

* See note, p. 18.

58. To the same, Lucerne, November 14th 1919 (unpub.)

58a. On the same day in a letter to Frau G. Nölke this remark about Mme Wunderly: 'I have come by several people, but only acquired a single one who was genuine and natural, a woman, mother of quite a big lad . . . but small, graceful, young.'

59. To Mme Nanny Wunderly-Volkart, Locarno, January 17th 1920 (unpub.)

60. To the same, Locarno, December 28th 1919 (unpub.)

61. To the same, Locarno, January 9th 1920 (unpub.)

62. To the same, Locarno, December 12th 1919 (unpub.). The woman in Locarno who aroused Rilke's pity, and whom he tried so hard to help that he reduced himself to a state of bewilderment, was called Angela Guttman. He did not continue this acquaintance.

63. To the same, Locarno, December 25th 1919 (unpub.)

64. To the same, Locarno, February 24th 1920 (unpub.)

65. 'Schönenberg' bei Pratteln (Basle-Land) belonged to Frau Burckhardt-Schazmann. Her daughter, Frau Dory von der Mühll, was anxious to help Rilke and offered him this house. With her son, Carl J. Burckhardt, Rilke also formed a close friendship. Cf. Regina Ullmann, *Erinnerungen an Rilke*, Tschudy-Verlag, St Gallen, 2nd ed. (no date), where a speech by Carl J. Burckhardt is printed in which he tells how Rilke at Schönenberg read aloud to his hosts Regina Ullmann's masterly story *Von einem alten Wirtshausschild*. It was at the house of these friends that Rilke met Hugo von Hofmannsthal in Basle.

66. To Frau G. Nölke, Schönenberg bei Pratteln, March 22nd 1920

67. To the same, Schönenberg bei Pratteln, April 20th 1920

68. Ibid.

69. Ibid.

70. *Briefwechsel Thurn und Taxis*, 602

71. To Frau G. Nölke, Venice, Palazzo Valmarana, June 24th 1920

72. *Briefwechsel Thurn und Taxis*, 611

73. Ibid.

74. Lou Andreas-Salomé, *Rainer Maria Rilke*, 73

75. To Mme Nanny Wunderly-Volkart, Venice, July 6th 1920 (unpub.)

76. Rilke developed these ideas during the course of a conversation with the author at Muzot. See also in a letter to Anton Kippenberg from Venice, G.Br., 306.

77. G.Br., VI, 306

78. To Mme Nanny Wunderly-Volkart, Venice, July 6th 1920 (unpub.)

79. To the same, Venice, July 8th 1920 (unpub.)

80. To the same, Geneva, August 20th 1920 (unpub.)

81. Rilke's letters to Mme Klossowska for the years 1919-22 have appeared in a selection with the title: *Lettres françaises à Merline*, Paris, Editions du Seuil, 1950. A more comprehensive, though still incomplete, edition of the correspondence between Rilke and Mme Klossowska is at present in preparation with the Max Niehans-Verlag in Zürich.

82. See 80

83. To Mme Nanny Wunderly-Volkart, Bern, August 22nd 1920 (unpub.)

84. Ibid.

85. To Mme Nanny Wunderly-Volkart, Bern, August 27th 1920 (unpub.)

86. Rainer Maria Rilke *Les Fenêtres*, with etchings by Baladine (Mme Klossowska), Librairie de France, Paris 1927 (and since reprinted in the volumes *Poèmes français* and *Gesammelte Gedichte*)

87. Rilke, who had to thank Mme Wunderly-Volkart's initiative for the hospitality of Schloss Berg am Irschel, lived there as the guest of Col. Richard Ziegler and his wife Frau Lily Ziegler to whom the castle belonged at the time.

88. To Frau Lily Ziegler, Bern, October 17th 1920 (unpub.)

89. Ibid.

90. G.Br., VI, 311. Rilke says in various letters that he stayed in Paris for six days. He arrived there on October 22nd 1920. On October 30th he was again writing from Geneva. He may have left on the 29th. It was characteristic of him that during those days he took no steps to find out what had happened to the belongings left behind in his 1914 flat and put up to auction during the war – a fate from which two boxes with papers and personal things were saved, thanks to the caretaker. A letter from Paris informed him of this rescue seven months later, when he was living in Switzerland.

91. G.Br., VI, 311
92. To Mme Nanny Wunderly-Volkart, Paris, Hôtel Foyot, 33 rue
    de Tournon, October 25th 1920 (unpub.). Rilke returned to
    the same hotel in 1925, when he spent several months in
    Paris. Since then the Hôtel Foyot has been pulled down.

HEALING AND NEW BEGINNING

1. Several letters from Berg am Irschel in the G.Br. IV and VI and
   in *Briefwechsel Thurn und Taxis*
2. *Der Kleine Bund* (Bern) for January 9th 1927
3. Ibid.
4. Ibid.
5. To Frau Lily Ziegler, Berg am Irschel, November 20th 1920
   (unpub.)
6. To Georg Reinhart, Berg am Irschel, December 30th 1920, in
   Das Graphische Kabinett, XII, Year 4, 1927 no. (Winterthur)
7. G.Br., IV, 345-346
8. *Briefwechsel Thurn und Taxis*, 627
9. Ibid., 628
10. See 5
11. See 5
12. To Frau Lily Ziegler, Berg am Irschel, December 2nd 1920
    (unpub.)
13. To the same, Berg am Irschel, December 26th 1920 (unpub.)
14. The coat of arms described by Rilke is that of the Hirzel family
    of Zürich.
15. See 7
16. See 7
17. To Mme Nanny Wunderly-Volkart, Berg am Irschel, November
    21st 1920 (unpub.)
18. To Frau Lily Ziegler, Berg am Irschel, December 23rd 1920
    (unpub.)
19. Cf. Robert Faesi, *Rilke der Briefschreiber*, in a publication in
    honour of Emil Ermatinger, *Dichtung und Forschung*, Huber
    & Co., Frauenfeld and Leipzig.
20. To Mme Nanny Wunderly-Volkart, Locarno, January 17th 1920
    (unpub.)
21. *Mitsou, Quarante images par Baltusz, Préface de Rainer Maria
    Rilke*, Rotapfel-Verlag, Erlenbach-Zürich and Leipzig, 1921

22. To Charles Vildrac, Berg am Irschel, December 13th 1920, original French, in *Les Lettres*, special Rainer Maria Rilke number, Paris 1952, p. 35.

23. Rilke first recounted this happening to Anton Kippenberg, when the latter visited him at Berg (January 22nd-24th 1921). After the poet's death Kippenberg repeated it to me. He has confirmed it again – with unimportant modifications – in the notes to Rilke's *Briefe an seinen Verleger*. Cf. G.Br., VI, note 326.

24. Now Poem X in the first part of the little book: Rainer Maria Rilke, *Aus dem Nachlass des Grafen C. W., Ein Gedichtkreis*, Insel-Verlag, 1950

25. The experience was noted down at the beginning of 1913, in A.W., II, 256.

26. Lou Andreas-Salomé, *Lebensrückblick*, Max-Niehans-Verlag Zürich and Insel-Verlag Wiesbaden, 1951, 167. For Rilke's attitude to the occult, see his detailed letter to Nora Purtscher-Wydenbruck, G.Br., V, 288, and his *Briefwechsel mit der Fürstin Thurn und Taxis*. Cf. the article by Gabriel Marcel, 'Rilke et l'occulte', in the special Rilke number of *Les Lettres*, Paris 1952, 136.

27. To Mme Nanny Wunderly-Volkart, Berg am Irschel, November 30th 1920 (unpub.)

28. Ibid.

29. Published in full in the little book mentioned in Note 24.

30. To Mme Nanny Wunderly-Volkart, Prieuré d'Etoy, May 26th and 27th 1921 (unpub.)

31. To Frau G. Nölke, Berg am Irschel, February 19th 1921

32. Ibid.

33. *Briefwechsel Thurn und Taxis*, 638-639. See also G.Br., IV, 380-381.

34. *Bassermann*, 205-206

35. G.Br., IV, 376-377

36. To Frau Lily Ziegler, Berg am Irschel, February 1921 (unpub.)

37. To the same, Berg am Irschel, November 23rd 1920

38. Ibid.

39. Rilke himself called the letters he wrote to Mme Wunderly-Volkart from Etoy 'journal' and 'diary-letters' (unpub.).

40. To Mme Nanny Wunderly-Volkart, Prieuré d'Etoy, Whit Monday (post-mark May 17th) 1921 (unpub.)

41. Ibid.

42. On February 3rd 1914 Rilke mentions the volume *Du côté de chez Swann* by Marcel Proust (published at that time by Bernard Grasset, Paris); he calls it 'an incomparable, strange book by a new author', and advises the Insel-Verlag to acquire the translation rights 'without delay'. Rilke mentions this novel to the Princess Taxis for the first time in a letter dated January 21st 1914, giving her a lengthy account of it (*Briefwechsel Thurn und Taxis*, 348). He converted the Princess into an enthusiastic admirer of Proust, and the volumes of Proust's *A la recherche du temps perdu* are mentioned over and over again in their correspondence. In Rilke's unpublished letters to Mme Wunderly-Volkart this writer is also mentioned several times, at greatest length on the occasion of Proust's death. An important evaluation of Proust may be found also in Rilke's letter to Prince Hohenlohe, where he writes: 'I was by chance . . . one of the first (1913!) to read *Du côté de chez Swann*, and therefore one of the first to admire Marcel Proust, which was the natural, immediate consequence of that reading. In connection with Proust's death, I reminded André Gide the other day that I had my place among the earliest admirers of that great poet . . .' (G.Br., 175-176).

43. The *Cahiers verts*, edited by Daniel Halévy, published by Bernard Grasset, Paris.

44. To Mme Nanny Wunderly-Volkart, undated, *Vendredi* (unpub.) Some of Rilke's letters to Pastor Rudolf Zimmermann appeared in a publication of the Olten Literary Circle, under the title: *Rainer Maria Rilke, Briefe*, Olten 1945.

45. *Briefwechsel Thurn und Taxis*, 662-663

46. To Frau G. Nölke, Prieuré d'Etoy, May 22nd 1921

47. See 40

48. *Treue und Ehre, Geschichte der Schweizer in fremden Diensten*, by P. de Valières, Verlag Zahn, Neuchâtel. (A new edition of this work has since been published.)

49. By the 'Almanach' is meant the *Schweizerische Geschlechterbuch* (*Almanach généalogue suisse*).

50. L. B. de Muralt, 1665-1749, author of the *Lettres sur les Anglais et les Français* (1728) and the *Lettres sur les voyages et sur l'esprit fort* (date 1753)

51. See 40

52. Rilke spoke to the author at Muzot of the great importance which Thomas Mann's novel about the downfall of a family had had for him in his youth. When it first appeared Rilke reviewed *Buddenbrooks* for the *Bremer Tageblatt* of April 16th 1902 (this article is included in the volume *Rainer Maria Rilke, Bücher, Theater, Kunst*, issued privately by Richard von Mises, 1934).

52a. Hans Egon Holthusen, *Der späte Rilke*, Verlag der Arche Zürich, 1949, 12-13

53. *Briefwechsel Thurn und Taxis*, 651

54. See 46. Lernet's *Kanzonnair* was published by the Insel-Verlag.

55. G.Br., IV, 400-403 and 419. Rolf Freiherr von Ungern-Sternberg's translation of Jean Moréas' poems was published by the Wir-Verlag, Berlin 1922.

56. Marie von Thurn und Taxis, *Erinnerungen an Rainer Maria Rilke*, Verlag Oldenbourg, Munich-Berlin-Zürich 1932, 89.

57. Ibid., 89-90. Cf. Rilke's letters to 'Merline' (Mme Klossowska), who is referred to here (cf. Note 81 to the previous chapter).

58. See 46. Rilke had never been to Carinthia.

59. G.Br., IV, 399

60. Marie Thurn und Taxis, *Erinnerungen*, 83

61. See 40

62. See 60

THE CHATEAU OF MUZOT AND THE COMPLETION OF THE DUINO ELEGIES

1. To Mme Nanny Wunderly-Volkart, Geneva, October 14th 1920 (unpub.)

2. To the same, Lausanne, July 4th 1921 (unpub.)

3. To the same, Sierre, July 15th 1921 (unpub.)

4. Ibid.

5. This is a description of Muzot at the time when Rilke was living there. Since then there have been various alterations, though none which affects the character of the house, while conveniences such as running water, electric light and telephone have been installed.

6. To Mme Nanny Wunderly-Volkart, Sierre, July 20th 1921 (unpub.)

7. To the same, Sierre, July 25th 1921 (unpub.)

8. Ibid.

9. G.Br., VI, 341, 348

10. To Mme Nanny Wunderly-Volkart, Muzot, July 30th 1921 (unpub.)

11. The reference is to a fifteen-year-old local boy called Alphonse Essayé.

12. See 10

13. Ibid.

14. G.Br., V, 15

15. G.Br., V, 25

16. To Guido von Salis-Seewis, Muzot, November 30th 1921 (unpub.)

17. *Briefwechsel Thurn und Taxis*, 677

18. G.Br., VI, 349. In the later editions of Rilke's letters to his publisher gaps occur which are probably due not only to the omission of family affairs and other things connected with Rilke's private life, but also of money matters. Anton Kippenberg, who was afraid of giving the impression that the Insel-Verlag had not made adequate provision for Rilke, wrote to me when the first edition of this book was published saying that he had 'sent our poet rather small amounts in francs, small from the Swiss point of view, very large if one takes into account the value in German currency at the time'. During the inflation period the Insel-Verlag had also looked after Rilke's dependents living in Germany. From 1924 onwards, until the end of his life, the Verlag had again been able to transfer quite large sums to him in Switzerland. Rilke told me at Muzot that during the inflation period it had been difficult and at times impossible to get money across to him. He said furthermore that Werner Reinhart had put Muzot at his disposal as a dwelling-place but that otherwise he had had to fend for himself. C. A. Mennicke, in his book *Der Mensch im All, eine Einführung in das Verständnis Rainer Maria Rilkes*, Amsterdam 1937, pp. 9-10, gives an accurate account of the poet's material circumstances: 'There is something improbable too, about the *outward* course of this life at a time when the pursuit of material security absorbs so much energy in the personal as well as the social sphere. But here is a man who obstinately refuses to follow any calling – and yet is very far

from being rich enough to live independently. Here is someone who insists on being allowed to work at the fulfilment of his nature and his creative vocation – his studies and his journeys, his impressions and his encounters, being in the last resort nothing but means to that end. By his lack of concern with the outward course of his life this man flung down a challenge to destiny – which is no discredit to him. His friends could not do otherwise than continue to provide him with conditions favourable to the fulfilment of his artistic . . . vocation – while he put their patience and their faith to ever harder and harder tests. In this life outward existence was sustained and determined from within, recalling modes of living which seem almost to have disappeared.'

19. G.Br., V, 51. In the same letter Rilke writes affectionately of his daughter Ruth to a mutual friend in Munich (ibid., pp. 46-47). Rilke's granddaughter Christine Sieber, whom he mentions in his letters, died at an early age after the Second World War. Both his other grandchildren, a girl and a boy, were born after his death.

20. Lou Andreas-Salomé, *Lebensrückblick*, 169

21. This poem has only recently become known. L. Albert-Lasard published it, together with fifteen other poems written during the war years, in her book *Wege mit Rilke* (1952), p. 82.

22. Ibid., 81

23. Quoted by Bassermann, 368

24. G.Br., V, 35-36

25. *Bassermann*, 248

26. Monique Saint-Hélier, *A Rilke pour Noël*, Berne, Editions du Chandelier, 1927, 21

27. G.Br., V, 83. The letter is from Muzot, dated December 29th 1921 and addressed to Lou Andreas-Salomé. Rilke does not mention this translation in another letter written on November 26th, although he has a great deal to say there about Valéry (G.Br., V, 53). Marie von Thurn und Taxis for her part speaks of Rilke reading the translation of the *Cimetière marin* aloud to her at Etoy (also in June 1921. *Erinnerungen an R. M. Rilke*, 89). It is probable, however, that there is a mistake here and that Rilke only translated this poem in December, at Muzot.

28. To Mme Nanny Wunderly-Volkart, undated, early in January 1922 (unpub.)

29. There is a detailed description of Rilke's relations with the Ouckama Knoop family in Bassermann, 428-436. Bassermann knew about Frau Ouckama Knoop's account of Wera's death, and how much Rilke's *Sonette an Orpheus* were influenced by that report on an illness.

30. This information is taken from the entry in Rilke's handwriting in Mme Nanny Wunderly-Volkart's copy of the *Duineser Elegien*. Normally when putting dates to Rilke's poems we follow Ernst Zinn's dating in the *Ausgewählte Werke*.

31. To Mme Nanny Wunderly-Volkart, Muzot, postmark February 8th 1922 (unpub.)

32. G.Br., V, 112. The telegram to this friend was handed in by Rilke at 5.10 p.m. on February 9th.

33. To Mme Nanny Wunderly-Volkart, Muzot, February 10th 1922, morning, *Vendredi* (unpub.). According to Ernst Zinn's dating (A.W., I, 423), the Sixth and Ninth Elegies were written on February 9th, as well as the original Fifth (*Gegenstrophen*) which he later replaced with the *Saltimbanques*. Earlier fragments of the Sixth, Ninth and Tenth Elegies were in existence, but not of the Eighth. Rilke began with the Seventh Elegy on February 7th, the Eighth followed on February 7th-8th, finally the Tenth Elegy on February 11th. The *Saltimbanques*, which replaced the *Gegenstrophen* as the Fifth Elegy, was written on February 14th.

34. G.Br., VI, 354-355

35. *Lettres françaises à Merline*, 179

36. See 33

37. *Briefwechsel Thurn und Taxis*, 697-698

38. To Mme Nanny Wunderly-Volkart, Muzot, February 12th 1922 (unpub.)

39. To the same, Muzot, February 15th 1922 (unpub.)

40. Rilke hardly ever mentioned Lou Andreas to other people, in letters or conversations; he preserved strict secrecy about his love-affair, dating back to 1897, with this woman fourteen years his senior. It was she who first gave the secret away in her posthumously published book *Lebensrückblick* (1951, p. 173 ff 'April, *our* month, Rainer . . .'). Apart, however, from the short interruption caused by Rilke's marriage to Clara Westhoff (1901), the relationship between Rilke and Lou, carried on by meetings and letters, continued until the poet's death. Rilke's boundless faith in this outstanding and

deeply wise woman, who had so much insight into his nature, and his well-founded admiration for her, are common knowledge today. From the poet's very rare utterances about Lou we may select the following, from the year 1913, as being thoroughly typical of his estimate of her: 'Then I was in Göttingen for a week with Lou Andreas-Salomé, of that I could tell you a great deal – the most wonderful things, what splendours that woman is able to perceive, how she turns everything that books or people bring her at the right moment to the most ecstatic comprehension, understands, loves, goes fearlessly among the most burning secrets, which do her no harm, which only cast a pure glow upon her. I know and have known since those distant years when I first met her, a meeting which was to be so infinitely important for me, no one else so entirely in harmony with life, recognising in what is gentlest and most terrible the *one* force, which conceals itself but always, even when it kills, wants to give . . .' (*Briefwechsel Thurn und Taxis*, 303-304).

If, from all the women who played a part in Rilke's life, it is possible to single out one and to say of her that she was *the* woman in his life, that person is certainly Lou Salomé. That the poet's opinion of her was not simply an emotional one is clear from the impression she made on other outstanding men of the time, among whom Nietzsche and Siegmund Freud are the best known. That Rilke was silent about Nietzsche and took no notice of him, inasmuch as he did not read his works, may have been connected with the unjust and mean attack on Lou made by Nietzsche's sister Elisabeth Foerster and her collaborator at the Nietzsche Archive, Peter Gast. The editor of Lou's *Lebensrückblick*, Ernst Pfeiffer, put these matters right, after that noble woman had kept silent about them all her life. It was Rilke's way, too, to keep silent when he encountered human ill-will and unpleasantness; he said nothing about the Foerster attack on Lou Andreas, while he shared approvingly, from a distance, her friendship with Siegmund Freud. It is a pity that serious Rilke commentators, among them even Bassermann, have continued this unjustified denigration of Lou Andreas's character, or else, like Dr Else Buddenberg, have failed through a dislike of the psychological approach to recognise the important contribution that Lou Andreas made to our knowledge of Rilke.

41. Rilke is referring here to an experience shared by Lou and

himself during their journey to Russia in 1900. Lou Andreas writes – in her *Lebensrückblick*, 177 – that they had seen 'the horse turned out to grass for the night with a cruel block of wood tied to its hoof' in a meadow outside the village of Kresta Bogoródskoje near Jaroslawl on the Upper Volga, where Rilke and Lou spent a few days together in an isbá.

42. Ernst Zinn in his epilogue to Rilke's *Ausgewählte Werke*, Vol. II, 408.

43. See 39

44. On February 20th 1922, G.Br., V, 119

45. Quoted by Bassermann, 476 (original in Rilke Archive)

46. G.Br., V, 50 (on June 28th 1915, Munich, Widenmayerstrasse 32). Pablo Picasso's painting belonged at that time to Frau Hertha König, to whom Rilke dedicated the Fifth Elegy. It is well known by the name *La famille des saltimbanques* and was painted in 1905. Now it belongs to the Art Institute of Chicago; cf. the essay by Peter H. von Blanckenhagen *Rilke und 'La famille des saltimbanques' von Picasso* in *R. M. Rilke und die bildende Kunst*, Volume 24 of the *Kunstwerk-Schriften*, Klein -Verlag, Baden-Baden 1951 (with a reproduction of the painting).

47. Hans Egon Holthusen, *Der späte Rilke*, Arche-Verlag, Zürich 1949, 18. After the great interpretations of the Elegies by E. Mason, D. Bassermann, R. Guardini, E. Buddenberg and others, we consider this short, closely packed little book, with its wide intellectual range, to be one of the best interpretations of Rilke's later work. This poetry found its true situation on the spiritual map when it was assigned an outstanding place not only in German poetry – though perhaps for the first time there with such sovereign certainty – but in the literature of the world, especially that of France, England and America.

48. Ibid., 19

49. To Mme Nanny Wunderly-Volkart, Muzot, Saturday, postmark February 18th 1922 (unpub.)

50. G.Br., V, 120 (to Lou Andreas-Salomé, on February 27th 1922)

51. See 47-48, p. 15

52. G.Br., V, 119-120

53. Lou Andreas-Salomé, *Rainer Maria Rilke*, 98-99

54. Ibid., 80

55. Inscription in Nanny Wunderly-Volkart's copy of the *Duineser Elegien*. Now: A.W. I, 404. Dated by Ernst Zinn: January 1922 and December 1923.

THE MAGIC TOWER

1. G.Br., V, 156

2. G.Br., V, 415

3. Maurice Martin du Gard, 'Une heure avec Rainer Maria Rilke', in the *Nouvelles Littéraires*, Paris 1925

4. To Mme Nanny Wunderly-Volkart, Sierre, June 28th 1922 (unpub.)

5. To Lulu Albert-Lasard, in *Wege mit Rilke*, 46. Rilke used much the same words in writing about this assassination to Mme Wunderly.

6. To Frau G. Nölke, Muzot, October 31st 1922. The active, practical care that Rilke bestowed on both the Klossowski boys appears in his letters to Frau Nölke, who at Rilke's suggestion had the elder of the two brothers, Pierre, to stay with her.

7. To Mme Nanny Wunderly-Volkart, Muzot, October 29th 1922 (unpub.)

8. To Frau G. Nölke, Muzot, December 1st 1922

9. To Mme Nanny Wunderly-Volkart, Muzot, postmark December 15th 1922 (unpub.)

10. Ibid.

11. To Frau G. Nölke, Locarno, February 22nd 1920

12. G.Br., V, 180-181

13. To Frau G. Nölke, Muzot, February 12th 1923

14. Ibid.

15. To Mme Nanny Wunderly-Volkart, Muzot, undated (January 1923) (unpub.)

16. Ibid.

17. To Mme Nanny Wunderly-Volkart, Muzot, February 11th 1923 (unpub.)

18. G.Br., V, 385 (December 18th 1925)

19. G.Br., V, 236 (February 15th 1924)

20. See 12

21. To Mme Nanny Wunderly-Volkart, Muzot, undated (January 1923) (unpub.)

22. In a special number of the *Neue Zürcher Zeitung*: 'In Memoriam R. M. Rilke', Zürich 1927.

23. Rudolf Kassner in the Rilke memorial number of the *Inselschiff*, April 1927, 121-122

24. Rilke's letter to Georges Brandes from Paris, November 28th 1909, is only printed in the first edition of Rilke's *Briefe aus den Jahren* 1907-1914 (Insel-Verlag, 1933). This letter to the Danish Jew Brandes no longer appears in the 'purged' edition of the *Gesammelte Briefe* published under the National-Socialist régime. A letter written to André Gide in 1914 is also left out of the G.Br. In our account of the relationship between Gide and Rilke we are following Mme Renée Lang's study in the special Rilke number of *Les Lettres* (1952), 148 ff. Mme Lang must today be regarded as the leading authority on Rilke's relationship with literary France, which is to say with Gide and Paul Valéry; a larger publication on this theme from the pen of the same literary historian is due to appear shortly.

25. *Les Lettres*, loc. cit., 150

26. J. Gebser had the merit of being the first to call attention to the 'a-perspective' element in Rilke's poetic vision, and to connect it with the change in modern man's conception of the universe, especially as seen by theoretic physics. Holthusen in his essay *Der späte Rilke* confirms this parallel between Rilke's strange new version of the poetic world-image and modern science's refusal to be bound by Euclidean geometry.

27. G.Br., V, 294

28. Renée Lang, *Les Lettres*, loc. cit. 154

29. André Gide, *Incidences*, Paris, Verlag N.R.F., 1924, 65

30. Ibid.

31. Ibid., 207

32. Bassermann, 415

33. Ibid. Unfortunately nothing is yet known of the correspondence between Rilke and Paul Valéry, which began in 1921.

34. See 13

35. To Mme Nanny Wunderly-Volkart, Muzot, March 26th 1923 (unpub.)

36. To the same, Muzot, May 16th 1923 (unpub.)

37. To the same, Kuranstalt Schöneck (Lake Lucerne), August 23rd 1923 (unpub.)

38. To the same, Lucerne, Grand Hôtel National, August 20th 1923 (unpub.)

39. 'Das Kleine Weinjahr' is printed in the periodical *Corona*, anno V, number 6, 1935 (none of these poems is included in the A.W.).

40. To Marie Elizabeth and Guido von Salis-Seewis, Muzot, March 3rd 1924 (unpub.)

41. These statements are taken from a letter to Mme Nanny Wunderly-Volkart, written entirely in French, which Rilke called a '*confession sans retenue*'. For the first time the hand-writing here is strikingly uneven and unsteady; the act of writing appears to have been a great effort to him.

42. To Mme Nanny Wunderly-Volkart, Muzot, February 8th 1924. Original German (unpub.)

43. Ibid.

44. Ibid.

45. Periodical *Commerce*, No. II, autumn 1924, 167 ff.

46. Foreword by Paul Valéry to R. M. Rilke, *Les Roses*, The Halcyon Press (Editor, A. A. M. Stols), Bussum 1927. German translation by Eduard Korrodi.

47. In the possession of Mme Nanny Wunderly-Volkart.

48. To Mme Nanny Wunderly-Volkart, Muzot, August 18th 1924. This letter is written in French, the postscript only being in German (unpub.)

49. To the same, Ouchy, September 9th 1924 (unpub.)

50. To the same, Muzot, October 4th 1924 (unpub.)

51. *Eupalinos oder die Architektur. Eingeleitet durch Die Seele und der Tanz*. This translation by Rilke was published by the Insel-Verlag after his death, in 1927. Cf. Marga Wertheimer, *Arbeitsstunden mit Rainer Maria Rilke*, Verlag Oprecht, Zürich-New York 1940. This is the secretary to whom Rilke dictated his Valéry translations in the autumn of 1924 at Muzot.

52. To Mme Nanny Wunderly-Volkart, October 1924 (unpub.)

53. To Mme Contat-Mercanton, late 1924, in *Der kleine Bund*, Bern December 24th 1929. Original in French. Not in the G.Br.

54. To Prof. Jonas Fränkel, Paris (spring) 1925, in the *Inselschiff*, April 1927.

55. O. F. Bollnow, 'Das Weltbild des reifen Rilke', *Universitas*, Stuttgart, July 1952

56. Gabriel Marcel, 'Rilke et l'occulte', *Les Lettres*, loc. cit., 141

57. We are quoting from the first edition of Rilke's French poems. They have since been published in the luxury edition of the *Gesammelte Gedichte*, Insel-Verlag of Leipzig 1933, and under the title *Poèmes français* by Verlag Paul Hartmann, Paris 1935.

58. Lou Andreas-Salomé, *Rainer Maria Rilke*, 90

59. J. Gebser, *Rilke und Spanien*, 2nd ed., Verlag Oprecht, Zürich 1946, where Rilke's letters to the painter Zuloaga were also published.

60. *Inselschiff*, April 1927, 125

61. To Mme Nanny Wunderly-Volkart, Locarno, February 1920 (unpub.)

62. See 53

63. 'Das Füllhorn, Geschrieben fur Hugo von Hofmannsthal', in R. M. Rilke, *Späte Gedichte*, Insel-Verlag of Leipzig 1934, 133 (not included in the A.W.). 'Corne d'abondance', in R. M. Rilke, *Vergers*, Verlag N.R.F., Paris 1926, 17.

64. Edmond Jaloux, *Rainer Maria Rilke*, Verlag Emile Paul, Paris 1927, 27 ff.

65. The unnamed poet in *Malte* is identified by a literary historian as Francis Jammes. Charles Guérin had sung of the window and the glass doors of the bookcase in Francis Jammes' house in the Pyrenees:

> Ta fenêtre pensive encadre l'horizon;
> Une vitrine ouverte auprès d'elle, reflète
> La campagne parmi tes livres de poète.

These three lines give a picture of the situation described in *Malte*, in the passage which refers to the poet living in the mountains. The window-motive sounded in the first of these lines was developed by Rilke in his French window poems.

66. Rilke's letters to Mme Jeanne de Sépibus-de-Preux are published by Maurice Zermatten, *Les années valaisannes de Rilke*, 2nd ed., Verlag O. Amacker, Sierre 1951.

67. See 53 and 57

68. Lou Andreas-Salomé, *Rainer Maria Rilke*, 88-89

69. See 56, p. 142

70. G.Br., V, 413 ff. (Valmont, March 20th 1926)

71. *Reconnaissance à Rilke*, Verlag Emile Paul, Paris 1926

72. E. Jaloux, loc. cit., 36

73. To Mme Nanny Wunderly-Volkart, Muzot, Christmas 1921 (unpub.)
74. G.Br., V, 178-179
75. E. Jaloux, loc. cit., 3
76. Pierre Jean Jouve, 'Souvenir', *Les Lettres*, loc. cit., 235
77. To the author, Sierre, April 24th 1924, 6.40 p.m. (unpub.)
78. To the author, Muzot, May 9th 1924 (unpub.)
79. To Mme Nanny Wunderly-Volkart, undated, postmark Pratteln, July 29th 1920 (unpub.)

ILLNESS AND DEATH

1. Cf. Maurice Betz, *Rilke in Paris*, translated by Willi Reich, Arche Verlag, Zürich 1948. The book contains valuable information about Rilke's 1925 Paris visit and about the assistance he gave to Betz in making his French translation of the *Aufzeichnungen des Malte Laurids Brigge*.
2. To Mme Nanny Wunderly-Volkart, Paris, Hôtel Foyot, postmark January 28th 1925. Original in French (unpub.). Mme Pozzi, a friend of Paul Valéry, who was a chronic invalid and therefore seldom received visitors, was the divorced wife of the dramatist Edouard Bourdet.
3. Ibid.
4. Maurice Betz, loc. cit., 95-96
5. To Mme Nanny Wunderly-Volkart, Paris, February 3rd 1925. Original in French (unpub.)
6. To the same, Paris, March 5th 1925. Original in French (unpub.)
7. To the same, Paris, June 26th 1925. Original in French (unpub.)
8. Maurice Betz, loc. cit., 129-130
9. To Mme Nanny Wunderly-Volkart, Paris, July 31st 1925 (unpub.)
10. Monique Saint-Hélier, 'Souvenir de Rilke', *Revue universelle*, Paris, April 15th 1935, 190. This is a description of the poet in his last years, at a time when, already ill, he used to visit Mme Saint-Hélier in Bern, before she became well known as a novelist. The author, who owed his acquaintance with Rilke to this lady, used to meet him often at her house, after first seeking him out at Muzot.
11. To Mme Nanny Wunderly-Volkart, Muzot, October 29th 1925 (unpub.)

12. To the same, Muzot, November 7th 1925 (unpub.)

13. To the same, Muzot, postmark November 12th 1925 (unpub.)

14. To the same, Muzot, postmark illegible, immediately after December 4th 1925 (unpub.)

15. The following sentences show us what Rilke had in mind in making his 'pious foundation' (*Stiftung*): '*Je suis tout heureux d'avoir pu exécuter cette petite action de dévotion qui se prolongera et dont profitera tout cet humble monde qui aime encore remettre son obole et sa prière a cet endroit sacré par l'intention de son pieux fondateur et par l'usage*' (to Mme Wunderly-Volkart, Muzot, December 10th 1925, unpub.).

16. E. Jaloux, loc. cit., 21-22

17. To Mme Nanny Wunderly-Volkart, Valmont, December 21st 1925 (unpub.)

18. To the same, Valmont, February 18th 1926. Original in French (unpub.)

19. Ibid.

20. To Mme Nanny Wunderly-Volkart, Valmont, Easter Monday, postmark April 6th 1926 (unpub.)

21. To the same, Valmont, April 26th 1926 (unpub.)

22. To the same, Valmont, May 11th 1926 (unpub.)

23. Ibid. Original in French.

24. To Mme Nanny Wunderly-Volkart, Etoy, undated (1921)

25. To Pastor Rudolf Zimmermann, Muzot, January 16th 1922, in R. M. Rilke, *Briefe*, Olten 1945, 57-58. A copy of this letter in Rilke's hand, sent to Mme Wunderly on January 19th 1922 contains the sentence, not included in this extract: 'There are such wonderful ways of grasping God.'

26. To Mme Nanny Wunderly-Volkart, Schönenberg bei Pratteln, 'Monday' (March 22nd 1920) (unpub.)

27. Ibid.

28. To Mme Nanny Wunderly-Volkart, Sierre, January 25th 1926 (unpub.)

29. Ibid.

30. *Bündner Monatsblatt*, Chur, September 1926. This poem has not hitherto been included in any of the editions of Rilke's poems.

31. Sent to the *Bündner Monatsblatt* (see 30) by Col. H. L. Gugelberg von Moos.

32. We only know of one other poem written at this time, on August 10th 1926, four days after the *Weide von Salenegg*. It is on a line by Karl Graf Lanckoronski: '*Nicht Geist, nicht Inbrunst wollen wir entbehren*' in A.W., I, 400-401. Up till now no poems have come to light written during the last four months of Rilke's life (September-December 1926); as far as we know those written in August at Ragaz were his last.

33. To Mme Contat-Mercanton, in *Der kleine Bund*, Berne, December 29th 1929 (original in French).

34. To Mme Nanny Wunderly-Volkart, Sierre, October 30th 1926 (unpub.)

35. To the same, Sierre, undated, first half of November 1926 (unpub.)

36. Genia Tschernoswitow to Mme Nanny Wunderly-Volkart, Glion, December 1926 (translated from the French). Rilke's last secretary recounts her memories of his last months in *Les Lettres* (loc. cit., 214 ff.). On October 15th he began his translation of Valéry's *Tante Berthe*. After that he put his correspondence in order with the secretary's help; with incredible patience, he arranged piles of letters he had received, and which she had brought from Muzot to the Hotel Bellevue in Sierre. They were put into big yellow envelopes, on each of which the secretary had to write the sender's name. As after Rilke's death a number of letters were found in green envelopes, with the sender's name written in his own hand, we must assume that Rilke had begun this work at an earlier date. He read Gide's newly published autobiography *Si le grain ne meurt* (translated into German under the title *Stirb und werde*). Mlle Tschernoswitow confirms that she read the Prince Wolkonsky's memoirs aloud to Rilke, as well as extracts from Turgeniev and finally, when he was confined to bed, Fromentin's *Dominique*. Then he got up again, and one evening the secretary found him pacing up and down in his hotel room; with a look of despair on his face he said to her: 'I can't stand it any longer, I can't stand it any longer – and no doctor on earth is going to be able to help me!' On November 30th she accompanied him to the Valmont clinic. On December 4th – his 51st birthday – he wrote to her in a letter from Valmont: '. . . *Je suis livré jour et nuit à d'indicibles tortures*'.

37. To Mme Nanny Wunderly-Volkart, Valmont, December 8th 1926. This was the last time that Rilke sent news of himself to

Mme Wunderly, as she at once hurried to Valmont and stayed with him until his death.

38. Dr Theodor Haemmerli-Schindler to the Princess Marie von Thurn und Taxis, Valmont, February 25th 1927. In *Briefwechsel Thurn und Taxis*, 954-958. Original in French. At a later date Dr Haemmerli dictated to the author his memories of Rilke's illness and death; Mme Wunderly-Volkart likewise recalled her impressions for me.

A strange and, if one goes to the bottom of it, doubtless senseless controversy has arisen, over the rumour that Lou Andreas-Salomé in her book on Rilke (p. 112) quoted as one of the sentences written from his sick-bed: 'Oh, but the hells!' The words have a resemblance to some that he wrote on December 8th to Mme Wunderly: '. . . *l'Enfer! on l'aura connu!*' – and: '*encore un autre chapitre d'Enfer depuis ma lettre de ce matin!*' In the year 1936 Ruth and Carl Sieber-Rilke asked Frau Andreas-Salomé for an explanation, as the impression had arisen that 'these were Rilke's last words'. Frau Andreas-Salomé in the kindness of her heart wrote a reassuring letter to the poet's worried daughter, in which she said that they were not 'last words', but had to do with memories of many conversations between the poet and herself. On behalf of the Rilke Archive, a German newspaper of 1936 published this 'correction', which Bassermann in his book *Der späte Rilke* (p. 529) calls 'a kind of corrective recantation'. Obviously it could not have been a 'recantation' on Lou Andreas's part, as she never asserts in her book that 'Oh, but the hells' were Rilke's last words. In fact, the poet did refer to the unspeakable sufferings he had to endure in his last weeks as 'torture' (*torture*) and 'hell' (*enfer*). The doctor who attended him and those who saw him die have told of the fearful pain he had to suffer before he could enter into the great rest.

39. As the author was not at Rilke's funeral, he has drawn upon Dr Eduard Korrodi's notes (*Inselschiff*, April 1927) and the spoken reminiscences of Mme Wunderly and of W. Reinhart, who has since died.

40. Korrodi's *Grabrede auf Rilke* in the private edition of the *Neue Zürcher Zeitung*, *In memoriam Rainer Maria Rilke*, Zürich 1927

41. Robert Faesi, 'Gedenkrede beim Tod Rainer Maria Rilkes', *Philobiblion*, 8th Year, No. 4, 1935, 7 ff.

GERMAN TITLES OF RILKE'S WORKS

The Book of Hours = Stundenbuch
 – If sometimes, neighbour God = Nachbar Gott
The Duino Elegies = Duineser Elegien
 – Antistrophes = Gegen-Strophen
 – 'All that rushed in the river' = 'Alle die Stimmen der Bäche'
From the Remains of Count C. W. = Aus dem Nachlass des Grafen
 C. W.
The Lay of the Love and Death of Cornet Christoph Rilke = Die
 Weise von Liebe und Tod des Cornets Christoph Rilke
The Little Wine Year = Das kleine Weinjahr
Military Novel = Militärroman
New Poems = Neue Gedichte
The Notebooks of Malte Laurids Brigge = Die Aufzeichnungen des
 Malte Laurids Brigge
Primeval Sound (Suggested Experiment) = Ur-Geräusch (Experiment-
 Vorschlag)
The Sonnets to Orpheus = Die Sonette an Orpheus
 – I, XX 'But what shall I offer . . .' = 'Dir aber, Herr, . . .'
 – I, XXV 'Now it is you, though . . .' = 'Dich aber will ich nun . . .'
 – I, XXI 'Spring has come again . . .' = 'Frühling is wieder
 gekommen . . .'
 – I, XVII 'Undermost he, the earthbound . . .' = 'Zu unterst der
 Alte, verworrn'
 – I, X 'Welcome, whose meaning in me so long' = 'Euch, die ihr nie
 mein Glück verliesst'
The Young Workman's Letter = Brief eines jungen Arbeiters
Miscellaneous Poems
 – 'Alas, my mother will demolish me' = 'Ach, wehe, meine
 Mutter reisst mich ein'
 – Cornucopia = Das Füllhorn
 – Early Spring = Vorfrühling
 – Hymn to Hölderlin = Hymne an Hölderlin
 – Imaginary Career = Imaginärer Lebenslauf

BIBLIOGRAPHY OF
REFERENCES TO RILKE'S WORKS

WORKS IN GERMAN